Archie Green

Sean Burns

The Making of a Working-Class Hero

UNIVERSITY OF ILLINOIS PRESS
Urbana, Chicago, and Springfield

Publication of this book was supported by a grant
from the L. J. and Mary C. Skaggs Folklore Fund

Manufactured in the United States of America
P 5 4 3 2 1
♾ This book is printed on acid-free paper.

Library of Congress Cataloging-in-Publication Data
Burns, Sean.
Archie Green : the making of a working-class hero / Sean Burns ;
foreword by David Roediger ; with a final interview conducted
by Nick Spitzer
p. cm.
Includes bibliographical references and index.
ISBN 978-0-252-07828-6 (pbk.)
1. Green, Archie. 2. Folklorists—United States—Biography.
3. Working class—United States—Folklore. 4. Labor unions—
United States—Folklore. 5. Folklore—United States. 6. United
States—Social life and customs. I. Title.
GR55.G693B87 2011
398.092—dc23
[B] 2011035134

Contents

Foreword

David Roediger

My strongest memory of Archie Green has him holding on to a hug, not letting go. The occasion was an event organized to honor and study the memory of the Southern Tenant Farmers Union (STFU) at University of Missouri during the 1980s. The academic talks, and a rollicking, reflective one by Archie, were punctuated by performances from the great African American socialist songwriter, poet, and singer John Handcox, who had memorialized STFU struggles in "Roll the Union On" and "The Planter and the Sharecropper" in the thirties. When the session had just ended, Archie and John found each other near the stage and embraced. Archie did not let go. The two hundred people in the audience saw something rare in U.S. culture and rarer still in academia—two men hugging, across the color line and for a long time. Archie was right to hold on; the Missouri event turned out to be one of Handcox's final public performances before his death in 1992.

Archie continued to hug and hold on throughout the 1990s and well into the twenty-first century. One of the highlights of the laborlore conversations—so well described in this wonderful biography—that Archie organized near the end of his life was him hugging and holding on to participants. This volume combines accounts of Green's life and times to describe the many ideas, actions, and people Archie embraced and held fast, whether from family to folk, left reformist politics to revolutionary working-class culture, craft traditions to creative breakthroughs, or individual passion to a profound desire to bring friends together in common projects.

Archie and I grew close initially and enduringly because of his penchant for holding on. We met during the 1980s when he sought me out because I was participating in cooperative efforts to preserve and revive the Charles

H. Kerr Publishing Company, the world's oldest socialist publisher, which had fallen on hard times. With the biologist Stephen Jay Gould, the novelist Jack Conroy, the artist Lenora Carrington, the poet Dennis Brutus, the historian George Rawick, and the wonderful Studs Terkel and others, Archie took a leading role in our modest Friends of the Charles H. Kerr Company, part of the improbable success of holding on to and reviving the press. At Kerr, the veteran Industrial Workers of the World (IWW) editor Fred Thompson and IWW/surrealists Franklin and Penelope Rosemont shared Archie's desire to maintain legends, examples, and, above all, songs of the Wobblies, as IWW members were called, and Thompson and the Rosemonts corresponded endlessly with him.

Thus when Archie visited the University of Missouri, where I was then teaching, we got together, although not without some suspicion on his part. My Kerr credentials did not fully override the fact that I was a writer, broadly speaking, within "new labor history," a subfield with which Archie rightly quarreled. I, like most labor historians meeting Archie, did not know at first that I was in the presence of a legend.

We quickly became friends around two circumstances. The first involved an event marking the donation, through Green, of the amazing papers of Peter Tamony, the working-class expert on U.S. slang, to the university's archives. The program (and to be fair, Archie) went on for a long time and became considerably behind schedule, but the moderator was still bent on following form by having several more scholars deliver formal remarks. Archie said, with no rancor but considerable firmness, that he was adjourning even if the event was not. He wanted, he added, to be outside for at least the end of a beautiful afternoon. The event ended then and there, and I, having never seen anything quite like this, followed him to watch the sunset. He opened up considerably, in part around a fear that occupational illness contracted on the waterfront left few sunsets for him to watch.

In fact, he was to live another remarkable quarter century, producing much of his most influential scholarship in very active retirement. For one of his books he interviewed me, in what proved to be the second circumstance cementing our friendship, on the origins of "Wobbly" as a name for IWW members. In contrast to Fred Thompson and Franklin Rosemont, whose brains he also picked, I had little to offer, coming along too late to know more than a few old Wobblies and having not yet written much on the union.

I talked not about the origin of Wobbly but about it being telling that IWW held on to the term. In contrast to the "scientific" socialism of the sectarian left that superseded the IWW, the working-class radicals of the "singingest" union in the United States reveled in the wobbles of the world and of themselves. Archie brightened greatly and republished the interview in his essay on "Wobbly." I had spoken to his, and our, passion for holding on to a politics suspicious of modernist straight lines—to his commitment to what Burns aptly discusses as "cultural pluralism" and more.

That love of multiplicity created contradictions that Archie characteristically and stylishly embraced. His concept of "laborlore" prioritized working lives insistently. When a large history conference convened in San Francisco during the 1990s, Archie celebrated his return to health after a series of setbacks by convening a tour of labor sites and walked a half-dozen eager invitees into the ground. We lingered forever at first in one small area as Archie stopped in every building, emphasizing that all were "labor sites" built by workers and every one deserved a marker detailing all who built it. When we moved on, it was to the marvelous Mechanics' Institute, a monument to a world beyond work and by then, much to Archie's delight, a chess center.

The same ability to see working-class experiences in the round, without minimizing the critical dimension of labor under capitalism, had Archie often eagerly asking me what would happen if workers were requested to name their roles and identities, and given no cues about the response. He predicted that identities such as *born-again Christian, guitar player, Giants fan, Filipina, Catholic,* and *lesbian* would very often come before *worker* or *union member* on resulting lists. The lesson was to deepen, not abandon, working-class studies.

We came to work together on various projects, including, with Franklin Rosemont and Salvatore Salerno, a massive collection of IWW songs, *The Big Red Songbook,* which Kerr published shortly before Archie died. Archie generously called what we did on the project coediting although the work and expertise were overwhelmingly his. As we did that work, I came to appreciate how rare Archie Green was. He had no need, as so much of the left sadly does, to be the most radical person in the room and divine, define, and personify what is called with great hubris the "left wing of the possible."

Archie was certainly very interested, as Burns demonstrates, especially in describing the creation of the American Folklife Center, in making concrete changes. He never assumed, however, that such pragmatism required looking only to the center. He sought conversation, including conversation and contention with radicals such as Thompson, Stan Weir, Bill Friedland, the Rosemonts, and myself, far more than certainty. He happily showed, and Sean Burns happily shows, how possible and necessary that it is to wobble, hold on, and move forward.

Illustrations

Following page 68

Abbreviations

AFL	American Federation of Labor
ASU	American Student Union
AVC	American Veterans Committee
CCC	Civilian Conservation Corps
CIO	Congress of Industrial Organizations
CPGB	Communist Party of Great Britain
CP/CPUSA	Communist Party of the United States of America
CWC	Clyde Workers Committee
EPIC	Ending Poverty in California
FLCH	Fund for Labor Culture and History
ILA	International Longshoremen's Association
ILWU	International Longshoremen's and Warehouse Union
IUMSWA	Industrial Union of Marine and Shipbuilding Workers of America
IWW	Industrial Workers of the World (Wobblies)
MFPC	Maritime Federation of the Pacific Coast
NMU	National Maritime Union
NYA	National Youth Administration
SD	Russian Social-Democratic Labor Party
SLP	Socialist Labor Party
SR	Socialist Revolutionary Party
SUP	Sailors' Union of the Pacific
RPC	Revolutionary Policy Committee
UBCJA	United Brotherhood of Carpenters and Joiners of America
UCLA	University of California, Los Angeles
VA	Veterans Administration
WPA	Works Progress Administration
YCL	Young Communist League

INTRODUCTION
Worker, Scholar, and Organizer

> Few scholars in their lifetime are entirely cognizant of the ramifications of their own contributions.
>
> —Archie Green, reflecting on his mentor, folklorist George Korson

"A working class hero is something to be," howls John Lennon in his famous post-Beatles polemic against authoritarianism of every kind.[1] As hard as it is to imagine today, there was a time, really not that long ago, when a generation of young people in the United States shared Lennon's conviction—a time when the social idea of "the worker," which is to say the coal miner, the builder, the mechanic, the longshoreman, conjured up pride, skill, accomplishment, even heroism. It was a time when broad currents of society began to associate manual work with social possibility and cultural significance. The time was the thirties and forties, an era that Michael Denning astutely refers to as the "age of the CIO."[2] Denning's reference invokes both the historic rise of the Congress of Industrial Organizations (CIO) as an unprecedented association of unionized workers and, very importantly, the widespread cultural shifts that accompanied labor's insurgence.

The age of the CIO, as with all historic junctures, formatively shaped many lives. And those lives, it must always be remembered, were the forces that shaped and reshaped the era. This is a book about an extraordinary worker, scholar, and organizer—Archie Green—and how he became, through a willful forging of his generations' ethos, a working-class hero. The central concern of the book is a discussion of Green's political and intellectual formation, how he came to understand the world as he did, how his political and intellectual commitments propelled a long life of action, and, perhaps most consequentially, how examination of Green's thoughts and public initiatives challenge contemporary understandings of the age of the CIO and the influence this period has flexed over subsequent U.S. history.

In 1962, when he was forty-four and yearning to redefine his professional career, Archie Green wrote to the president of the American Folklore Society, Richard Dorson, "If I stay with the rebels, the hillbillies, the coal miners, the lint-heads, and the discographers I'll be busy for a lifetime to come."[3] A self-fulfilling prophecy if there ever was one. For the next fifty years Green worked tirelessly to redefine and invigorate American democracy through combining his groundbreaking research on the traditions and cultural practices of working people with innovative public-sector advocacy on behalf of workers' culture and the labor movement.

Green's upbringing, set against the backdrop of the age of the CIO, prepared him for this lifelong work. The son of Jewish-Ukrainian socialists who fled the Russian Cossacks in the aftermath of the 1905 Revolution, Green was born in Winnipeg, Canada, raised in a multi-ethnic, working-class neighborhood of East Los Angeles, and educated at University of California, Berkeley in the late thirties. In 1939, degree fresh in hand and captivated by the rise of industrial unionism and the emergent cultural glorification of the worker, Green immediately signed up for a Civilian Conservation Corps (CCC) work camp. Following a year of surveying roads and fighting fires with the CCC he returned to the Bay Area and, in January of 1941 at the age of twenty-three, landed a shipwright apprenticeship on the bustling dry docks of South San Francisco. Surely the most pivotal event of his professional life, Green began a consuming journey into both the skills of hand and the abundant cultural practices that define and sustain American work traditions. He became a dedicated student of work songs and labor yarns as much as stem and stern.

When Green wrote to Dorson in 1962 about sticking with the rebels, hillbillies, and coal miners, he had just begun to parlay his twenty-year career as a shipwright and carpenter into an unconventional academic career as a folklorist and labor historian. His long-time hobbies of work-song discography and cataloging the lore and rituals of shop-floor cultures needed fuller expression. As a scholar, Green would go on to coin the term *laborlore*; write voluminously on worker folklife, vernacular music, and labor history; and become one of the most respected folklorists of the twentieth century. On March 22, 2009, at the age of ninety-one, Green died peacefully in his long-time San Francisco home. He was surrounded by his wife of sixty-six years, Louanne; many of their children and grandchildren; and sprawling shelves of books, files, letters, and records, including seven books and more than a hundred articles he had written.

To mark his lifetime's achievements, the Library of Congress in 2007 bestowed on Green its highest honor: the Living Legend Award. Speaker Nancy Pelosi rose to the House floor to pay tribute:

> Dr. Green has devoted most of his ninety years to the study and celebration of people, and to the texture and meaning of their lives as expressed in song, story, custom, belief, ritual, and craft. . . . Decades ago, believing that the Federal Government had a vital role to play in documenting, supporting, revitalizing, and disseminating America's grassroots knowledge and arts, Dr. Green envisioned a national center that would preserve and present American folklife. He then spent ten years walking the halls of Congress, explaining to every Senator and every Representative, and to their staffs, why the folk traditions in their States and districts mattered, and why the ordinary citizens who carry them on deserved our recognition.[4]

The national center to which Pelosi referred is today's American Folklife Center. On January 2, 1976, President Gerald R. Ford signed into law the American Folklife Preservation Act—a successful culmination to Green's decade of lobbying. Arguably the most significant cultural policy ever enacted at the federal level, the law established the American Folklife Center at the Library of Congress.[5] Today, the center houses more than four million items in its archive and each year spearheads dozens of public folklife programs. These programs, reflective of Green's vision, highlight a kaleidoscope of cultural expressions from the fullest range of ethnic and work communities in the United States.

As the Living Legend Award exemplifies, Archie Green, in the last decades of his life, garnered substantial and well-deserved praise for his contributions to public folklore. Given the importance and visibility of the American Folklife Center, it makes sense that the majority of people who are familiar with Green know of him because of his Herculean efforts to legislate its creation. Sandra Gross Bressler's 1995 doctoral dissertation, "Culture and Politics: A Legislative Chronicle of the American Folklife Preservation Act," traces in detail this history. Her narrative consistently highlights Green's central role in the passage of the American Folklife Preservation Act and the subsequent formation of the American Folklife Center. Green's celebrated years of congressional lobbying, however, represent only one passage in his long and remarkably influential life. Taking a fuller view of Green's life history, the development of his political identity, and the numerous educational initiatives he launched, will not only help in understanding Green's passion for projects such as the American Folklife Center but also offer a productive entry into many central questions of politics and culture in twentieth-century American social history.

The Origins and Motivations of This Study

When I first met Green in the spring of 2005 I had no idea of his significance as a major American public intellectual. Green's long-time friend Paul Buhle had come to the University of California, Santa Cruz to discuss his latest book, *Wobblies: A Graphic History of the Industrial Workers of the World.*[6] Buhle brought Green along to share a few introductory stories about the IWW. At the time I was a third-year graduate student in the history of consciousness and beginning to formulate a dissertation on political education processes in several U.S. social movements. California Wobblies were to be the focus of my first chapter. I attended the book event with great anticipation. Green mesmerized me with his tales. He employed obscure colloquialisms and spoke with soft force, humor, and, most of all, political urgency. He was eighty-eight at the time. Before a packed room of students and professors, Green asked, "Why can't we get this many of you to a local union hall?" He insisted that in looking to the Wobblies academics cannot just be "sweepers in the saloon sifting through old sawdust for a few good coins." Instead, they must direct their work "to bear meaningfully on today's struggles." That resonated with my own intellectual and political imperatives. After the event, I introduced myself to Green and told him of my idea for a dissertation chapter on the Wobblies. He immediately shot it down. "You'll find no sources," he insisted. "All the original Wobblies are dead, and they left little behind. But come to my house in San Francisco, we can talk labor history."

A week later I made the panoramic drive up Highway 1 to visit Archie and Louanne Green. I hardly got a word in on that first visit. He filled my mind with anecdotes, and he filled my belly with a strange Ukrainian peasant stew. I returned the following week with a digital recorder, camera, and sandwiches—then again the next week, and the next, and the next. After five or six lengthy visits, and upon discovering that very little had been written about him, I decided to defer my initial project and focus my dissertation on Archie Green. This book is a product of that decision.

On a personal level Green represented an invaluable connection with a past beyond my experience. In my years of schooling, nearly all of my teachers have been intellectuals politicized through the insurgencies of the sixties; I have had regular contact with the legacies of the "New Left" in many community struggles and university classrooms. Archie Green, born in 1917, spoke from a different, earlier era—one largely cut off to my generation because of the enduring, repressive silencing of McCarthyism on his generation, known as the "Old Left," and the particular political preoccupations of New Left participants who most often mentor my generation.[7] When I began recording fifty-plus hours of Green's oral history I encountered a man whose political cosmography revolved around the Bolshevik Revolution, Stalin's Moscow Trials, the 1934 General Strike in San Francisco, the Spanish civil war, the Popular Front, the New Deal, and the rise of the CIO. In short, Green was my first living contact with the Old Left. He had mourned the executions of Sacco and Vanzetti as a school boy, played in the streets of Boyle Heights with children of exiled Magónistas, heard Eugene Debs's final speaking tour, campaigned door to door for Upton Sinclair, built World War II battleships with militant Scottish syndicalists, and debated feverishly with Communists, Trotskyists, anarchists, and liberals in a heightened period of American radicalism. For me, a young U.S. social movement historian, dialogue with Green was metabolic.

Intellectually, I came to see that Green's life history—his particular political genealogy and activist trajectory—constitutes a neglected area of study for social historians of the American left. Politically baptized in the contradictory waters of the age of the CIO, Green forged a left, anti-Communist politics.[8] His loyalties, polemics, and ideals offer an investigative tributary alternative to the main currents of Popular Front scholarship—*Popular Front* being a term historians use to reference certain elements of the larger age of the CIO.[9] In the opening to his landmark study *The Cultural Front*, Denning aligns with David Roediger in a call for more studies of independent, rank-and-file political figures from this era. Archie Green fits the bill. I agree with Denning when he says, "I take issue with most accounts of the Popular Front, sympathetic or hostile, which have seen it through a core-periphery model, in which the core was the Communist Party and the periphery was the surrounding circles of 'fellow travelers' with greater or lesser affiliation to the Party. This view leads to a remarkably inadequate understanding of the depth and breadth of the [Popular Front and Cultural Front] social movement. . . . The heart of the Popular Front as a social movement lay among those who were non-Communist socialists and independent leftists, working with Communists and with liberals, but marking out a culture that was neither a Party one nor a liberal New Deal culture."[10]

Green worked vigorously for much of the twentieth century to open an independent left political space best defined through unwavering commitment to cultural pluralism and against the ideological hegemonies (what Green would call "monisms") of fascism and Stalinism. To forge this space, Green drew from and grappled deeply with the often-conflicting traditions of anarcho-syndicalism, philosophical pragmatism, and New Deal liberalism—social visions messily constitutive of the Popular Front and the age of the CIO. By his own account, Green's political positions, and the projects born of them, were sometimes contradictory and unsuccessful. Yet, as with so many social movements and their participants, his most resonant legacy may lie in the questions he asked. Through his scholarship, lobbying, and organization building, Green raised questions about democracy; the production of knowledge, modernity, tradition, identity, difference, and leadership; and the transmission of cultural meaning, which, to return to his own measure of relevance, continues "to bear meaningfully on today's struggles."

Methodology, Scope, and Emphasis

This book is the most extensive examination of Archie Green to date. Despite innumerable references to him in scholarly literatures spanning folklore, anthropology, musicology, American studies, labor history, public history, oral history, Appalachian studies, and cultural studies, only two essays have been published on Green previous to this work.[11] I extend appreciation to Brian Finnegan and Robert Cantwell for these insightful essays and cite their ideas intermittently throughout the book. In 1998, Finnegan, then a doctoral student in American studies at George Washington University, wrote a journal article titled "Only a Folklorist, or Cult Stud? Archie Green's Contributions to American Folklore and Cultural Studies."[12] Chapter 12 expands Finnegan's proposition that we see Green as vitally contributing to American cultural studies. Cantwell, a well-known scholar of folk revival, compiled an excellent, representative volume of Green's writings in 2001. *Torching the Fink Books and Other Essays on Vernacular Culture* begins with a foreword as poetic as it is thought-provoking. During the weeks after I met Green, Cantwell's essay confirmed that my instincts for researching his life and scholarship were trustworthy and important.

During my years of research, many of Green's friends and colleagues suggested that my project was a version of something they had repeatedly proposed that Green himself should undertake: an overarching, theoretical examination of his political views and their historical origins. It is unfortunate that he never took up his friends' requests, but as my investigations took shape I concluded that the most productive contribution I could make was a book on the development of Green's political and intellectual commitments. I am keenly aware that this deliberate emphasis leaves many important biographical and scholarly questions for others to pursue—questions that, in many cases, I feel other scholars are better positioned to address. Much like Barbara Ransby's approach to investigating Ella Baker, I encourage and welcome additional studies of Green's life and work.[13] Like Baker, the extent of Green's productivity and the complexity of his intellectual and activist interventions call for multiple investigations and interpretations. It is my hope that this study catalyzes such future inquiry.

A cultural and intellectual biography of Archie Green fits within my larger research concerns about how political identities take shape, and, more specifically, how participation in social movement cultures can transform people's identity in their views of history, sense of self, experience of community and world, and desire for alternative futures. Such questions necessarily position my research at the intersection of multiple disciplines. To understand Green's political and intellectual formation I draw from history, sociology, political theory, and philosophy. To measure the nature of Green's intellectual and activist contributions requires engagement with the history of folklore studies, cultural anthropology, musicology, labor history, and American cultural studies. As George Lipsitz recognized in his examination of Ivory Perry's political activism, certain disciplinary frameworks illuminate one dimension of a person's identity and choices yet obscure others.[14] Therefore, I examine the social and structural determinants of Green's development as well as the more individual and subjective conditions that formatively shaped his political and intellectual identity.

This book, informed and inspired by a generation of social historians before me, illuminates how Green's life choices and political formation emerged from specific historical encounters in which social conditions shaped his actions and his actions shaped and reshaped the social conditions within which he lived. My method for getting at this situated encounter is interweaving, and at times counter-positioning, oral history with multiple other forms of archival and secondary historical research. Green's thirty linear feet of personal papers at the University of North Carolina's Southern Folklife Center are therefore essential, as were more than a hundred hours of interviews with Green's friends and colleagues. Throughout the book the conversation between print and oral sources generates fundamental historiographic questions about what counts as history.

The method of constructing social history from the register of the individual—placing oral history in relation to a range of primary and secondary written sources—serves many functions. First, in the spirit of W. E. B. Du Bois, E. P. Thompson, Herbert Gutman, and C. L. R. James, it facilitates the return of narrative into historical work.[15] That becomes doubly prominent when investigating Archie Green, one of the great storytellers of the twentieth century. The book's historical narrative becomes a product of what Alessandro Portelli calls "plural authorship," a method that helps in understanding how Green negotiated multiple and often contending narratives of who he was and the nature of the eras through which he lived.[16] In that sense this study aspires to reflect Green's nuanced understanding of how identity is plural and developmental. David Roediger understands that well when he suggests that Green's work on laborlore importantly supplements Edward Said's conception of the individual as multiple, "never only one thing."[17] Drawing on Green's oral history helps get at how he, like all of us, experiences and articulates identity through a dynamic intersection of narratives, associations, cultural paradigms, and blinders. To have concern for Green's formation is to take up how deeply relational ethnicity, class, race, gender, and political ideology are, from the most intimate levels of subjectivity to the most macro structures of social representation and cultural reproduction. This unconventional biography, drawing significantly from Green's letters, personal essays, and oral history, is an effective way of accessing how, for example, an individual experiences ethnicity in relation to class, or class through racial identity, or gender through work.

Making Green's voice integral to this study of his life and labor should remind us of his vigilant efforts to create spaces where workers could speak for themselves.[18] Strongly influenced by the social-political philosophy of syndicalism, Green's considerable intellectual and activist contributions might be best summarized as an effort to assert the intelligence and dignity of workers within a social order that consistently denies and silences their voices.[19] My consistent use of oral history brings personal and social meaning into the center of a quest to determine historical facticity. When Green shared his history he relayed his past and provided interpretation of it in relation to concerns he had during the final years of life, among them concerns for what I, a younger scholar and activist, should know and think about history, concerns for the nature of his legacy, and concerns for building a humane world. All along, I, too, had motivations for talking with Green. My questions directed, redirected, and challenged his narratives. Ultimately, my political, cultural, and intellectual contextualization of his oral history reflects my concerns for my generation of scholars and activists and our students. I agree with Staughton Lynd that this kind of multigenerational, dialogic encounter can be extremely generative. During Lynd's interview for the landmark book on new social historiography *Visions of History,* he says, "Just from the standpoint of knowledge I think that a much more satisfactory, three-dimensional feeling about your product is possible if you are able to use both oral and written sources. Then, when you add to that the dimension of talking to people still alive, you have an opportunity to assist them in making their lives useful to younger comrades, it seems to me the method has very strong claims."[20] As Lynd adds, it takes "history from the bottom up to another level."

As I have implied, Green's voice does not go unchallenged in this book. As I understand it, my task as a historian and biographer is to develop arguments about what I perceive to be his strengths as well as his shortcomings, his victories and defeats, and, most significantly, to draw questions and lessons from the full spectrum of his experiences. The cross-generational dimension of this study is as much about sustaining historical continuities and invigorating social memory as it is about recognizing what has been left behind, buried, and dissolved. I believe the life-nourishing quality of radical social imagination draws both from sustained memory and, as Milan Kundera understands, laughter and forgetting.[21] I am often less interested in judging the merit of Green's ideas, decisions, and projects than showing how and why he arrived at them.[22] In the case of Archie Green's life, such inquiry engages numerable central questions of twentieth-century social, political, and cultural history in the United States.

Beginning with the story of his father's recollection of the 1905 Russian Revolution, Part 1 explores issues of how Old World immigrants negotiated political and cultural identity in the New World. That cultural brokerage sets the stage for a prominent theme throughout the book—how the radical social imaginary travels, reconfigures, dies, and sustains. Related with this, Green's upbringing in the working-class immigrant enclave of Boyle Heights during the 1920s offers perspective on the shifting, and not-so-shifting, conceptions of normative American citizenry and how that ideology reconfigures around issues of race, culture, gender, class, and geography.

Green attended high school and college during the height of post-depression New Deal politics, and his fervent engagement with student politics forced him to confront the left's age-old quandary: the relationship between reform and revolution. He was exposed to many strains of left politics through contact with groups such as the Workmen's Circle, the Young Communist League, the Young People's Socialist League, and the Young Democrats (chapter 2). Negotiating tension between syndicalist ideals and the era's newfound confidence in large-scale organizations, state bureaucracies, and political coalitions created energy that for the next seventy years propelled Green's quest to root American democracy in cultural pluralism and working-class dignity—two antidotes for the era's haunting specters of fascism and Stalinism.

Part 2 traces how his formative family upbringing and liberal education translated into surviving the explosive political climate of the San Francisco waterfront in the early 1940s and the legendary union leadership struggle between Harry Bridges and Harry Lundeberg. I offer a framework for understanding how Green's interpretation of this conflict deeply shaped his political philosophy. Central to his interpretation were the perspectives of Scottish radical shipwrights—notably the left, anti-Communist nationalist Benny Carwardine—who mentored Green through his encounters with waterfront Communists, Trotskyists, Wobblies, racketeers, and goon squads. Green's experiences shed needed light on the political terrain for non-Communist radicals during one of San Francisco's most defining eras of social struggle. At stake all along were the consequences of Popular Front nationalism and New Deal business unionism on prospects for a culturally plural, working-class-rooted American left in the second half of the twentieth century. Green's many decades of challenging the labor movement to take seriously workers' culture—a conviction born out of the cultural climate of the thirties and forties—offer a window into the fundamental implications of the business unionism model. After all, where is the space for workers' culture in the cloistered, guarded boardrooms of collective bargaining negotiations? The concluding chapter of Part 2, chapter 7, tracks Green's service in World War II as a carpenter's mate in the U.S. Navy and, with the war's end, his passionate commitment to organizing for the newly formed American Veterans Committee (AVC). Green's AVC years reveal how he negotiated his political progressivism, and particularly the lessons he learned on the waterfront, within the rising tide of cold war consensus.

Part 3 shifts focus to another of Green's sustained passions—vernacular music—all the while noting that folk revivalism constituted a site of political and cultural contest that resembled and at times mirrored the struggles of the waterfront. On April 19, 1965, reflecting on his twenty years as a trade unionist, Green explained to Pete Seeger, "I am eager to set down my personal growth in the labor-radical movement as it correlated with my interest in folksong."[23] Part 3 interprets how Green forged the correlation between his trade union history and his love for traditional music. One cannot understand his unyielding positions on vernacular authenticity without knowledge of his critiques of Popular Front cultural politics. To get at this conjunction requires discussion of how a small group of Communist-affiliated musicologists, folklorists, and performers from the late 1920s through the early 1940s definitively reshaped the conventions and representations of American folk song. As Green moved from a career in the trades to becoming a professor of folklore and labor history, his perspectives on vernacular music offered a unique window into understanding the relationship between the American folk revival of the World War II era and the larger, more familiar revival of the late 1950s and early 1960s. Archie Green's views become a counter-narrative to the most publicly familiar symbol linking the two revivals—the iconic Pete Seeger. The contrast between their political and aesthetic commitments invites reconsideration of the prevailing views on the legacy and lessons of the Popular Front's cultural politics.

In the final section, Part 4, I interpret Green's laborlore scholarship and public projects in light of his life story, specifically how he significantly contributed to folklore studies, labor history, and American cultural studies. Green's astounding productivity late in life (he wrote most of his books in his seventies and eighties) can obscure the ways in which the social forces and cultural imaginary of the age of the CIO deeply animated his work. The fact that he so vehemently criticized the Popular Front is further proof for how his life and work can expand understanding of that era and the variety of ways its social warrants traveled into the second half of the twentieth century. Informed by the ethnographic sensibilities of a folklorist, Green's vision for where and how worker culture and consciousness take shape in everyday life opens an important horizon of inquiry for labor history and cultural studies. Mostly recognized for his contributions to public folklore, Green should be centrally placed in the historiography of New Labor history and American cultural studies. More important, his emphasis on folklife as an integrative, reflexive, and public-oriented practice should continue to serve as a signpost for the futures of these interdisciplinary traditions.

Archie Green spent the better part of his long life building what I term a *pedagogy of culture* and a *culture of pedagogy* for understanding and illuminating the cultural expressiveness of working people. Part 4 is an exploration of how these two categories can guide an understanding of laborlore and support building upon Green's work. His mission over seventy years, whether expressed through May Day speeches, innovative university courses, congressional lobbying, or years of heading up the Fund for Labor Culture and History, was, at its core, educational. Thousands of people directly and personally benefited from his incredible intellectual generosity. I am deeply grateful to have been one of them. In addition to the stories, questions, and analysis that compose this volume, my research has taught me that it is intellectually, politically, culturally, and emotionally critical for young people to be in close relation to elders. This study was possible, first and foremost, because of Green's unwavering commitment to share his life and the lessons, both bitter and sweet, he had learned. I honor him, in the critical spirit he championed, with this book. Archie Green, never far from the rebels, hillbillies, and coal miners, taught us much about the virtues of the examined life and the demanding quest to translate vision into collective social action.

Part 1 Of Shreds and Patches

Early Political Formation

When I read Du Bois on double identity,
I realized that at five, six, or seven years old
in Los Angeles, hearing my father's stories,
I was dealing with quadruple identity.

—Archie Green

Archie Green was a lifelong student of stories. As a folklorist, he exercised an exceptional capacity for tracking how stories lay claim upon people and how people turn to stories and adapt them to make sense of their lives and world. During the four years that I recorded Green telling his own history, I considered how a lifetime spent collecting others' stories would influence the manner in which he told his own. His longtime friend and editor Judith McCulloh emphasizes that when Green wanted to understand something he would work hard to place it in the largest context possible. Observations became meaningfully couched within larger observations, just as an Euler diagram locates each circle within a larger circle. Green's accounts of his youth and adolescence demonstrate this practice. He relayed to me a constellation of people and events that substantively influenced his life's direction. This part of the book is an exploration of those people and events, and, mirroring Green's intellectual orientation, places these influences within larger historical and cultural contexts.

The central concern of Part 1 is Green's intellectual, moral, and political development during the twenties and thirties, decades framed by the cataclysmic tragedies of the First and Second World Wars and a period during which Green frequently characterized himself as a "thing of shreds and patches." More than any other section of the book, Part 1 draws significantly from interviews with Green, particularly his adolescence and young adult life in the context of major American events between the wars: the Great Depression, the Popular Front, and the New Deal. Green offers a window into the ways in which events and social conditions of international proportion registered at an individual level. The narrative unfolds where memory, history, society, and self intersect. My interest in the early formation of Green's political identity specifically raises questions about how his class identity took shape in relation to experiences of ethnicity, race, gender, family, school, and community. Beginning with the conditions of his parents' emigration to the United States and the nature of their political and cultural commitments, the chapters in Part 1 address issues of culture and community in East Los Angeles during the twenties, left student politics during the thirties, and Green's college graduation in 1939.

Chapter 1 Family, Revolution, and Emigration

Archie Green was born on June 29, 1917, in Winnipeg, Canada. When he was six years old, Samuel and Rose Green "bundled up" young Archie along with his two sisters and got on a train, leaving "snowy Canada for sunny California."[1] Family lore holds that Rose disliked the severe Winnipeg winters, but Archie suspected that the post–World War I recession also contributed to the relocation.[2] The continental excursion marked a definitive rupture in his early life. Green insisted that he had no conscious memories of life in Winnipeg but perhaps the "train ride might have been such a cutting and traumatic break" that none of his early childhood memories survived. What Green knew of his early life he knew mostly through the stories of his father. Samuel Green's stories served as a foundation for Archie's identity in multiple ways. On one hand, the stories politically and culturally linked Archie to "the Old Country," specifically, the Chernigov Province of Czarist Russia (north of Kiev in modern-day Ukraine). On the other hand, Samuel's tales structured his son's encounter with American culture as an immigrant child. The stories, therefore, offer an important starting point for exploring experiences that formatively shaped Archie's political orientation and commitments.

In late October of 1905, Nicholas II, the Russian czar, implemented martial law in several of the most politically tumultuous provinces of his empire.[3] Revolutionary calls for economic justice and political representation were spreading through rural and urban areas alike. In the cities, workers held mass strikes. In the countryside, peasants organized to seize land, looting and burning massive estates. Russian Cossacks stormed into these regions, looking to imprison anyone associated with radical challenges to the czar's power or the stability of rural land holdings. These political upheavals, commonly referred to as the Russian Revolution of 1905, were a heightened manifestation of long-term struggles to defeat monarchical absolutism and overcome feudal serfdom. Samuel Green, sixteen at the time, lived in Chernigov and was inspired to support these revolutionary causes.

No one political party spearheaded the Russian Revolution of 1905. Numerous parties debated whether social change should proceed through leadership from the emergent urban proletariat or be rooted in the vast peasantry of agrarian Russia. The most established of these parties were the Socialist Revolutionary Party (SRs) and the Russian Social-Democratic Labor Party (SDs), the latter ultimately produced the split that became the Mensheviks and Bolsheviks. The SRs promoted agrarian revolt while the SDs focused on organizing the urban proletariat, as explored in V. I. Lenin's *What Is to Be Done?*[4]

Green had few details on his father's early life and regretted not recording him talking about his youth. What he did know about young Samuel, however, formatively influenced his own political identity. The father's political values served as a kind of north star for the son's constellation of commitments. Samuel was born around 1889 and spent his adolescence in Chernigov Province. His family name was Canterovich, and his given name Shmuel. Both would be changed during immigration.[5] The men of his extended family were all connected to trades. They were tailors, tinsmiths, and foundry workers. Samuel had little contact with city life and in his early teens began apprenticing as a harness maker, being that horses were still the prevailing mode of transportation. He also began to engage with revolutionary political groups in the years preceding the Revolution of 1905 and was likely familiar with the competing platforms of the main revolutionary parties by the time he was sixteen. According to Archie's sister, Mitzie Green, Samuel hid a primitive mimeograph under the floorboards of the family house and used it to run off socialist broadsides.[6]

Green portrayed his father as a politically sophisticated young radical who, like many other East European Jews, was captured by ideals of the French Revolution, particularly the challenge to orthodox religion by scientific rationality. Samuel told Archie that he identified as an agnostic at a young age. He also conveyed that the decision of whether to affiliate with either the SRs or SDs during the years leading up to the 1905 Revolution was deeply entangled with questions of ethnicity and nationalism. Of his Jewish Ukrainian father, living in a Russian, Christian Orthodox empire, Archie explained:

> Minorities had the choice to be either with the SD or SR and affect revolution against the Czar. But the wiser position was, we may achieve revolution,

> but the great Russians may still discriminate against Poles, Finns, or Balts, or Ukrainians or Jews. If you wanted to be safe, you ought to combine some form of socialism with some form of nationalism. Now, in modern times we think of socialist nationalism as so negative because that's a Nazi experiment. I now recoil against the phrase and against the thought. But then it meant an ideal combination of socialist values and ethnic, linguistic, nationalist identity. My dad was early influenced by socialist Zionism, but in his thinking there wasn't much stress on Zionism, yet still it meant you couldn't place your full confidence in Moscow. Even if you had a socialist revolution in Russia, whoever emerged in power would likely discriminate against Ukrainians or Jews. Many Jews, Poles, Latvians, Ukrainians, and Estonians believed that when socialism would come there would be no oppression. Others in these minorities saw that the patterns of oppression are such that when Russian Bolsheviks rule they [would] continue to discriminate . . . and this proved true.[7]

Russian Jews within the Bolshevik Party, for example, took the position that ethnic discrimination would end after the revolution. Other Jews argued that ethnic discrimination had a life autonomous from class-consciousness and that its deep roots could persist beyond a working-class revolution. These Jews promoted radical politics combining socialism and ethnic nationalism.

Samuel Green wrestled with political decisions that foreshadowed perennial challenges of revolutionary politics in the twentieth century. Looking back on his father's youth, Green said, "I realized later that at age seventeen, my father already faced some of the central problems of revolutionary or Marxist thought, that is: how to make a combination of your identity as a member of a minority with revolutionary activity?"[8] Versions of this question have deeply challenged many U.S. social movements. For decades, the relationship between the African American freedom struggle and the Socialist and Communist Parties (as well as other sectors of the labor movement) was rigorously contested by blacks and whites alike. Similarly, multiple waves of the feminist movement faced challenges around the place of different forms of racial, class, and sexual identity. At root, the issues concerned the capacity for difference in solidarity. Like participants in more recent movements, Green recognized that "for my dad and his friends, those were not theoretical questions as they are for university students. They were living questions. They meant when you went out on the street whether you'd get clobbered or not."[9] When Archie reflected on his father's experiences in Czarist Russia he often linked them to contemporary sovereignty struggles in Chechnya, Tibet, or Palestine. His message, in short, was that when one hears a call for freedom, the attendant question must always be, Freedom for whom?

Samuel told Archie that at the height of the 1905 Revolution, the SDs and SRs seized power in Chernigov Province and for several days ran the area through a joint administrative council until Cossacks reestablished control through martial law. Revolutionaries were shot, sent off to Siberian prisons, or escaped the region via an underground railroad.[10] It was during this phase of political purging that Samuel fled Chernigov. As Archie told it, "In the dark of night, my dad escaped in the back of a wagon covered by straw. The closest port going south would have been Odessa, but for some reason he went north to Helsinki, Finland, . . . The movement was significantly organized in that they could get people out—helpers at various locations, fake documents, etc." Samuel's escape was, in fact, facilitated by fake documents. Archie did not know whether the documents were forged or if they belonged to someone who had died. In either case, Samuel made his way from the port of Helsinki, across the Baltic Sea, and to Hull, England, with papers designating the surname *Greenstein.* Shmuel Canterovich became Samuel Greenstein, and, as Archie observed, "Greenstein translates as green stone, emerald, or green stein like beer stein. We're not sure of the exact etymology."[11]

Although it is now easy to romanticize such a tale of political contest and escape, Samuel emphasized to Archie that he was part of a generation that fled repression.[12] "[Samuel] was careful to point out that his adventure was not unique, it was quite common for the young radicals to be smuggled out of the country." In Hull, he began work at textile and shoe factories, gradually picking up English. "My father was very good with language," Archie said. "Ukrainian was the language of the community, Russian of the state, Hebrew of the synagogue, and Yiddish was the language at home. Then he added English. Dad was well read in four languages."[13] Samuel spent no more than a year in England before moving further west to Canada, which encouraged immigrant labor through cheap Atlantic crossings. Archie believed that his father paid $10 to get to North America and first settled in the forested areas surrounding the Hudson Bay, where lumber camps proliferated. Before the advent of motorized transportation the timber industry required huge numbers of oxen and horses. The work of a skilled harnesser was in constant demand; all the draft animals needed their harnesses prepared for hauling work. The steady income enabled Samuel to send money back to his young sweetheart, Raisel Goosen, in Chernigov, and in 1907 she joined him in Winnipeg, where they married shortly thereafter.[14] The harness work continued for years, but Samuel had shifted to factory labor by the time of World War I. He first built wooden containers in which butter could be shipped, and then he began doing repair work at a small secondhand furniture store.

During World War I, Samuel made the transition from working-class labor (i.e., following a manual trade) to becoming, in Archie's words, a "cockroach capitalist" or small business owner. In the nineteenth and early twentieth century, "Jewish people were not thought of as professionals, they were workers. Although this is supposed to be a big theoretical jump [worker to professional], for many Jewish workers in the trades, this transition wasn't severe."[15] Archie emphasized that his father was never successful as a business owner but did make enough to support their family of five. Judy, Archie's older sister, was born in 1913, and Mitzie, his younger sister, was born in 1919. In addition, Samuel subsidized the emigration of several more Ukrainian family members to Canada, including his parents and brothers and sisters.[16]

Chapter 2 Boyle Heights in the 1920s

If being uprooted to California severed Archie Green from his earliest sources of memory, his family's arrival in the East Los Angeles neighborhood of Boyle Heights vividly marked the beginning of a new life. Boyle Heights in the 1920s was a diverse, working-class neighborhood that attracted immigrants from all over the world. It is illuminating to situate Green's many stories about adolescence in Boyle Heights against the backdrop of George Sanchez's seminal essay "What's Good for Boyle Heights Is Good for the Jews" (2004).[1] Sanchez focuses on the decline in Boyle Heights's ethnic diversity in the 1950s, but his argument rests on data revealing the multicultural character of the neighborhood in the first half of the twentieth century. Green's family arrived in 1923, and Sanchez tracks how changing racial politics in the decades that followed catalyzed significant demographic shifts in Boyle Heights. Green's memories of East Los Angeles align with Sanchez's claims about shifting racial categories in this period and the geographies through which they were reinforced. In sociopolitical terms, therefore, Sanchez's work effectively contextualizes many of Green's memories of adolescence.

When the Green family moved to Boyle Heights, Jewish immigrants were the largest ethnic group in the area. They constituted a vibrant, working-class community infused with many European radical traditions and fervor for trade unionism.[2] As Green accurately remembered, Boyle Heights also had significant populations of Mexicans, Armenians, Serbs, Slavs, Bosnians, and Japanese. That ethnic mix was not accidental. "Local officials attempted to keep two discrete migrant streams—one of Midwestern 'folks' and another of distinctly working class and ethnic newcomers—carefully separated from one another in Los Angeles through an intricate residential segregation that placed American-born Anglo newcomers on the west side of the city, while foreign-born and nonwhite residents found themselves largely confined to the east side."[3]

Samuel and Rose welcomed neighbors of all ethnicities into their home, and the long-term impact of doing so on Archie's personality and political commitments cannot be overemphasized.[4] "My dad had solidarity with people of other castes," he recalled. "That was part of his pluralism."[5] Visitors frequently came and went, and Green's anecdotes of this period paint a picture of a home that provided a vibrant intersection for ethnically diverse, working-class intellectuals. "The discussions around the living room were philosophical and political," he said. "They didn't talk about fashion, or Super Bowls, or the stock market, and in that sense they were unassimilated into American life."[6]

Although many visitors were other Jews from the neighborhood, most of whom worked in the garment industry, other communities were also present. He remembered "some interesting meetings in the 1920s in L.A.: political refugees of the Diaz leadership in Mexico—followers of the Magon brothers, Magónistas; a lot of Wobblies and anarcho-syndicalists. I was always intrigued by the Jewish immigrants speaking a broken English, talking to the Mexican immigrants speaking a broken English. They were debating anarchism versus socialism, Wobblyism versus trade unionism. I have a vague memory of meetings like this in the house before I started going out around town on my own."[7] Some memories were quite specific. On one occasion, "Some visitors argued Mussolini made the trains run on time. Others argued it [didn't] matter if the trains r[a]n on time. He's a bad man."[8] Another poignant memory concerned Japanese youngsters in kimonos, going door to door to ask for donations for victims of the Great Kanto Earthquake of 1923 in which more than a hundred thousand died. Samuel gave them money and then emphasized to Archie and his sisters that "Jewish people have an obligation to be generous and charitable."[9]

Green portrayed his parents as maintaining a lifestyle that combined material austerity with cultural sophistication—a mix that defies popular class assumptions in the United States today. When I asked him, for example, to describe the impact of the Depression on his family, he responded, "Our family standard of living never changed substantially before and after 1929. We always had lentil soup before and after the [D]epression. Hobos would come to the door, and mother never turned away anyone. Always enough to feed us, but it was basic. Mom sewed and repaired all our clothing. I don't remember breadlines or soup kitchens."[10] Samuel and Rose did not place much emphasis on making money, but Archie hesitated to characterize that purely as political principle or a consequence of their modest income. Instead, he viewed his parents as embodying qualities common to first-generation Jews from the Old Country. "Jewish life," he said, "emphasizes an interesting combination of Puritanism and hedonism—joie de vive. Mom never drank coffee, never smoked or played cards, no makeup. She raised the girls as virtuous. My parents were not religious fundamentalists. All three of us were early on exposed to *culturenzachen*—cultural things."[11]

When the famous Russian baritone Feodor Chaliapen toured the United States in the early 1920s the Greens took the children. Rose loved his rendition of "The Volga Boatmen." On the political front, Samuel brought Archie to the Zelig Zoo to hear Eugene V. Debs on his 1924 campaign tour for U.S. president. Years later Samuel was baffled at Archie's inability to remember hearing the legendary American orator. Green's recollection had nothing to do with Debs's fiery polemics but of sneaking off to imitate Tarzan in the thick bamboo forest surrounding the gorilla section of the zoo.

Another important expression of the Greens' cultural values can be found in their decision to enroll Archie in a nearby after-school program at the Workmen's Circle or, as it was called in Yiddish, *Arbeter Ring*. The Workmen's Circle was and is an American Jewish fraternal organization committed to cultural education and social justice work, but the after-school program did not promote Jewish Orthodoxy or revolutionary ideas. Its focus was on cultural identity, *yiddishkeit*. That suited Samuel and Rose. "Our family didn't observe the holidays or dietary guidelines," Archie stated. "My mother and father felt emancipated from orthodox religion, and they didn't subscribe to any orthodox Marxism. Their politics were reformist with a strong emphasis on culture. It was good for Jewish children to learn the language." Young Archie did not find these reasons compelling. He resisted attending the Workmen's Circle program, a disagreement that caused the first family conflict in memory. Ultimately, however, Samuel and Rose prevailed and Archie spent two years in the program.

One early fall day in 1927, Green arrived at the after-school to find a haunting wall display. Two black and white framed portraits of young men hung in the school entry. Dark veils were draped around the perimeters of the frames. The men were Nicola Sacco and Bartolomeo Vanzetti, and the display was a memorial to their execution by the state.[12] According to Green, it was the first time he became conscious of the repercussions of political belief. This impact, most likely, was less a rational association and more the kind of intuitive correlation that so often characterizes a child's emotional development. And all the more vivid an image it is to picture ten-year-old Green, a recent immigrant, peering up at a memorial to Sacco and Vanzetti in the corridor of his socialist after-school program.[13] One could feel the country's tensions as rising nativism, new deportation programs, union busting, and soon the Palmer Raids heavily targeted immigrant communities and the politically progressive.

The diversity of Green's neighborhood as well as cultural tensions around the nation's shifting population were mirrored in his experiences at Bridge Street Elementary School and Hollenbeck Junior High School. Much like the visitors he remembered in his parents' living room, most students at both schools were recent immigrants. Green's classes were filled with Japanese, Mexican, and Russian children. The few white, Anglo-Saxon, Protestant students were from families that likely settled on the East Side close to the turn of the century and had not followed the trend to relocate to West Los Angeles. A favorite childhood story reveals the implications of that student demographic. The date was March 4, 1929. Herbert Hoover was being inaugurated president, and the Bridge Street School's principal, Ms. McCann, wanted to mark the ceremony with a special outdoor assembly. Her challenge, according to Green, was to find a student speaker who would be symbolically appropriate for marking the inauguration. "There was one kid in our elementary school named Adams, Billy Adams. That was a good American name with two presidents and many novelists behind it. Ms. McCann asked Billy to speak. There were no other kids with the name Roosevelt, Fillmore, or Wilson. More likely Schuben, Metechoff, or Hernandez. So Billy Adams spoke, and I've been asked many times: Was Ms. McCann prejudiced? I say no, she was trying to serve all of us. When she analyzed her situation, Billy seemed the appropriate one to speak. Years later, Billy went to work for the *Los Angeles Times* right out of high school. This indicated he had connections. I just took this for granted, not as discrimination. I've often wondered what happened to Billy Adams."[14]

In addition to Green's collegial curiosity, the question of what happened to Billy Adams concerns identity and power. Like so many children, he was sensitive to who hung out with whom, who lived where, what parents held which jobs, where families moved, and who did what socially. The visible answers to these questions, mapped out over the shifting social geographies of Los Angeles, reveal a dynamic intersection of race, ethnicity, class, and gender in relation to the transforming conception of American national identity in the first half of the twentieth century. In other words, those decades saw a change in who was perceived as a legitimate American citizen, and that legitimacy found expression through all kinds of forms of identity, including surnames, skin color, home address, recreation, and employment. Referring to childhood memories, Green said, "I was conscious that I was Jewish, that I grew up in Boyle Heights. I was conscious that I *wasn't* an American—in the sense of WASP . . . I had white skin, but I didn't think of myself as WASP. WASP is made up of ethnicity, language, culture, politics and race."[15] By extension, Green recognized the historically shifting category of whiteness—an insight that undergirds the important and growing field of whiteness studies.[16] "I didn't think of Jews or Mexicans as white," he continued. "I say white meaning WASP. Everyone else *wasn't* American: Jewish, Mexican, or Slavic, or Armenian, Persian, Arab, or Bolivians. Billy Adams was American. Ms. Perkins the librarian, Ms. Butterfield. Mr. Bagwell, Mr. Swanson. Ms. McCann. They were American." In other words, Green, as a ten-year-old Jew in Boyle Heights in 1927, associated being an American with being Protestant and white, and white meant being Protestant and American; it was not determined or expressed just as a matter of skin color.

Green's experience of friends and neighbors was that they were fundamentally unassimilated. "All of my friends, Mexican friends, Japanese friends, assorted Europeans," he observed, "were identified by nationality or ethnicity and that stems from earliest childhood. It was like existence, you just knew that Max Moreno was Mexican. Peter Schubin was Molokan Russian. Mitch Kunitani was Japanese. It was just existential reality. Billy Adams was the only American from school, and we knew he was destined for greatness. He went to the *LA Times*."[17] These last references further suggest how Green as a child experienced working-class identity through the modes of race and ethnicity. He and his friends, just like Principal McCann, assumed that Billy Adams was "destined for greatness."

George Sanchez helps in understanding that while Green's parents circulated among Jewish working-class immigrants who recognized and celebrated ethnic differences, another emergent sector of the city's Jewish community actively promoted and pursued a form of assimilation. What distinguishes the two groups, Sanchez argues, were differing class notions of identity and mobility. "The two poles of Jewish ethnic identity—the separate world of working-class ethnicity and the middle-class ideal of assimilation—were mapped onto the very geography of the city of Los Angeles."[18] A significant portion of Jews in Boyle Heights moved to areas in West Los Angeles and the San Fernando Valley between the thirties and fifties. That, too, was about identity and power. Referring to the historical work of Matthew Jacobson and Karen Brodkin, Sanchez connects the relocation with the aim to position oneself within the boundaries of a new definition of Caucasian.[19] The boundaries were cultural, ideological, and geographic. The title of Brodkin's book captures the transformation succinctly: *How Jews Became White Folks and What That Says about Race in America*. Green's stories about fellow students—those who transferred to new schools in different neighborhoods and those who did not—support Sanchez's argument that certain Jews moved more quickly into a new racial ideology and the privileges it conferred.

Boyle Heights, during Green's youth, was sometimes referred to as the Lower East Side of Los Angeles.[20] The prevalence of Jewish cultural life may have provided a supportive atmosphere for Green, but he was not immune from experiences of marginality. By his own account, he spent a large amount of time in middle and high school doing two favorite things: hiking and reading. Both offered discovery and escape. Talking to rangers on the winding trails of Mt. Wilson, Green was at home in ways he could not be around the athletes and socialites who garnered popularity at school. "In junior high I became very fond of camping. I early on got into hermiting," he recalled. "This seems crazy that my parents let me. I never encountered wild animals, rattlesnakes, or perverts. I knew every trail on Mt. Wilson. It could be that I had a rich enough life in camping and hiking to compensate for the lack of a social life." In junior high school he joined the Boy Scouts. Deflecting any image of young patriots in training, he said, "It was pretty autonomous unlike now. Our group was run by Nisei Japanese . . . we did a lot of camping in Angeles National Forest, beyond Santa Anita before the race track was built."[21] Mitzie, Archie's younger sister, recalls that he had considerable adventures, and, she is quick to emphasize, the gender expectations within the family enabled him to do so. While Archie wandered the hills Mitzie worked in the family's used luggage shop on First Street near St. Louis Avenue, a venue Archie described as being "dull as dishwater."[22]

Green's hikes did not just take him to the wooded periphery of developing Los Angeles; he also spoke of venturous city walks. Many times he made his way to the central branch of Los Angeles's public library at Fifth and Olive, and on some days he would stroll by Pershing Square and listen to the polemical soapboxers. Fiery communists, socialists, and Wobblies would wrangle over "New Deal panaceas, socialist utopias, and EPIC" in what became known as the "spit and argue club."[23] More than forty years later Green's reading of Hyman Weintraub's study of California Wobblies triggered memories of specific men such as Dan Buckley whom he heard address the Pershing Square crowd.[24] A few particularly memorable walks involved Ester Hernandez, the one girl for whom Green expressed romantic feelings in high school. He offered to walk her home a few times, a circuitous, three-hour journey toward Evergreen on the other side of town. The courtship ended quickly, however, when she informed him of her interest in a football player.

Green was candid about his social marginality in junior high and high school: "The Jewish kids who would go into business, et cetera, they had lots of social clubs and a rich social life. They dated, went to dances. Some of us not in the clubs were either rejected or not invited." He said that, however, within the context of a narrative that emphasized a confidence gestated in being an underdog who prized intellect. "Those of us who came from enlightened or emancipated families, whether on the left, or liberal, or cultural," he maintained, "we felt superior to kids in the clubs, but we paid a heavy price for our feelings of superiority because all of us were late in our social development. I had no girlfriends. I didn't go to high school prom. I thought it was too bourgeois."[25] That statement is particularly interesting because its language recalls the political climate of Samuel Green's Old Country. *Enlightened*, *emancipated*, and *bourgeois*, terms that had particular resonance in revolutionary Russia, were being articulated by an immigrant youngster finding his way in East Los Angeles.

Like so many young people, one of the ways Green forged an identity in high school was through ventures with a best friend. Norman Granz and he shared a liking for theater and public lectures. They attended a speaker series at the Los Angeles Philharmonic, where fifteen years later Granz would begin hosting his famous "Jazz at the Philharmonic" series. By 1934 the Works Progress Administration (WPA) wing of the New Deal was sponsoring a myriad of cultural events open to the public, and Green and Granz attended several performances of *The Mikado* by black theater troupes within the WPA. Green also remembered a staging of Sinclair Lewis's play *It Can't Happen Here* as well as the Hal Johnson Choir performing African American spirituals and work songs. Granz went on to become one of the era's most successful jazz impresarios noted for his defiance of racial segregation patterns in the entertainment world. "Norman [by this time in his early twenties] knew almost all the jazz/blues musicians in L.A," Green recalled. "He rented a nightclub in Hollywood that was open on Sunday—Billy's Band Box—and put on jam sessions. Norman took Central Avenue black musicians and brought them to Hollywood to do genuine jam sessions for white urbanites, intellectuals, Hollywood people who wanted to 'dig' real black music."[26]

These ventures introduced Green to public live performance, and pursuing it, primarily in its musical form, would become central to his life both recreationally and professionally. The first musical concerts Green witnessed were at the Workmen's Circle school, where small groups would perform traditional Yiddish songs for the children. This material resembled the Yiddish and Ukrainian songs he remembered his mother singing at home. Ethnic street festivals in Boyle Heights also exposed Green to a variety of traditional performance. One weekend his young Japanese neighbors might perform a moon dance, and the following weekend he would see Mexican friends dancing under sombreros. In 1925 the Greens purchased a radio, and for the first time he regularly heard popular music. He was immediately drawn to a West Coast variety program, *The Blue Monday Jamboree*, which showcased cowboy songs. At ninety-one Green could still hum the first country and western melodies he heard from Vernon Dalhart and his favorite Wobbly cowboy, Haywire Mac (Harry McClintock).

Reading was valued in the Green home. As Archie put it, "We thought of ourselves as a working-class family, and yet we read the *American Mercury*. We didn't think this was unusual."[27] Mitzie Green recalls that high stacks of magazines cluttered several rooms, including the children's. One day a friend came over and gawked at the collection, suggesting that they should throw away older issues. To Mitzie, it was a shocking idea. Why would one ever get rid of reading material?[28] The stacks included a range of prominent national periodicals, including *The Nation*, *American Mercury*, and *American Republic*. Green supplemented these materials with books from the school library at Hollenbeck Junior High School. At Hollenbeck, he volunteered to assist librarian Alice Butterfield with her inventory duties. While putting shellac on the hard covers of new books one day he came across John Lomax's *Cowboy Songs*. The book referred to music Green recognized from radio shows, and for the first time he consciously recognized cowboy songs as a genre worthy of study. On the political front, Green was by high school a fan of Louis Adamic's essays in the *American Mercury*. Adamic, a Slovenian immigrant, regularly wrote of militant industrial labor struggles, and his work left vivid impressions of itinerant Wobblies courageously fighting free-speech battles in the Northwest or defiant strikers in the canneries of nearby San Pedro. Adamic's *Dynamite: The Story of Class Violence in America* was the first serious history text Green read, and shortly thereafter, in 1932, he heard Adamic lecture in Los Angeles. "When I read *Dynamite*," he exclaimed, "I was hooked on labor history, and that's been with me up until today."[29]

Chapter 3 Student Politics and Labor in the Thirties

The San Francisco General Strike of 1934 reverberated throughout the U.S. labor movement. It was the most significant confrontation between labor and capital on the West Coast since the 1916 Mooney-Billings case. Despite the scale of the strike—a strike that would become of significant political interest to Green—he did not learn of it while in his junior year of high school. Boyle Heights was too far removed from San Pedro, the southern California port where longshoremen had joined the work stoppage. There were, however, two significant experiences in 1934 that were important to Green's developing political sensibility. The first was a fleeting episode that made a lasting symbolic impression.

In the spring of Green's junior year at Roosevelt High School, a student ran through the halls during class time yelling for classmates to strike. The young man was Barnie Stringerman, and Green, looking back, suspected he was a member of the Young Communist League (YCL), a youth division of the Communist Party quite active in East Los Angeles at the time. Barnie was likely part of the first national, student-led peace strike called during the Depression years to advance a U.S. foreign policy of isolationism and nonintervention. In the early thirties, before the birth of the Popular Front, left-wing national student groups such as the National Student League (Communist influenced) and the Student League for Industrial Democracy (Socialist influenced) promoted isolationism based on their critique of World War I as imperialist.[1] What struck Green as he sat in class listening to Barnie was not the purpose of the protest call but the form it took. "From Bernie's point of view, it must have been brave or adventurous," he recalled, "but I didn't relate to his fervor. I knew, experientially, that I was not going to be like Barnie Stingerman. I didn't know what he was affiliated with, but whatever I was going to do with my life, I wasn't going to run through the hall and shout 'revolution' or 'to the barricades'. It just didn't seem like the right way to put a point of view across. This was a formative experience for me."[2] Perhaps the critical phrase in this narrative is "the right way to put a point of view across." Although Green went on to generally avoid sectarian identification, he never shied from political advocacy. Indeed, that very year he found a form of political expression that did suit his sensibilities.

Five years into the Depression, muckraking journalist Upton Sinclair launched the Ending Poverty in California campaign (EPIC) to address unprecedented levels of unemployment throughout the state. Sinclair had long been a member of the Socialist Party, but his strategy in the 1934 contest for governor was to implement socialist reforms through the Democratic Party. The foundation of Sinclair's platform was a program intended to turn dormant factories and farmland into productive cooperatives for the million plus unemployed of California. Sinclair's analysis of the causes of the Depression, and his strategy for overcoming the "permanent crisis," attracted a groundswell of popular support. In Green's words, great numbers of socialists "voted with their feet" by moving into the Democratic Party.[3] Clubs popped up all over California to promote the EPIC campaign. Inspired by Sinclair's social vision, Samuel Green began to sell 5 cent EPIC newsletters in Boyle Heights, and Archie joined his father in the door-to-door precinct work. "It's my first memory of doing political work. . . . Everyone in the neighborhood was into him."[4] Samuel and Archie attended nearly a dozen of Sinclair's speeches during the campaign. Archie never found out if his parents voted Socialist or Democrat in 1932, but by 1934 his parents were solid supporters of Roosevelt's New Deal, and, as the door-to-door advocacy suggests, they fervently backed Upton Sinclair.

Green thought of his family as being poor, but they were never made desperate through unemployment in the manner faced by millions of working-class Americans in the Depression years. Samuel Green had a small used furniture and appliance store and would occasionally sell an icebox or kitchen stove. In addition, on weekends he used his truck to find work as an "expressman." As people arrived at train stops in Los Angeles, Samuel would load their luggage and transport it to their houses. The passengers themselves would get home via a separate taxi, as was the practice of the day. Although Green considered time spent at the store uneventful, the train stations along the river offered excitement and romance.

Samuel never expressed any expectation that Archie would follow his line of work. At the same time, Archie never felt encouraged, let alone pressured, by his parents to attend college. On Samuel's recommendation he did take up a few odd manual jobs around town, but they never lasted long. At one point Archie sorted piles of junk at a new factory, but he quit at the end of the day because of the boss's hostility and the fact that no water was available for the workers. "Dad was quite disappointed," he recalled, "but he didn't punish or spank me. That never happened." Instead, Samuel began to see a different path for Archie's future. "When my dad saw that I wasn't strong or enterprising enough to get my own job, he realized in his mind that I should go to college. If I had found a job as an office boy trade apprentice, he would have been fine, he didn't express any ambition for me. He couldn't make me go to college, but I went. What else was I going to do?"[5]

In fact, Green did have strong feelings about what he wanted to do after high school. All those years of talking to rangers in the parks bordering Los Angeles had piqued his interest in working for the Forest Service. He wanted to learn about firefighting and road construction. As part of the New Deal, the Civilian Conservation Corps (CCC) gave young people the opportunity to enter into outdoor environmental preservation work and park maintenance. Corps members labored hard on maintaining public trails and educating communities about ecology. After graduating from high school, Green went down to the CCC office in Los Angeles and submitted an application, but two circumstances thwarted his efforts. The CCC prioritized families on relief, and Green's family did not receive relief. More personally, professional forest rangers were required to have a significant background in science, which frightened him. His interests were history and literature, and he had struggled with science and mathematics courses at Roosevelt High School. His dream was the physical, outdoor work of a ranger, but the science required intimidated him.

With the CCC ruled out, Green turned his attention to college. By this time his older sister, Judy, had made her way through Los Angeles Community College and earned a B.A. in one of UCLA's earliest graduating classes. Judy's efforts helped pave the way for Archie. He applied to UCLA and was admitted for the winter term, leaving six open months before university challenges would begin. He spent most of these months at home, voraciously reading and occasionally walking uptown to replenish his materials at the central library.

It was rare for young people in Green's neighborhood to attend college. In fact, for the nation as a whole only 10 percent of the college-age population enrolled. Economic hardship combined with minimal financial aid opportunities and different cultural expectations barred college education as an option for most young people in the Depression decade. Contrary to these trends, Green emphasized that it was not unusual for children of working-class Jews to receive a college education during the 1940s. The tuition when he began UCLA was $27 a semester—not a strain for the Green family. To save money, however, Green continued to live at home. If he could not find rides to school with neighborhood friends then he would take the Pico Line streetcar. Either way, the twenty-mile commute to Westwood made engagement in college campus life difficult. Green responded by diving into UCLA's scholastic resources, and most courses he took were in the humanities and social sciences. When asked what he read at that point, Green responded, "It's almost easier to say the things I didn't read. I didn't read James Joyce. I didn't read science."[6] In his first year of college he fostered a deep appreciation for American literature; the work of authors such as Ernest Hemingway, Carl Sandburg, and Sinclair Lewis filled his days. Again and again he read the *USA* trilogy by John Dos Passos, whose experimental style stretched his sense of narrative possibility. Green's first philosophy professor, Donald Piatt, was a committed pragmatist and turned students on to the work of William James and John Dewey. That influence would be lasting. Similarly, a young professor in literature, Bradford Boothe, encouraged Green to pursue his concerns for labor history. In the pages of *The Nation* and *New Republic,* Green had learned of John L. Lewis's new Congress of Industrial Unions (CIO), and he focused his final paper for Boothe's course on the "The Rise of the CIO." He earned an A along with a rather clairvoyant commentary from Boothe: "Continue to do your research in this fascinating area, and prepare yourself to make a contribution some day."[7]

As a freshman, Green kept focused on schoolwork and earned As in nearly all his courses. By the time his sophomore year rolled around, however, he grew curious about campus politics, no surprise given that UCLA's student activism in the mid-thirties reflected larger national trends toward more progressive student political activity. In the early thirties, student government at UCLA, like those at many other campuses around the country, was a conservative extension of the fraternity and sorority system. By the mid-thirties, however, the sustained impact of the Depression and a heightened awareness of international political crisis rattled campus apathy. According to Robert Cohen, it was less economic hardship and more international instability—most vividly symbolized by the civil war in Spain—that really catalyzed campus activism in the thirties.[8]

The year 1934 saw the UCLA campus embroiled in a free speech battle when Provost Ernest C. Moore expelled students for promoting antiwar messages, including actively discouraging other students from enrolling in mandatory military training courses. The conflict went all the way to the U.S. Supreme Court and catalyzed the "largest campus free speech movement on the West Coast" to date.[9] The legacy of the struggle combined with the militant California maritime strikes of 1934 and Upton Sinclair's gubernatorial campaign to influence UCLA's campus political climate. Green engaged in the growing fight to challenge conservative hegemony over student government politics. His new captivation with "sandbox politics" quickly eroded his academic consistency. Although he maintained some As, he skipped other courses and did not pass. Sandbox politics is Green's term for situations like student government that introduce people to the dynamics of politics. That was the case for Green when the campus chapter of the American Student Union (ASU) became his training ground. "Whatever bent I had toward organizing came to the surface then," he recalled. The ASU provided information on how organizations are structured in general and offered a valuable glimpse of the prominent competing political tendencies of the day.

Founded in 1935, the ASU was a college-based manifestation of the Popular Front political climate. Most students involved in the ASU came from the main left organizations of the day: the Young Communist League (YCL), Young People's Socialist League, National Student League, Student League for Industrial Democracy, and various liberal organizations. At UCLA meetings took place at a local YMCA, and on those occasions Green began to hone a skill that would serve him for decades—quickness in identifying a speaker's political orientation. This was valuable because many students, even during this relatively nonsectarian period of the Popular Front, did not openly admit their connection to socialist or communist groups, particularly when (or precisely because) the political agenda of the groups significantly influenced participation. Many speeches before the ASU impressed Green, including one by Joe Lash, the ASU's national executive secretary, who visited UCLA. Lash toured college campuses promoting "collective security" as a U.S. foreign policy orientation after he had spent several months with the Abraham Lincoln Brigade in the Spanish civil war.[10] On a more regular basis, Green heard presentations by campus YCL leader Joe Guatanolo, a precocious and dynamic speaker. Like Lash, Guatanolo, the son of a gardener, inspired Green through fiery anti-imperialist speeches condemning Benito Mussolini's invasion of Ethiopia and Adolf Hitler's support of Spanish fascists. Here was a young white Communist speaking publicly for world peace, the spread of democracy, and, on the domestic front, equality for blacks. When Guatanolo later invited Green to attend a YCL meeting he enthusiastically accepted. It was an overture that set the stage for a pivotal experience in Green's early political development.

Every Friday evening, the UCLA chapter of the YCL would meet in a private residence in Westwood made available for meetings by a local Communist sympathetic to the group's efforts. These meetings were the first time Green had substantively interacted with Communists. Up to this point, he had always viewed them as "weird and mysterious," a natural reaction given that the FBI, State Department, and Hearst Press had run national anti-Communist propaganda campaigns for years. Around twenty students consistently attended the Friday night meetings. While the meetings largely consisted of political discussions and organizational planning, what Green remembered most was the lively group singing. With great passion students sang tunes including "Song of the Red Air Fleet" with the chorus "fly higher and higher and higher; our emblem is the Soviet star. And every propeller is shouting *Red Front,* defending the USSR."[11] At the time, Green was genuinely moved by these sing outs, but in retrospect, he wondered, "Why did they sing the songs they did?" and, "How did these American students get a bang out of singing a song about a red Soviet airplane flying high into the sky?"[12] Seventy years removed from the experience Green could make claims about how these episodes revealed the troubling distance many Communists, even during the Popular Front, had from day-to-day working-class struggles. But in 1936 he was at the meetings. He was singing, too. After two months of engaging with the YCL, what ultimately caused Green to distance himself from the young Communists was not group songs but a more dramatic episode of ideology and organizational structure.

One Friday evening in the fall of 1936, the officers of the YCL chapter at UCLA opened the meeting and announced that the main order of business was the questionable loyalty of one of their members, Aria Schwartz. Green remembered Schwartz as a "tall, thin, intellectual Jewish guy with talent for music."[13] Apparently, Schwartz had been found reading materials by Trotsky and attending meetings with other students interested in that internationally known critic of Stalin. The YCL officers considered this a violation of membership. That night's meeting would include a mini-trial of Schwartz for his actions. The proceedings enraptured Green. What he observed, and how he reacted to the trial, are as revealing of Green's character as they are of aspects of the CPUSA:

> The problem was raised that Schwartz was dangerous, a "class enemy." This middle-class group, meeting in a luxury Westwood home, went through a

> trial like the Soviet trials. . . . It was so top down . . . imitating [Communist International] ideology and form/structure. He was accused of being a Trot. I'm ashamed to say this, but instead of identifying with the victim—Aria—an early tendency of mine was identifying with organizations. I believe in organizations. I like to bring people together. I like programs and constitutions. I liked Joe Guatanolo. I remember thinking to myself, if this guy Aria is an enemy of the group: throw the son of a bitch out. That revealed to me that I had (and all radicals have) a tremendous capacity to be mean, dictatorial, and murderous. If we had been in Moscow or St. Petersburg we would have put Aria up to a firing squad . . . as they did. But all we could do was expel him. In the YCL, I sided with the majority against this isolated radical, and I've been ashamed of myself (at age nineteen) ever since.[14]

For days the events of the trial consumed Green. He felt his behavior was incriminating and revealed how "unstable and untrustworthy" he was politically. Reflecting on the event, Green contrasted his behavior with that of two later, long-time friends, Bill Friedland and Stan Weir. Although he wished he had acted differently, his emphasis, ultimately, was on how formative the incident was to his future choices:

> I wish I had the brains and feelings to say to the organization: you are wrong. I wish I identified with the guy that was being railroaded. I wish I said, "My comradeship was with Aria." I wished I had defied the Stalinist dictators. What could a musician at UCLA have done to hurt the working class? He wasn't a labor spy. He just had checked out another meeting. I often think back that Bill Friedland and Stan Weir . . . they were heroic in their understanding of Stalinism, and they wouldn't have accepted that bad position. But anyhow, it had a good consequence. After thinking about it for about twenty-four hours I turned against myself—instead of saying the YCL, or Stalinism, or democratic centralism was wrong I internalized. If I have the capacity to identify with this machine against an isolated figure, there must be something wrong with me. I have the capacity to be part of the dictatorship, part of the machine, and injustice. So I said the hell with YCL, and fly higher and higher and higher, and Joe Guatanolo. I quit the meetings. If machine guns get turned, I'm gonna turn it against those kids singing fly higher and higher. I can proudly say I've been anti-Stalinist ever since.[15]

Shortly after he stopped attending YCL meetings Green decided that UCLA was not what he wanted. The twenty-mile commute wore on him, and he yearned for experience beyond home life. For years Green had known about UC Berkeley because of its reputable Department of Forestry. Although forestry was no longer his focus, Berkeley seemed like an ideal escape from the familiarity of Boyle Heights. In 1937, Green transferred to Berkeley, moved into a campus dormitory, and began his junior year in a new context of intellectual, social, and political resources. He continued to load his schedule with humanities and social sciences courses. The growth of the CIO's industrial union challenge to the craft-based AFL was at the exciting front of the labor movement. Green hung a poster of John L. Lewis on his dormitory room wall and quickly found that Professors Paul Taylor and Ira Cross offered the best courses on labor economics, history, and politics.

Both men came out of the paradigmatic Wisconsin School of labor economics. Their advisor had been John Commons, the liberal pragmatist who defined the Wisconsin School of thought. When it came to the central questions of the relationship of capital and labor, the Wisconsin School emphasized the potential for class cooperation and collaboration. Workers and bosses could find common ground through the process of collective bargaining. The school considered the revolutionary workers' struggles of the late nineteenth and early twentieth centuries as failed efforts. Although their courses appealed to radical students, Taylor and Cross offered a perspective that challenged orthodox Marxism. For Green, this was an extension of, rather than a challenge to, the labor history reading he had done independently so far. Both teachers had an impact on him but in different ways. Cross was "elderly, urbane, humorous, a good lecturer. He was a Shakespearean man and class was exciting."[16] Taylor wrote on topics that Green found fascinating; his dissertation, for example, was on Andrew Furuseth and the formation of the Sailors' Union of the Pacific. Through Taylor's work Green was introduced to the Norwegian syndicalism that defined young Furuseth. Taylor also wrote about Mexican laborers in California in the 1920s. He explored Mexican folklore and talked about the *corridos* that Green first had heard wafting out of his neighbor's windows in the ethnically mixed Boyle Heights. For all these reasons, Green aspired to major in economics, the discipline under which labor studies existed at the time. There was, however, one problem. The major required a passing grade in statistics, and Green did not make the cut. His best alternative was political science, and that was the degree with which he was graduated from UCB.

Everything about Berkeley worked well for Green. He considered the student body to be motivated and intellectual, but, unlike Ivy League schools at the time, he remembered that many working-class students attended Berkeley. In contrast with memories of other left student activists of the era, Green never felt alienated from other students. When asked about class relations on campus, he responded, "There were so many students that I liked and got along with that I didn't waste any time being antagonistic to anyone."[17] That attitude conformed to Green's liberal assumption that "Cal was democratic. I thought that anyone could go there. All you had to do was study hard, and you could be anything you wanted to be. I was optimistic and accepted the premises of democratic education."[18] In contrast, Pauline Kael, reflecting on her experience at UC Berkeley in the thirties, offered Studs Terkel a very different portrayal of campus class relations: "There was a real division between the poor who were trying to improve things on campus and the rich kids who didn't give a damn."[19]

Robert Cohen's research indicates that no simplistic analysis of the class composition of the left student movement in the thirties can hold weight. The best studies of who was active on college campuses and why show that working-class, middle-class, and affluent students all played important, often different, roles in the movement.[20] Aspects of Green's experience exemplify the limitations of reductive claims about student politicization in the thirties. Green grew up working-class, yet his politics did not grow out of witnessing severe economic hardship through the Depression. He did not witness the breadlines, evictions, and migrant camps that politicized many of his generation. Instead, his mother and father's history and exposure to left politics through books and organizations proved much more influential.

At Berkeley, Green increasingly embraced the premises of the Democratic Party. In 1938 the Young Democrats on campus blossomed with the national stabilization of the New Deal and the state's election of a democratic governor, Culbert Olson, who came to office on a Roosevelt-backed ticket promoting reconciliation of national productive capacity with just distribution of wealth. In his inaugural address Olson emphasized that business enterprise aimed at the overall social good and not exploitation was important in the struggle between democracy and fascism.[21] A Democrat had not been governor in California since 1898 and would not be again until 1958.

The UCB chapter of Young Democrats was the largest in the state with some five hundred members. Green actively participated at the local and state levels, and by his senior year the phase of U.S. left politics known as the Popular Front or Democratic Front was in full swing. From 1935 until the Hitler-Stalin pact in 1939 the international Communist Party platform emphasized strategically forming broad alliances with other left, liberal, and centrist political parties in order to consolidate defense against emergent fascism. In the United States that meant the CP actively worked on building the CIO and, for a period, backed Roosevelt and the New Deal. Consequentially, the membership of the Berkeley chapter of the Young Democrats during Green's participation would have represented a broad range of left-oriented political positions. The group likely included young Communists who took inspiration from the Bolshevik emphasis on a vanguard leading a proletariat revolution; socialists who envisioned state ownership of all means of production; and a considerable group of social democrats, a political philosophy that stresses the reform of capitalism toward better social ends through representational democracy. There may even have been a handful of anarcho-syndicalists inspired by American Wobblies or labor federations in the Spanish civil war to build a society around self-managed groups of workers. Green, who began to develop a fascination with other political ideologies while attending UCLA's chapter of the American Student Union, was becoming adept at scrutinizing individuals who took the floor at Young Democrat meetings. "When a person would speak on the floor," he recalled, "we were so sophisticated politically we were able to identify all the factions and count the votes in advance. . . . We would predict votes. I think we were pretty sophisticated for college seniors in politics."[22]

The New Deal ethos and federal programs influenced Green's college life in a number of ways beyond involvement in the Young Democrats. He participated in building the "Fair Bear" campaign of the Welfare Council of the Associated Students of the University of California. The concept was straightforward and foreshadowed contemporary living-wage campaign strategies. The council investigated student-employee working conditions on and off campus and organized for increased wages. It also established a labor board that determined a minimum wage and reasonable work conditions. Local businesses that upheld these standards earned a Fair Bear sticker to be placed in their front windows. Students would then pass the word to patronize these businesses and boycott others that failed to meet the criterion. The Fair Bear immediately proved effective, and other campuses emulated the reform program.[23] The New Deal also touched Green's life in terms of his first campus job. Funded through the National Youth Administration (NYA), a wing of the New Deal dedicated to creating jobs and training for young people, he conducted library research work for Professor George Steward of the English department. Steward was writing a book on the history of storms in California, and Green spent his work hours combing old newspapers at Berkeley's Bancroft library for relevant clippings. The NYA provided $15 a month jobs to more than a hundred thousand undergraduates each year during the second half of the thirties.[24] This kind of New Deal youth program was a direct result of pressure on Washington from groups such as the American Student

Union. In a concrete sense Green was being rewarded for some of his earlier political advocacy.

Most important, the political and cultural climate of the New Deal shaped the way in which Green viewed options for life after graduation. Working-class identity and the contributions of labor to society were celebrated in unprecedented ways during the New Deal era, what Michael Denning alternatively refers to as the Age of the CIO. Denning uses the concept of a "laboring of American culture" to capture a multiplicity of ways in which struggles to reconfigure U.S. society occurred during the thirties and forties. He argues that "the culture of the CIO working class was marked by a sustained sense of class consciousness and a new rhetoric of class, by a new moral economy, and by the emergence of a working-class ethnic Americanism."[25] Living and studying in Berkeley in the late thirties, Green experienced these shifts. Left-wing student politics influenced by Marxist philosophy glorified the role of the worker in social change processes. The rapid expansion of CIO unions engendered new cultural capital for America's workers. Together, radical artists and intellectuals infused working-class perspectives into mainstream American culture to a degree unknown earlier.

Another historian of this era, Robert Cohen, pointedly captures the influence of these national dynamics on college students' visions of their future. "The reverence for labor, which the student movement preached—and which was particularly strong among communist and socialist students, ideologically wedded to the ideal of a heroic proletariat—made a career in the labor movement seem very attractive," Cohen observes. "To join the labor movement meant serving on the front lines of the struggle for social change."[26] Green possessed that kind of respect for a working-class life. Reflecting on his thoughts before graduation, he said,"In '39, when I got out of school, I didn't want to be a doctor, or lawyer, or teacher, or any kind of professional. I knew that I didn't want to fit into middle class life . . . I wanted to be a worker. I wanted to be a worker ever since I read about workers in Adamic's *Dynamite*."[27]

Faced with job hunting in a still lagging economy, Green remembered his earlier desire for outdoor work with the Civilian Conservation Corps. In the four years that had passed since he first applied the CCC had eased hiring restrictions. Degree in hand, Green visited the Oakland office of the CCC and was hired on the spot. In the winter of 1940 he went north to the canyons of the Klamath River with a working-class crew of Italian, Irish, Portuguese, and Spanish young men. Green's life was on the verge of significant change and so was the world. In a few short months German troops would occupy Paris; World War II was underway.

Part 2 Triangle of Commitments

San Francisco Maritime Politics of the Thirties

I remember when I first started working on the waterfront in 1941, a real popular saying was, "The waterfront isn't big enough for two Harrys."

—Archie Green

In her essential political memoir on the American left in the twentieth century, Grace Lee Boggs describes her ambivalence when first introduced to the Workers Party. "It was a strange and bewildering experience," she writes about the 1942 party convention, "to be in a hall on the Lower East Side of New York City with several hundred people, most of whom seemed to be Jewish and all of whom seemed to know each other. People were caucusing all over the place. The main bone of contention was the nature of the Soviet Union or what was called the 'Russian Question.'" Boggs was new to organized political activity and ten to twenty years younger than most other party members. She stresses that the "Russian Question did not particularly engage" her because "unlike those who had been around since the twenties and thirties, [she] had been drawn to the radical movement—not by the Russian Revolution but by the Black struggle."[1]

Boggs's reflection points to a number of important factors in considering processes of political identity formation. When we try, as I do, to make sense of another's intellectual and political development, we must pay attention to questions that shaped the historical and cultural milieu within which a subject commenced political activity. I take Boggs's insight to be both a statement about the role of timing in life and a recognition that often (but not inevitably) the questions resonant during periods of formative political development can exert a particularly lasting imprint on long-term concerns and modes of thinking. If that is true in general, it is particularly true for Green's generation of the Old Left. A confluence of the Russian Revolution, the Great Depression, the New Deal, the rise of fascism internationally, the building of the CIO, and the outbreak of World War II defined that era.

When I began recording Green's oral history, my feelings resembled those of Grace Lee Boggs. I was frustrated with how frequently he circled back to lengthy stories about particular left political contests during the thirties and forties. I could not at first relate to the debates he described or, more precisely, the level of consequence he ascribed to them. His extended, visceral excoriations of American Communists were fascinating (on the level of "how did Archie come to feel so strongly about this?"), but I also felt alienation from, and sadness for, the infighting and factionalism of the left reflected in his convictions. After all, some sixty years had passed since the events he described, and yet Green, ninety, would readily vituperate Harry Bridges and other so-called Stalinists with blood-boiling, sweat-ringing, hand-waving intensity.

Green's charged emotions and trenchant convictions were not just free-floating and abstract. They had a specific history born at the meeting of national and world events with local and personal circumstances. This part of the book describes that complicated meeting place in Green's early work life between 1939 and 1943, four years that profoundly shaped his political identity and life path. He began working on San Francisco's waterfront, where some of the most decisive labor struggles of the thirties occurred. To step into maritime work when he did was to confront the central events, personalities, and ideological legacies of that era, specifically the heated, protracted struggle between maritime labor leaders Harry Bridges and Harry Lundeberg. Understanding Green's interpretation of that contest, the origins of which predated his arrival on the waterfront, is critical to understanding the larger contours of his lifelong political commitments. For that reason I will examine many histories in this section that Green did not experience firsthand but that were critical in determining his political identity. Those less familiar with U.S. labor history might find the level of detail challenging if not frustrating at times. I wrestled with that issue as well and can only emphasize the centrality and consequence of these stories for understanding Archie Green.

Chapter 4 From Berkeley Stacks to Stake-Side Trucks

In the early 1940s, with concerns rising about U.S. entry into World War II, some sectors of the Marxist left encouraged young men to move to industrial centers, take up shop-floor jobs, and help organize the rank and file. Internal bulletins of the Socialist Workers Party and Workers Party, for example, encouraged young Trotskyists to see that "the place for the party is in the front ranks of the revolutionary struggle against the war. Every party member must find his place in the mass movement. The party must be deeply rooted in the ranks of its class."[1] Bill Friedland, a contemporary of Green and years later one of his closest friends, was compelled by this directive. Friedland was a member of the Workers Party—the Max Shachtman–led formation that split from the Socialist Workers Party. In 1942, at age nineteen, Friedland moved from Staten Island to Detroit to become an autoworker and radical union organizer. The Workers Party, he observed, labeled men like him "colonizers." Although it may be hard to believe now, the term at the time was not being used in a pejorative, critical, or ironic way. "Colonizers" was a descriptive and prescriptive reference. Young men like Friedland were sent out from New York City in a cluster to form a "colony" in Detroit.[2] Reflecting on his and Green's life, Friedland stressed how different the processes were that led them both to pursue industrial labor in the early 1940s. Whereas Friedland was persuaded through Workers Party political strategy, "Archie became a worker out of his own volition; his own long time desires to be a worker."[3]

Even though Green's ambitions to become an industrial worker were in the broader national context of the laboring of American culture, Friedland is right to highlight the exceptional quality of his decision. In January 1940, when Green went to the far northern counties of California as a new enrollee in the CCC, he held a bachelor's degree from the most prestigious public university in the country. The CCC did not typically attract such young men; only 2 percent of the some three hundred thousand Corps members had received a college education.[4] The difference between Green and other CCC enrollees could be seen as class-based, but considering the modest earnings of his family and the area in East Los Angeles where he grew up, the more relevant distinction is cultural. As Green put it, "I was the only Jewish kid in the whole camp. Jewish kids didn't go into the CCC. They went into law school or medical school. Or they would go into their dad's business. I wasn't about to go that route. I was obviously the only college grad at CCC camp. Well, there was one other guy, but he walked right over the hill and left after two weeks. He couldn't take it."[5] For Green, the issue was not whether he could endure the CCC. He relished it. The learning and personal transformation the Corps afforded were immense.

Recruiting brochures for the CCC emphasized the program's motto: "A young man's opportunity to work, to live, to learn, to build, and to conserve our national resources."[6] The agency saw its conservation mission as multifaceted. The CCC would create and maintain national recreational areas, and in the process the Roosevelt Administration believed it would uplift the spirits of Depression-era youths, foster civic virtue, and help preserve American families through a $22 monthly remittance officially earmarked to be sent home.

In many ways Green's experience in the CCC largely matched the program's promise. His assignment to a road construction crew in Siskiyou County exposed him to single jacking, firefighting, and the fundamentals of surveying. It was a refreshing change from the library stacks of Berkeley, and Green enjoyed the long workdays in the forests of the Seiad Valley, describing the period as transforming him from "an intellectual to working class." Developing trade skills and a renewed love for nature was just one facet of the transformation. His stories of the CCC camp also emphasize how eye-opening it was to be surrounded by a plurality of working-class youths. The camp drew from three populations: "First, Bay Area kids from mostly Spanish, Italian, Portuguese, Irish and Mexican families. Then we had kids that had been on the road from Oklahoma to California, and last we had enrollees from the local Klamath River area."[7] That cultural mix made for lively conversations about favorite movies, neighborhoods, and women as well as no shortage of "bawdy jokes." Green heard all kinds of new slang and witnessed unfamiliar ethnic traditions from Corps members and their leadership. His foreman, Lawrence Roberts, was a Native American and informed Green about the history and culture of the Yurok and Karok tribes around the Klamath River.

While Green had not yet been formally introduced to folklore, the CCC work camp, much like the neighborhood streets of Boyle Heights, immersed him in the plurality of American cultural expression. Workers traded stories on the job, exchanged barbs and jokes over their three square meals, and every other Saturday night a stake-side truck would carry half the crew to a nearby gold-mining town, Happy Camp, which Green remembered as having ten to fifteen families and one saloon dating back to 1849. On Saturday nights a ragtag string band would get together and play country music. It was the first time Green heard live country music, an important moment for a man who went on to help establish the legitimacy of American roots music scholarship. "One of my regrets," he said, "is that I didn't keep a list of the songs, but I never thought I'd end up as a ballad scholar. One doesn't know what one is going to do in life. The one song I remember is 'Little Brown Jug.' I infer that the repertoire of this group was standard Appalachian music coming west through the South, including Jimmie Rodgers, the Shelton Brothers, and Carter family."[8]

The ten-mile trip from the Seiad Valley to Happy Camp was not Green's only off-site adventure in the Northwest. He did not return home to Los Angeles for the entire year and so accumulated leave days. In the fall of 1940 he set off for a ten-day solo trip, hitchhiking north through Oregon; winding through Medford, Eugene, and Portland; and then traveling to northern parts of Idaho mining country. Ultimately, he arrived in Wenatchee, Washington, where his father's youngest brother, Bill Green, had settled after emigrating from the Ukraine to Canada and then making his way to the northwestern part of the United States. Bill Green was a Wobbly and painted Great Northern Railroad cars before catching the attention of Rufus Woods, a local populist editor and publisher of the *Wenatchee Daily World*. Woods gave Bill Green a chance to report the news, and he went on to develop a career in local journalism. After leaving his uncle's, Green traveled south through Seattle and returned to camp for three more months of work.

Along with hitchhiking, new friends, surveying tools, and country music, Green was introduced to one more notable experience at the CCC camp: Jim Crow. Like the armed services at the time, the CCC was segregated. African Americans could only enlist in designated work camps in the South. There were no African Americans at Green's camp, at least not after the violent incident he witnessed in the spring of 1940. One young man in camp, from Mississippi, was part African American. Most Corpsmen from the West Coast did not care that his skin was light enough for him to pass, nor did they talk about it. One Sunday afternoon Green and a group of other workers, including the man from Mississippi, sat in the back of a large, open, stake-side truck as they were driven to another camp for a baseball game. On the way back, Fox, a strapping worker from Kansas, began to harass the young black man. "Fox got into an argument with 'Mississippi' on the matter of 'Mississippi's' identity," Green recalled. "'Mississippi' denied he was black—even though his tight curly hair and skin made it likely. Fox pushed him completely off the truck into the road. Mississippi never came back to camp again. This was the first time in my life I experienced southern violence against a race."[9] The experience revealed another face of American racism. Green did nothing in the moment to intervene, but the violence provoked awareness that would inform future political commitments.

In December 1940, after a year of CCC work in Siskiyou County, Green returned to Los Angeles to visit with his family. Due to financial necessity and Green's need for space and autonomy the stay was brief, and in January 1941 Green returned to the Bay Area in search of work.

Red Clydeside Meets Green Shipwright

Green's year in the CCC confirmed his desire to work in mass industry and "toughened" him for the demands of industrial labor. Leaving the CCC, he did not pursue work in a specific trade but rather searched for what was available. "If I had been in Pittsburgh," Green said, "I would have joined a steel mill. In North Carolina, I would have joined textiles—in Detroit, an auto plant. In California, it was maritime. The structure of the economy determined the trade."[10] When Green began walking the San Francisco waterfront in search of work the shipbuilding industries of the Bay were expanding, but this was not yet the explosive economy of wartime ship production. Living at a YMCA on the San Francisco Embarcadero, Green had no luck for a week; then a connection from college got him in the door at Western Pipe and Steel, a small yard in South San Francisco that produced Type C3 cargo ships.[11] He immediately began work as a shipwrights' helper and proudly received his first union card in Local 2116–Dry Dock, Marine Waysmen, Stage Riggers and Helpers. "Local 2116," Green wrote, "attracted an unusual mix of men—waterfront drifters, castaways, casualties of the labor wars of the thirties. We had a large contingent of former seamen and longshoremen who found safe haven in the area's shipyards."[12]

As an apprentice, Green was assigned to work under one of the veterans of the waterfront, shipwright Benny Carwardine, and the ensuing relationship proved formative. Not only did Carwardine introduce Green to stem and stern but he also offered a very specific orientation to the complicated and contentious politics of the San Francisco waterfront. When Green arrived in 1941 to work on the docks he stepped into a space in which some of the fiercest worker-employer-state struggles of the thirties had occurred. The insurgent General Strike of 1934, catalyzed by maritime worker militancy, expressed an emergent "social warrant" demanded by workers nationwide.[13] The era gave birth to industrial unions, union leaders, and bold new experiments in worker solidarity such as the Maritime Federation of the Pacific. The '34 strike was followed by an even longer, ninety-nine-day maritime strike in winter of 1936–37. These monumental waterfront struggles took place within a larger context of battles to define the nature and scope of American unionism. As Bruce Nelson persuasively argues, these struggles were fundamentally about defining Americanism and the place of workers in the larger social order.[14] Specifically, West Coast maritime, like the automobile industries of the Midwest, became a site at which larger contests between the American Federation of Labor (AFL) and the CIO, craft unionism and industrial unionism, and social democrats and communists were all played out.

Because of this relationship between the microscopic and the macroscopic in terms of the connection of the waterfront to larger national union politics and how his early experiences on the waterfront shaped the rest of Green's life, an examination of how waterfront politics during the thirties and forties influenced him must begin with discussion of Benny Carwardine. Understanding his political orientation is vital to this study because of his deep and lasting imprint on Green's interpretation of thirties and forties Bay Area maritime politics. By extension, Green's experience of maritime politics, and the ideological loyalties woven through his analysis of Harry Bridges and Harry Lundeberg, shaped his philosophical and political commitments for more than seventy years.

Carwardine, like most seasoned shipwrights Green encountered at Western Pipe and Steel, was a "Clydesider," a term that can refer to radicals from all over the west coast of Scotland. More often, *Clydesider* specifically designates Scottish shipbuilders who learned their craft on the docks of the river Clyde outside Glasgow.[15] Clydesiders were vital to British naval production in World War I, but after the war reduced production drove many to emigrate to the United States. Revered for their engineering skills, Clydesiders were equally known for their unique brand of militant industrial unionism and Scottish cultural pride. "They were blue collar, overall wearing, whiskey drinking, haggis eating, and camber throwing," Green recalled. "They went to the Scottish games. They would go out to the St. Andrew's Society and recite Robert

Burns. I can't express the amount of admiration I had for these men: salt of the earth, good mechanics, revolutionists, and nationalists—proud of one's heritage."[16] As he suggests, the mentorship was not limited to craft and politics but style and manner as well. As veteran Clydesider Andy Mahon, told him, "If you want to be a shipwright, you've got to look like a shipwright." That meant white cap, blue overalls and always your union button.[17] Green frequently and energetically highlighted Carwardine's and other Clydesiders' influence, and when he did so he quickly emphasized that Carwardine's political education, like that of many other immigrant Scottish shipwrights, stemmed from association with the legendary Scottish socialist John Maclean.

Maclean was a teacher and Marxist revolutionary who devoted all his spare time to educating the industrial workers of Scotland, notably the Clydesiders. Early in his career Maclean embraced the "founding father" of British social democracy, Henry Hyndman, who advocated the primacy of political education as the means for achieving social revolution.[18] Maclean began offering courses in the basics of Marxist economics to shipyard workers, and after participating in the 1907 Belfast dock strike began to espouse a form of industrial militancy that questioned the tenets of British social democracy.[19] The critical divide grew, and, as with Rosa Luxemburg, the events of World War I definitively turned him away from social democracy.

Maclean became quite famous for his outspoken resistance to the war. His criticisms of British militarism as imperialist led to being arrested three times and advanced his heroic stature among workers. During this period Maclean founded the Scottish Labour College. With the exception of his unequivocal anti-imperialist position, historians differ on the character of Maclean's political philosophy between the World War I and his death in 1923. Some deemphasize his turn to Scottish nationalism whereas others highlight it as a defining contribution.[20] For our purposes, it is important to have a sense of how Carwardine underscored for Green that John Maclean combined commitments to syndicalism, communism, and Scottish nationalism.

Within the shop stewards' movements of Clydebank during the war, syndicalism exerted tremendous influence on shipbuilders.[21] A branch of Daniel DeLeon's Socialist Labor Party (SLP) in Scotland had encouraged shipbuilders since 1903 to embrace a syndicalist political philosophy. Many Clydesiders adopted the SLP's strain of syndicalism, which emphasized the revolutionary potential of building worker control on shop floors. The belief was that transforming social relations at the point of production would have the greatest revolutionary impact on the larger social structure.[22] DeLeon's followers were less interested in, if not averse to, labor trying to build strength through

Parliament. John Maclean shared that syndicalist vision of direct action and worker autonomy. He stayed committed, however, to the need for worker organizing on the political and electoral front as well. For decades Maclean played a central role in the British Socialist Party, which after the October Revolution became a springboard for the establishment of the Communist Party of Great Britain (CPGB).

According to John McHugh and B. J. Ripley, Maclean was always committed to his vision of the Communist International—the international wing of the Bolshevik Party. His personal differences with its leaders, however, combined with his commitment to an autonomous Scottish communist party, alienated him from the CPGB. Instead of supporting it, Maclean devoted his energies to founding the Scottish Workers Republican Party in 1921, an organization that combined communism with a movement for Scottish independence. The call for independence stemmed in part from Maclean's view that British imperialism was the greatest threat to the new Russian workers' state.[23] His admiration for the Bolsheviks, however, was not unqualified. He strongly criticized aspects of the relationship between Moscow and the CPGB, saying in 1920 that "the [British] Communist Party has sold itself to Moscow with disastrous results both to the Russian and the British Revolution."[24] Such criticism had much to do with Maclean's suspicion that the CPGB depended on money from Russia.[25]

In 1941, in the yard of Western Pipe and Steel, Benny Carwardine spoke to Green about his personal relationship with John Maclean. Although I have found no information documenting the nature of their friendship, it is likely that Carwardine as a young worker-student met Maclean in one of his hugely popular courses on Marxism. Maclean's courses and public lectures during the war would sometimes draw more than two thousand participants.[26] In addition, Maclean frequently consulted weekly delegate meetings of the Clyde Workers Committee (CWC), the central organizing body of the shop stewards' movement in the Scottish shipyards. Whether Carwardine attended the CWC in person or was influenced by its role in the larger movement, it is certain that he would have been exposed to the most pressing challenge of the CWC—how to link the concerns of skilled craft unionists with the newfound momentum for organizing unskilled workers.[27]

This challenge was, of course, not limited to the banks of the Clyde. In the United States the competing principles of craft and industrial unionism fueled the struggles between the traditional AFL and the emergent CIO. Benny Carwardine, who had since immigrated to the shipyards of northern California, found himself enmeshed in the struggle. He became a regional leader in the formation of Local 7 in the newly formed Industrial Union of Marine and Shipbuilding Workers of America (IUMSWA). Activist workers at the New York Shipbuilding Corporation in Camden, New Jersey, founded the IUMSWA in 1933.[28] John Green, who had also recently immigrated from Clydebank to the United States, significantly contributed to this unprecedented campaign and became the union's first president. The IUMSWA was an independent industrial union that later became a charter member of the CIO. Much of its leadership associated with the Revolutionary Policy Committee (RPC), a left-wing faction of the Socialist Party that challenged old guard leaders such as Morris Hillquit. According to David Palmer, who has written the only book on the IUMSWA, John Green and the RPC were critical of the Communist Party's Third Period uncompromising suspicion of the U.S. government. In the eyes of Communists at the time, that qualified the RPC as "social fascists."[29]

The preamble to the first constitution of the IUMSWA, written in 1933, exhibits a unique blend of Wobbly syndicalism, social-democratic tendencies in the Socialist Party, and even language lifted directly from the Declaration of Independence.[30] The preamble is quoted here because this radical political syncretism expresses the orientation of Carwardine and many other Clydesiders such as Jock McGiver, Benny Dean, and Arthur Ross who mentored young Archie Green.

> We, Marine and Shipbuilding Workers of America, believing in the solidarity of all workers, irrespective of race, color, creed or national origin, hereby declare our purpose of joining in one strong union to win our just demands for a fuller life, liberty and the pursuit of happiness. These rights are today denied us. Experience of the past has taught us that rights are not won without struggle. Through our Union we prepare ourselves for the Workers' struggle, not merely to win concessions of higher wages and shorter hours, but to abolish forever the system of exploitation that compels us to support with our labor an idle owning class.[31]

By the time Green began apprenticing with Carwardine in 1941 John Green had dissolved Local 7 of the IUMSWA. Local 7 ended in the context of the rapid expansion of the shipbuilding industries before World War II and fierce jurisdictional battles over which unions would represent the growing workforce. This is a complex history, and very little has been written about it. Its details extend beyond a focus on Green's political education, but some of the story is relevant for understanding why Green developed a scathing dislike for longshoreman Harry Bridges.

Correspondence from Bernard Mergen, longtime labor historian and an early scholar of the IUMSWA, succinctly captures these complicated twists.[32] Referring to Carwardine as president of Local 7 before it dissolved, Mergen observed, "Carwardine realized early on that they [Local 7] were a pawn in a bigger game being played for control of American labor by John L. Lewis, Harry Bridges, the AFL, and the Communists." With regard to the immediate jurisdictional union struggles of the San Francisco waterfront of the later thirties and forties and how Carwardine, and, by extension, Green, would view those contests, Mergen added, "On the West Coast, Bridges' ILWU and Harry Lundeberg's Sailors' Union of the Pacific (SUP) were vying for control of all maritime labor. Unemployed longshoremen and sailors often did shipbuilding and ship repair in competition with shipbuilders who belonged to the various craft unions, or, after 1935, to IUMSWA. John Green was suspicious of Bridges and favored Lundeberg, but he had to go along with Lewis and others who supported Bridges for tactical reasons. Carwardine, Archie Green, and all west coast shipyard workers had good reasons to hate Bridges. His union was poaching on their territory, he was Communist, and he wasn't a Scotsman." Finally, Mergen noted that after Local 7 was shut down "Carwardine and Archie Green had good reasons to hate John Green too."[33]

Mergen is right about Carwardine's animosity toward John Green. Carwardine's challenges to the IUMSWA leadership had, in fact, resulted in him being blacklisted from working in the San Francisco shipyards. Western Pipe and Steel so desperately needed experienced shipbuilders to oversee ramped-up war production that it disregarded the blacklisting and gave Carwardine a special foreman role that was not under the jurisdiction of the AFL Carpenter's local (No. 1149) that now represented workers.[34] While he was an independent foreman at Western Pipe and Steel, Carwardine began mentoring Green. Their work focused on early steps in the iron shipbuilding process—measuring out template battens that would guide construction of a hull.[35]

The stories of John Maclean, socialist Clydesiders, and workers like Benny Carwardine who brought a particular radical genealogy and sensibility to the shipyards of the United States are essential to understanding Archie Green because they form a foundation to Green's own political amalgam of syndicalism, New Deal social democracy, cultural sovereignty, and virulent anticommunism. Looking back on his first years as a shipwright apprentice, Green said, "I consciously or unconsciously modeled myself after Benny," and then added, "In many ways, the rest of my life, I've continued to try and maintain his triangle of commitments."[36] By "triangle of commitments," Green meant:

- the practice of and reverence for excellent craftsmanship;
- upholding an independent socialist radicalism (foundational to Green's anticommunism);
- and celebrating Scottish nationalism, which for Green translated more broadly into an unwavering conviction for cultural sovereignty and deeply pluralist societies.[37]

Later chapters expand upon and connect all three commitments. In the next chapter it is important to offer more perspective on how these principles assist in making sense of Green's experience of waterfront politics in the 1940s. As with his mentor Benny Carwardine, Green's admiration for skilled crafts did not entail rejection of industrial unionism. Quite the contrary, as on the Clydebank, admiration for craft fused with a syndicalist advocacy of organizing all workers through an industrial union vision. The implications of that vision, with its independent socialist and culturally pluralist positions, return us to the San Francisco waterfront, specifically, to the legendary battle between the two Harrys.

Chapter 5 "Brother Slugging Brother"

Sailors, Longshoremen, and Legacies of the '34 Strike

Young workers who arrived in the Bay Area in the early forties to labor in the expanding maritime industries encountered a highly politicized generation of veteran waterfront workers that have come to be known as the "thirty-four men." In the wake of the Depression, and emboldened by the 1933 shift in federal government policy supporting union representation, workers across the country organized for union recognition, higher wages, and greater shop-floor control. This 1934 surge of activism produced general strikes in Toledo, Minneapolis, and San Francisco. In turn, these strikes catalyzed an era of worker militancy, the age of the CIO, that would last through World War II and into the late forties.[1] On the West Coast, the thirty-four men were maritime workers—predominantly longshoremen and sailors—who sustained an eighty-three-day strike in the face of brutal employer and state violence. The Big Strike, as it came to be known, produced new forms of worker solidarity, new forms of political consciousness, and new rank-and-file union leaders who would come to symbolize those advancements. Harry Bridges and Harry Lundeberg, two workers who would ultimately become union presidents, were the most legendary, controversial, beloved, and despised militants of the San Francisco waterfront.

Their careers, in combination with the politics of the different maritime unions they led, have been examined by historians of the dramatic events constituting Bay Area waterfront political history after 1934.[2] Those histories are significant to this study for two reasons. First, it was a complicated terrain of events and personalities into which Archie Green stepped when he began waterfront work in 1941. Second, Bridges and Lundeberg, two union leaders who became arch-enemies, acted out central roles in a sustained morality play through which Green understood and communicated his own political identity. Green regularly referred to the men. It is unrealistic to overview waterfront political history in this period but essential to have some feel for the jurisdictional and ideological battle of the two Harrys. In order to do so I first summarize the Big Strike of 1934 and then discuss the politics of the pathbreaking maritime coalition forged out of the strike—the Maritime Federation of the Pacific Coast (MFPC). The chapter concludes with a characterization of the aggressive feud between the two Harrys that, after disintegration of the MFPC, took on an infamous life of its own.[3]

Nearly seventy-five years after these events, Green still frequently discussed the high stakes and enduring implications of waterfront politics in the Bay Area during the thirties and forties. He may not have been on the waterfront for the two big strikes of the thirties, but the still-cooling lava of those two volcanic episodes confronted him when he arrived in 1941. Exemplified through Benny Carwardine, Green knew many sailors, longshoremen, and shipwrights who experienced the waterfront firsthand during the thirties. Like many of these veterans, Green interpreted labor struggles in a very specific, unequivocal manner. His interpretations must be understood in light of four factors:

- the particular vein of socialism advocated by his Jewish-Ukrainian parents;
- his experiences in the college student politics of the late thirties ;
- the political orientation of his Scottish shipbuilding mentor Benny Carwardine;
- and, finally, how Green's folk music scholarship after the war solidified his critical assessment of the cultural politics of the Communist Party during the thirties and forties.

Some historical literature supports Green's interpretations of Bay Area waterfront politics in the thirties. Other scholarship refutes his claims. Given that opposing, discrepant historical accounts, and resulting interpretative legacies, are largely the product of the pragmatic and ideological loyalties of their authors, some of Green's opinions of Harry Bridges and Harry Lundeberg were sound and some were questionable. What is of interest is why he held such opinions and how they relate with his other political and intellectual commitments.

* * *

The pro-business, open-shop climate of the postwar era decimated waterfront unions such as the International Longshoremen's Association (ILA). A concerted assault by industry and government left many San Francisco maritime workers frustrated with the company-backed organizations called "Blue Book" unions. Rampant antiunionism, however, could not fully abolish longstanding radical traditions on the waterfront. The extensive studies of Howard Kimeldorf and Bruce Nelson both illustrate how, particularly on the Pacific Coast, the syndicalism of the Wobblies endured the conservative twenties and made an important contribution to the surge in worker militancy during the thirties.[4] One example can be found in the 1933 formation of a caucus of longshoremen who were interested in fostering rank-and-file leadership in the newly resurrected ILA. Based on the location of their meetings, the caucus was known as the Albion Hall group, and Harry Bridges was one of their most intelligent and outspoken members.[5] Bridges was Australian by birth, but at sixteen he left home as a merchant seaman. Joining the Australian sailor's union and briefly the IWW, he was exposed at sea to the syndicalist emphasis on building worker control at the job site. In 1922 Bridges settled down to do longshore work in San Francisco.[6] At this point no one could foresee that he would become one of most celebrated and controversial labor leaders in U.S. history.

Bridges and his coworkers in the Albion Hall group supported an ILA referendum conducted in March 1934 that called for a coastwide strike. The overwhelming vote, 6,616 in favor and 699 opposed, set the stage for the Big Strike and reflected the extent to which Albion Hall, in concert with organizing efforts of the Communist Party, influenced stevedores along the Pacific Coast. During the nearly three-month strike, Bridges became the predominant voice and symbol of longshoremen militancy. Bruce Nelson emphasizes that his leadership should be understood as "very much a product of the rank-and-file movement." Nelson also gathers considerable evidence to confirm that Bridges was an extremely smart and charismatic worker who "became the stevedores' spokesman through his unique 'ability to verbalize their yearnings and concretize their goal.'"[7]

Longshoremen initiated the strike but their position was significantly strengthened in the second week of the conflict when West Coast sailors officially joined them. Like the longshoremen, the West Coast sailors had seen a severe weakening of their union during the 1920s. By 1934, aggressive tactics by ship owners to control hiring halls combined with the growth of other, competitive East Coast maritime unions to significantly lower numbers within the AFL-affiliated Sailors' Union of the Pacific (SUP).[8] Nonetheless, SUP sailors drew from a longstanding pride in skill best symbolized by their mythical president, Andrew Furuseth, and a tradition of job actions rooted in the rich syndicalist culture of Norwegian sailors, one of whom was Harry Lundeberg.

Lundeberg was born in Oslo in 1901 to parents actively involved in the Norwegian labor movement. Drawn to the sea, he began deck work at fifteen and by twenty had sailed much of the world. After stints in the Norwegian Seaman's Union and the Seaman's Union of Australia, he signed on in 1923 to a Seattle local of the SUP. Like Bridges, Lundeberg's early years at sea exposed him to a variety of militant work cultures, often Wobbly-influenced, that stressed the importance of direct action at a work site. When the West Coast longshoremen struck in May 1934, Lundeberg was one of the fifty-four Seattle sailors who voted unanimously against the pressure of their international and in favor of supporting the strike.

The '34 strike produced relationships of solidarity that workers in West Coast maritime had never seen but for which they had long yearned. "After more than three decades of craft separation," writes Nelson, "the militants' dream of maritime unity had emerged as a powerful reality during the strike."[9] The conclusion of the strike nearly dashed those hopes. Against the wishes of Bridges, the longshoremen agreed to arbitration whereas the sailors were committed to maintaining the pickets. Ultimately, on July 31, a day after sailors ritualistically burned their company "fink books" in a bonfire outside the Sailor's Union hall, they joined the longshoremen in returning to work.

Gains of the '34 strike were at first uneven. The longshoremen, for example, won sole right to select job dispatchers well before the sailors gained full control of their hiring halls. Although the immediate benefits of arbitration varied, Nelson argues that the most significant outcome of the strike was a coastwide "syndicalist renaissance" in which on-the-spot work stoppages proliferated and the basic power struggle between worker and employer shifted toward worker advantage for years to come. The fullest expression of this newly galvanized union solidarity was the creation of the Maritime Federation of the Pacific Coast (MFPC) in 1935. Bridges and other members of the Albion Hall group broadcast their vision of such a coalition through the rank-and-file newspaper *Waterfront Worker*. The MFPC can be viewed as a CIO-era experiment in building industrial unionism within maritime industries where divisive craft union loyalties had traditionally thrived. Sadly, the experiment would prove short-lived. Opposing interpretations of the MFPC's break-up are important to this project because they revolve around the struggle of the two Harrys and, ultimately, help explain Green's veneration of Lundeberg and abhorrence for Bridges.

When an April 1935 convention in Seattle established the MFPC, Harry Bridges endorsed Harry Lundeberg for president of the federation, and Lundeberg defeated several conservative rivals for the position. At the time he was a relatively unknown SUP patrolman, but his courageous actions during the strike had garnered Bridges's respect. Lundeberg quickly demonstrated his capacity as a union leader.[10] He would soon become president of the SUP and lead it through a defining period of independence as it rejected affiliation with the growing CIO after having been expelled by the increasingly reactionary, AFL-affiliated International Sailor's Union. Despite its One Big Union motto—"An Injury to One Is an Injury to All"—the federation between 1935 and 1938 would crumble under the weight of jurisdictional disputes (reflective of old craft loyalties), contract discrepancies, and, most notably, an intensifying battle between the trade unionist strategies and ideologies of Bridges and Lundeberg.[11]

There are reasons to think that the men could have been supportive allies. Both began sailing internationally at a young age and absorbed a syndicalist political sensibility through contact with militant sailor cultures around the world. Both went on to become presidents of their unions and, within the same two-year period, lead those unions to independence from previous international affiliations. Lundeberg's SUP briefly broke away from the AFL, and Bridges, in 1937, helped establish the International Longshoremen's and Warehouse Union (ILWU) which left the ILA and quickly joined the CIO.[12] Bridges in 1934 described Lundeberg as "a fine trade unionist."[13] In this same period, many sailors "warmly received" Bridges when he appealed to them at the SUP hall in October 1935 to preserve MFPC unity.[14]

These anecdotes, however, are now obscure, lost behind the densely clouded smoke of a two-decade fiery feud. By 1936 differences over the role of job actions, efficacy of government arbitration, and connection to the Communist Party spoiled relations between Lundeberg and Bridges. That rift found its primary expression through never-ending mudslinging between stevedores and sailors over the presumed, devious communist agenda of Bridges and the reported gangster racketeering of Lundberg's sailors. As Green remembered, maritime workers commonly exclaimed, "This waterfront isn't big enough for two Harrys."

The lines in this infamous battle of San Francisco labor leaders are drawn in blood, and few participant accounts of the era attempt, let alone succeed, in transcending partisan loyalty to one of the sides. Expressive of the worst sectarianism of the Old Left, most sailors' accounts of Bridges and the ILWU reduce their history unequivocally to "Stalinism," and most longshoremen's accounts of Lundeberg and the SUP come back again and again to tales of "goon squads" and "gangsterism." The official SUP history written by Stephen Schwartz in 1986 reads at times like a manual in red-baiting. Although not as hyperbolic, the ILWU's publication, *The Dispatcher*, abounds in demagogic portrayals of Lundeberg.[15]

Two studies stand out as the best examples of scholarship attempting to break from these partisan tendencies: Bruce Nelson's detailed study of maritime political history in the thirties, *Workers on the Waterfront*, and Jane Record's 1955 dissertation, "Ideologies and Trade Union Leadership: The Case of Harry Bridges and Harry Lundeberg."[16] Both studies detail the leaders' strengths and weaknesses. The authors relay episodes of both acting in an autocratic manner but do so within a framework that recognizes that each leader sustained a courageous, lifelong commitment to improving the conditions of waterfront workers. As her title indicates, Record focuses on their distinct political philosophies and asks if those ideologies were expressed in the men's day-to-day choices.

Record establishes that Bridges and Lundeberg at times articulated "diametrically opposed perspectives concerning the role of the state in social reform," but their leadership behaviors over time indicate more commonality than one would think.[17] Bridges "view[ed] political action as a primary instrument—if, indeed, not *the* primary instrument—of social change. He welcome[d] the expansion of government ownership; he often called for the establishment of a labor party."[18] As a result, for much of his early career Bridges advocated NLRB arbitration and settlement of labor disputes. By contrast, Lundeberg "recoil[ed] from any suggestion of government arbitration for the industry, let alone government ownership; he consider[ed] the idea of a labor party to be ridiculous."[19] He believed that "shipowners, as bad as they are, are still to be preferred to government bureaucrats."[20] These differences manifested in friction between the ILWU and the SUP in the late thirties as each union's leadership argued over the degree to which job actions should be regulated within the Maritime Federation of the Pacific Coast. Lundeberg's view, expressed in a 1935 editorial from the federation's paper, was unwavering: "How to plan job action is NEVER DECIDED BY COMMITTEES OR CONFERENCES AND NEVER WILL BE. The workers on the job know best when the time is right for job action. . . . Those who try to put job action in committee's hands or in conferences are people who are trying their damnedness to kill the seaman's strongest weapon."[21]

Record's emphasis is that neither leader maintained consistency in actual leadership decisions (as opposed to ideological rhetoric). For both Harry Bridges and Harry Lundeberg, "Principle yield[ed] readily to expediency." From a long historic perspective, their maneuvers to expand union numbers, squash internal dissension, and, retain tight control over their respective unions make them more alike than different. As Record concludes:

> In large areas of their behavior there has been little to distinguish the one from the other—or the two taken together from the typical orthodox union chief. Both Bridges and Lundeberg have vigorously defended their jurisdictional borders—and just as vigorously invaded those of rival organizations. Each, once firmly in control of his union's government, has displayed impatience toward dissent. One might have expected Lundeberg's anarcho-syndicalist leanings to result in a consistently particularist position and Bridges's Stalinist orientation in a consistently centralist stand. One finds, however, that Lundeberg has behaved as a states-righter in union coalitions and as a federalist in internal government; whereas Bridges, despite a centralist bent in most of his interunion and intraunion relations, invoked the precept of local autonomy when the ILWU found itself in a minority position within the CIO after the Second World War. Principle appears to yield readily to expediency in this sphere.[22]

When Green arrived on the waterfront in January 1941, the Maritime Federation of the Pacific Coast was officially still alive, its ambitious vision having ended in June 1938 when Lundeberg's SUP withdrew. Many discrepant historical accounts exist of what led to the dissolve, most are organized around loyalty to Bridges or to Lundeberg. Bruce Nelson's study serves as an effective check for discussion of several episodes from this era that regularly surface in the crossfire between SUP and ILWU defenders, Green included.

In 1937, with Furuseth's International Seamen's Union attempting to crush the SUP, Lundeberg and his sailors faced the question of who to affiliate with nationally. The CIO was growing rapidly at this time and working to establish dominance in maritime industries. Initially, Lundeberg supported CIO affiliation for the SUP but changed course when it became clear that Bridges was warming up to John L. Lewis and would likely take the Pacific District of the ILA into the CIO. A referendum vote had already been put to the SUP on whether to affiliate with the CIO. Several historical accounts concur that the sailors voted overwhelmingly to join the CIO. The exact numbers will never be known because the SUP's leadership nullified the ballots, or, as is more commonly described in circles critical of the SUP, Lundeberg burned them.

Stephen Schwartz's official history of the SUP does not in any way discuss this event. Ottilie Markholt's detailed, SUP-sympathetic history, states that a June 14 SUP headquarters meeting voted to "hold up the results of the referendum ballot" and that several weeks later branch meetings "voted to burn the ballots."[23] All accounts agree that rabid anticommunism was emerging in the SUP, and Lundeberg wanted to steer clear of what he saw as the increasingly CP-influenced Bridges and CIO. Accounts vary considerably, however, in terms of explaining Lundeberg's action. Markholt, working from the assumption that anything connected to the Communist Party should be understood as antidemocratic, implies that disqualifying the referendum was a way to protect SUP rank-and-file democracy from outside forces, specifically the "Communist bloc." ILWU historian Harvey Schwartz sees it differently: "Markholt's anti-Communist bias leads her to rationalize one of the era's most embarrassing episodes. In 1937 Harry Lundeberg and his fellow SUP officers burned their union members referendum ballots on possible affiliation with the CIO. . . . Thus Lundeberg, who ultimately stifled union democracy in the SUP to a degree unimaginable to a democratic leader like Bridges, remains an unimpeachable figure in Markholt's mind."[24]

Benny Carwardine was shipbuilding on the waterfront in the midst of the escalating struggle between Bridges and Lundeberg several years before Green showed up to work on the docks. Carwardine astutely pointed out that "opposition to the CIO on the west coast is now based on personal opposition to Bridges, and even more, on antagonism to the Communist Party . . . all enemies of Bridges and his faction have now automatically become enemies of the CIO."[25] With a tinge of pride Green often remarked that Carwardine was one of the first on the waterfront to write criticisms of Harry Bridges. Given his education under John Maclean, it makes sense that Carwardine would be particularly sensitized to the relationship of the Communist Party with trade unions. He objected to CP influence on the waterfront and, like so many in the anti-Communist left, projected Bridges as the embodiment of this trend. Green fully adopted Carwardine's anti-Communist, anti-Bridges perspective. Events on the waterfront in the late thirties are just one dimension of Green's critique of the CP, but they form a cornerstone of his politics and are effectively revealed in his interpretation of the famous "*Shepard Line* beef."[26]

The MFPC, despite a seemingly continuous series of crises since its inception, survived through another major maritime strike in 1936–37. The strike preserved many gains of the 1934 strike and advanced SUP control of the hiring process. In terms of the life of the MFPC, however, the future did not seem hopeful. Escalating inter-union conflicts significantly threatened the federation's vision of solidarity, a process that culminated in a series of events in the spring of 1938 known as the *Shepard Line* beef.

The *Shepard Line* beef centered on a contest over what maritime union rightfully held a contract with the bicoastal Shepard Line Freight Company. The SUP claimed jurisdiction over all Shepard Line boats based on a closed-shop agreement signed in 1937. However, the National Maritime Union (NMU), a fast-growing, CIO-sponsored maritime union based on the East Coast, had won an NLRB election for representation on all East Coast shipping lines. On April 19, 1938, the jurisdictional battle culminated when fifty-four ILWU longshoremen, ostensibly supporting their fellow CIO workers, violently broke through an SUP picket line protesting the presence of an NMU crew on the newly arrived *Sea Thrush*, a Shepard Line freighter. A hefty police presence aligned with the longshoremen. Standing at the entrance to Pier 41, Lundeberg stressed to his sailors that this was a battle for "protection of seaman's hiring halls."[27] He also provided fifty baseball bats to assist them in the brawl with longshoremen that followed.[28] In an often-quoted reflection on the battle, MFPC secretary John Kucin lamented, "Who struck the first blow, no one will ever know and each side blames the other. The fact remains that regardless of who was right or who was wrong we found brother slugging brother. Men who were the best of friends before, became bitter enemies latter. Men who had suffered side by side and stood shoulder to shoulder on other picket lines now were battering each other down."[29] Markholt, who devotes a full chapter to the Shepard Line beef, maintains that the violence of the longshoremen emblemized the larger intent of the Communist Party to attain control of all maritime unions through raiding.[30] Similarly, Stephen Schwartz writes, "In the Shepard controversy the Communist faction in the C.I.O. had united with the employers, and with the police, to fight the S.U.P."[31] Green agreed with Markholt and Schwartz.

These interpretations express Lundeberg's assessment of the growing threat of communism on the waterfront. Shortly after the *Shepard Line* beef, the SUP withdrew from the MFPC. This move encapsulates what would become Lundeberg's defining motivation through the 1940s: protecting SUP autonomy from outside control (read: Communists) under the banner of tried and true syndicalism. Ironically, this "path of independence" was untenable in the heated jurisdictional strife of the time, and the SUP was forced to reaffiliate with the AFL.[32] Nelson maintains that "although the rhetoric of syndicalism remained more or less constant, in practice the SUP was moving toward the hardheaded business unionism of Andrew Furuseth and the AFL."[33] That certainly became the opinion of Harry Bridges and many longshoremen. In a 1952 reflection on waterfront events between 1936 and 1938, Bridges claimed that Lundeberg had teamed with the president of the Waterfront Employers Association, T. G. (Tear Gas) Plant, to undermine maritime solidarity. "[Plant] worked with Lundeberg to split the strike and the strike program of the Maritime Federation of the Pacific."[34]

For the next twenty years the ILWU's *Dispatcher* consistently portrayed Lundeberg as a "fifth column" support for ship owners. Among a litany of accusations, Lundeberg was viewed as befriending Sen. Robert Taft in the pursuit of stacking an anti-Communist NLRB, hiring goon squads to violently discipline dissenting sailors and other threatening trade unionists, and (indisputably) maintaining racist hiring practices that barred African Americans for decades from working deck and engine room departments. Bridges's long-time claims that Lundeberg was "running a machine dictatorially crushing worker autonomy" found judicial support in 1951 when a Seattle judge ruled in favor of John Mahoney, who had been expelled from the SUP for refusing to break through the picket line of an independent sailors union.[35] Those criticisms of Lundeberg and the culture of the SUP are not found in Markholt's or Stephen Schwartz's histories. As for Archie Green's oral history of the era, he knew well the history of SUP racism and would make passing references to the hired thugs of the waterfront. His primary focus, however, was on critiquing the enemy—Harry Bridges and the Communist Party. In his long, ninety-one-year life filled at every turn with engaging conversations, few rhetorical battles were returned to as frequently or with more zeal. Green, like SUP-allied historians such as Markholt and Schwartz, constantly criticized the "Stalinist" orientation of Harry Bridges, the ILWU, and the Communist Party.

Chapter 6 Harry Bridges and Reconsiderations of Communist Party History

Americans are well aware of the tradition of demonizing the Soviet Union and the Communist Party that liberal, conservative, and reactionary forces promulgated through much of the twentieth century. The famous faces of this history are Richard Nixon, Joseph McCarthy, and Ronald Reagan. Much less known is the history of critiquing the Soviet Union and the Communist International rooted in left politics, whether socialist, Marxist-Leninist, or anarchist. This left tradition of critique is far from homogenous and is referred to in various ways. My preferred reference is "left anticommunism."[1] One genealogy of left anticommunism can be traced to the Trotsky-associated left Opposition, a political position that believed Stalin, after Lenin's death in 1924, began to destroy the truly revolutionary Bolshevik Party Lenin had led. In order to do that, Stalin had to defeat and discredit another prominent Bolshevik, Leon Trotsky. The followers of Trotsky defined themselves—and continue to do so—as the true heirs of Lenin's authentically radical program.[2] Other genealogies of left anticommunism identify with Wobbly history or the social-democratic tradition.[3]

It may now seem distant and obscure to grapple with the early history of the Soviet Union, but it is vital to recognize that for Green's generation of the Old Left the question of the nature of the Soviet state was the paramount political concern. It was that question which caused Grace Lee Boggs to feel disengaged from her first meeting of the Workers Party. Those who worked on the San Francisco waterfront in the thirties, however, likely had their position on this issue colored by how they interpreted local labor upsurges as well as other consequential world events such as the Spanish civil war. Trotskyism, for example, strongly influenced SUP members on issues ranging from policies of the MFPC to the Bolshevik-led massacre at Kronstadt.[4]

The anti-Communist left is most commonly associated with Trotskyist parties, but not everyone who identified with this critical position was affiliated with the Trotskyist Socialist Workers Party or its offshoots. "Was Archie a Trot?" many have asked. He was not. But given the passion and frequency with which Green condemned the Communist Party it is understandable why people make this connection. Although never a party member, Green was, without doubt, influenced by the Trotskyist political perspectives of the waterfront.

Before U.S. entrance into World War II, Trotskyist critiques on the waterfront revolved around two themes. The first, the purported antidemocratic nature of Communist-associated unions, grew out of the more general belief that these unions followed directives from Moscow. That critique closely links with an attitude that Communist-associated unions, which for Green most immediately meant the ILWU, would go to any length to build their numbers through raiding other union's workforces. The second common theme was that Trotskyists argued the class-collaborationist nature of Communist-influenced trade unionism. That critique again grew out of more general disapproval with the Communist Party's shift from the dual unionism of the Third Period to a priority on coalition-building during the United Front–Popular Front. As Tom Kerry, a Trotskyist, maintains, "Every aspect of 'Communist' Party politics is designed to suck the workers into the camp of their class enemies. If there are only two kinds of politics, working class and boss class, then, by definition, a 'People's Front' of the two classes is a betrayal of the workers."[5] In the specific context of the waterfront, that critique is found in repeated attacks on Harry Bridges's embrace of government arbitration to determine work contracts.[6] Asher Harer, a long-time SWP member and dissident ILWU longshoreman, stresses in his essay "The Trouble with Harry Bridges" that Bridges too willingly accepted compulsory government arbitration to protect gains made in the 1934 strike.[7] Of these two recurring critiques, Green only shared the first. He consistently portrayed Bridges as exercising authoritarian control over the ILWU and framed that as an extension of subservience to policies of the CP. I never, however, heard Green emphasize that Harry Bridges was a class-collaborationist, perhaps because Green's New Deal sensibility upheld compromise through arbitration.

By the late thirties the pressing question for the left, and the nation as a whole, was whether the United States should involve itself in another European war. In that context, Trotskyist critiques of the CP shifted toward focusing on the severe vacillations of the CP on the war question. Trotskyists argued that the clearest proof of American Communist subservience to

Moscow was the sequence of reversals in their attitude toward World War II. Communists, they emphasized, went from spearheading the antifascist build-up in the Popular Front (1935–39), to condemning any involvement in war as imperialist after the Hitler-Stalin Pact of August 22, 1939, to, finally, following Hitler's June 1941 attacks on Russia, advocating a full-bore war effort. Based on these events, Trotskyists claimed Harry Bridges's promotion of a plan to increase war production and pledge to not strike was simultaneously class-collaborationist, supportive of imperialism, and representative of a disavowal of rank-and-file militant unionism.[8] Green, like most critics of the CP whether from the left or right, stressed the party's inconsistency during this period, by far the most emphasized and widely shared critique of the left anti-Communists. Unlike Trotskyists, however, Green used these inconsistencies only to support his claims of the hierarchical and authoritarian culture within the CP. He did not subscribe to the Trotskyist appraisal of the war as imperialist but supported U.S. intervention.

In terms of industrial unionism, Green's particular strain of left anticommunism was grounded in a commitment to rank-and-file democracy. The anarcho-syndicalism of the Wobblies was his ideal—an ideal well circulated by the older Scottish seamen working the shipyards when Green arrived in 1941. He often spoke angrily about the gulags and imperialism of the Soviet Union, but his critique of the party in the United States had more to do with his interpretation of its relationship to the working class. It was, Green believed, fundamentally utilitarian. He insisted that the predominantly middle-class, intellectual party leaders and bureaucrats viewed the working class as a population to recruit and co-opt in the pursuit of party expansion, an orientation that rubbed him as audacious, elitist, and, at root, a betrayal.

As Green's friend and collaborator Franklin Rosemont has documented, this attitude toward Communists was pervasive in Wobbly circles.[9] The IWW "was wholly sympathetic to the Bolshevik Revolution and its leading figures" from 1917 to 1921, Rosemont maintains, but after 1921 "many Wobs were troubled by the increasingly statist character of the Revolution, and by the consequently diminished role of the workers' own organizations."[10] Furthermore, Rosemont specifies that Wobbly criticisms were born out of the fusion of political, cultural, and aesthetic aversions to the party. In that respect Rosemont's interpretation, which Green respected and shared, is central to understanding Green's deep-seated aversion to Stalinism:

> The Wobbly expose of . . . Stalinism tended to avoid gossip and *ad hominem* attacks, and stuck to essentials: the Communists' massive ignorance of the U.S.

> working class; the Party's naïve and muddled misconceptions of Marxism; its servile acceptance of each and every dictate from Russian bureaucrats whose understanding of the U.S. workers' movement was even more defective than its own; and, by no means least, its obnoxious bullying arrogance and cynical disregard for proletarian democracy. Much more than "style" is involved here, but it is not without interest that the style of the IWW—as characterized by rank-and-file democracy ("We're *all* leaders!"), spontaneity, direction action, playfulness, songs, and humor—had virtually *nothing in common* with that of the CP, with its overriding emphasis on the Central Committee, authority, obedience, total control, and that holy-of-holies, the "Correct Line."[11]

Green drew from this twofold critique—both political and aesthetic—and reserved his fiercest denunciations of the party for the manner in which it related to American folk artists, beginning in the Popular Front era.

As a labor historian, Green was not ignorant of the fact that Communists vitally contributed to building sectors of the American labor movement. He expressed respect, for example, for the party's overall commitment to championing African American rights, in glaring contrast to the long-time, racist exclusion practiced by the SUP and his own Carpenter's Union. But even as he honored the CP's support for the Scottsboro Boys' defense and the role of the CP in winning inclusion of African Americans in the CIO he pointed to the aftermath of the Port Chicago explosion as a reason to question the degree of party commitment to African Americans.

On July 17, 1944, at the Port Chicago Naval base north of the San Francisco Bay, an ammunition explosion killed 320 people—202 of whom were black ammunition loaders. The U.S. Navy was still segregated at the time. All commissioned officers at Port Chicago were white, and every man who handled ammunition loading was black. Just three weeks after the tragedy more than three hundred surviving ammunition loaders were ordered to stock another ship. They refused the order, and officers responded by detaining 258 of them on a nearby barge. "Eventually," writes Robert Allen, "fifty men were singled out, charged with mutiny, court-martialed, convicted, and handed sentences ranging from eight to fifteen years."[12]

The NAACP, whose chief council at the time was future U.S. Supreme Court justice Thurgood Marshall, claimed that the men had been imprisoned because of their race and led a campaign to overturn the verdict. All the sailors were granted clemency in 1946. When Marshall came to the Bay Area to speak on behalf of the campaign, Green attended the public meeting with fellow shipyard worker Ray Thompson, an African American and member of the Communist Party. The CP at the time was vigorously advancing no-strike pledges aimed at securing wartime production. According to Green, Thompson reported that black communists were angry with the CP for withholding support for "mutineers" based on their priority of backing the war effort. Thompson decided to leave the CP because, he maintained, it betrayed black workers during the United Front. Green interpreted the aftermath of Port Chicago as evidence of his claim that the CP had utilitarian reasons for advancing African American rights. Similarly, Stan Weir, another vocal left anti-Communist of Green's generation, argues that the CP used "blacks as political footballs by patronizing them and using them."[13] This emphasis on instrumentality encapsulates many left anti-Communists' view of how the CP related with the working class.

Green and other left anti-Communists raise important questions about the CPUSA, whether in relation to waterfront politics of the post '34 strike or, more generally, dynamics on the American left. Their questions and accusations, however, are often accompanied by an ideological fervor that distorts the larger issue of the party's relation to trade unions and the directives of the Communist International. Like so many other forms of sectarianism, left anti-Communist diatriabes can begin to take on the attributes they fervently critique in others. As the anti-Communist historian Robert Zeiger has observed, "The fight by 'anti-Stalinist leftists' against the Communists and their allies in the CIO did not consist only of vigorous, democratic competition on the shop floor and in the union halls; rather, it was characterized by sordid episodes of reckless charges, personal violence and intimidation, and collaboration on the part of anti-communists with some of the most disreputable congressional witch hunters and anti-labor publications."[14] Zeiger's perspective is important because he highlights the contradictory, paradoxical record of left anti-Communists—a movement that birthed militant rank-and-file democratic organizing as well as reactionary racketeers. The best studies of the CPUSA, Harry Bridges, and the ILWU produce equally complex histories.

Since the mid-seventies a community of historians has challenged reductive assessments, whether from the left or the right, of the CPUSA.[15] The work of Robin D. G. Kelley, Maurice Isserman, Bert Cochran, Mark Naison, and Nell Irvin Painter refutes any uniform portrayal of rank-and-file Communists as lacking agency in the face of top-down directives from New York central committees or the Kremlin.[16] Although the studies do not speak directly to the politics of the San Francisco waterfront, they are useful in understanding and assessing Green's critique of Harry Bridges and the ILWU. They are also reminders that all historical assessments reflect the conditions within which they are produced. Archie Green worked from a definitively left anti-Communist position.

As Green recognized, "Waterfront history is encrusted in mythology."[17] By that he mostly meant a mythology of Harry Bridges that, from his perspective, wrongly elevated Bridges to a godlike status in the annals of progressive labor. Several comprehensive studies of Bridges and the ILWU, among them Jane Record's work, offer evidence of a leader who had admirable qualities and accomplishments as well as shortcomings and contradictions. Putting aside the debate of whether Bridges was actually a member of the Communist Party, many historians have concluded that he never relinquished control of the ILWU policy to the CP or any other outside political force.[18] Robert Cherny, the foremost scholar on Harry Bridges, argues that "he often did not do what the party wanted him to do, and when he went his own way—for instance, in taking the Pacific Coast ILA locals out of the AFL into the CIO—they promptly decided he was right and made his views or actions, or both, into party policy."[19] In addition, the University of Washington working group Union Democracy Reexamined (UDR) concludes that the ILWU had an uninterrupted "strong rank-and-file democracy, whose leaders are responsive and accountable to membership."[20] The UDR's statement is drawn from studies developed by Judith Stepan-Norris and Maurice Zeitlin in *Left Out: Reds and America's Industrial Unions* that extensively analyze union constitutions, levels of democratic contestation in convention proceedings, and electoral challenges to leadership.[21]

When Green, with valid skepticism, asked how the ILWU and Bridges could be democratic when Bridges held on to the presidency of the International for forty years the UDR study argued that "Harry Bridges and Louis Goldblatt were able to stay in power for so long because they were successful organizers, negotiators and strategists. They delivered improved wages, working conditions, and job security. Other unions' leaders also deliver material benefits and are popular among many members while relying on decidedly anti-democratic methods. Bridges and Goldblatt, on the other hand, built on contract success to construct a rank-and-file democracy. They did this by developing a set of rules that limited their power while empowering the members: the recall, direct elections of officers, and procedures by which members could voice their meaningful preferences about policy."[22] At the same time, the study says nothing of the lengthy fight Stan Weir led against Bridges to gain full union recognition for a group of longshoremen, the majority of them African American, known as "B-men." For Weir, a former sailor turned longshoreman and also a long-time friend of Green, Bridges's leadership of the ILWU represented the worst form of vanguard authoritarianism.[23]

I have no concern with trying to "get to the bottom" of the struggle between Harry Bridges and Harry Lundeberg. I simply maintain that in order to understand what colored Green's left oppositional interpretation of such struggles it is essential to understand the basic contours and culture of the political struggles taking place on the San Francisco waterfront during the thirties and forties as well as the particular circumstances of Green's life and the people and values he embraced. Many detractors of Harry Bridges and Harry Lundeberg share a tendency to exaggerate the authoritarianism of their opponents and, conversely, deify whomever they are loyal to, a tendency born of the need to survive politically—indeed, physically—in an atmosphere that carried significant consequences for having particular union loyalties.

With all the attention Green paid to the two Harrys of the waterfront it is easy to forget that he was not actually a member of either the SUP or the ILWU. In 1941 the workers at Western Pipe and Steel were organized through Local 1149 of the United Brotherhood of Carpenters and Joiners. The two Harrys may have vied for his ideological loyalty, but it was conservative union president William Hutcheson who unsuccessfully sought his vote.

Chapter 7 Union Service and Organizing World War II Veterans

The United Brotherhood of Carpenters and Joiners of America (UBCJA) dates back to the late nineteenth century. Instrumental in the founding of the AFL, the Brotherhood historically represented unwavering commitment to craft unionism as well as, for generations, the deeply racist culture that often accompanied such pride. On one hand, carpenters vitally contributed to the struggle for the eight-hour workday and helped sustain the AFL through its early embattled years. On the other, locals such as San Francisco's 22 enthusiastically supported successive Chinese Exclusion Acts.[1] David Roediger and Alexander Saxton offer critical, historical frameworks for seeing such histories as fundamentally related.[2] Skilled carpenters built social power—union power—through a cultural identity implicated in whiteness and the exclusion of other ethnic workers. Some of this contentious history played out in the CIO's late-thirties' affront to AFL craft unionism.

When John L. Lewis threw his famous right hook at the 1935 AFL convention it landed on the chin of William Hutcheson, the conservative, cocksure president of the UBCJA. The scuffle foreshadowed the looming contest over the shape of American unionism. Old Guard business unionists like Hutcheson felt that the push to organize the expanding industrial workforce was a threat to craft union strength. Ironically, the struggle catalyzed massive growth in the industrial sector for unions in both federations. As Paul Bullock notes, "Despite Hutcheson's misgivings and forebodings, the competition ultimately proved to be beneficial. Whenever the CIO even approached the Brotherhood's jurisdiction, the leaders reacted immediately and strongly. Fearful of encroachment by newly-organized CIO international unions, the UBCJA moved into industrial areas which it had never before sought to organize. In the process the union itself became relatively more industrial in character."[3] In northern California, the most heated jurisdictional battles occurred in the lumber and sawmill industries, but the waterfront was not immune to these tensions. The CIO made inroads with some UBCJA pile driver and shipbuilding locals. Dissident union organizers like Jack Wagner of Pile Drivers Local 34 led efforts to abandon the AFL.[4] Hutcheson responded with expulsions and an overall fortification of his control within the Carpenter's international.

When Green began working as a shipwright, the Bay Area waterfront writhed with the legacies of the 1934 and 1936–37 maritime strikes. These legacies, because they were in part organized around competing CIO and AFL loyalties, were not just about Harry Bridges and Harry Lundeberg. Other major union leaders like John L. Lewis, John Brophy, Andrew Furuseth, and William Hutcheson were involved. Benny Carwardine's leadership within the initially independent shipbuilder's local of the IUMSWA placed him in this pressure cooker of union affiliations. His political perspectives in the early 1940s bore the scars. Carwardine hated Hutcheson as much as he distrusted Bridges. Once again, his apprentice, Green, followed suit. "I took Benny's position," Green said, "which was to be anti-Huntcheson, anti-corruption, but also anti-Bridges, and this was early in my union career."[5] Green's animosity for Hutcheson was based on a critique of his antidemocratic machine politics and conservative Republican Party loyalties.

When I first began to interview Green, his enthusiasm for Wobbly syndicalism made it appear that he had kept his distance from the business unionism of the AFL and later CIO during a life of militant direct action and hearty suspicion for organized labor and union politics. In reality, Green's political path, as exhibited in his student years before the waterfront and in decisions he made during his first years as a shipwright, expressed an unlikely blending of idealism and pragmatism. The New Deal had a lasting impact on him. When Upton Sinclair infused the Democratic Party with socialist commitments in his EPIC campaign in 1934, Green was there with his father to organize at the precinct level, and at UC Berkeley he maintained an active commitment to Roosevelt through the College Democrats. Between 1941 and 1944, as a union shipwright, Green continued to engage with political organizations for a reformist agenda. Troubled with the conservatism of his union's International, he challenged the reactionary forces of the Hutcheson machine. In an interview with folklorist John Vlach, Green described one of these political projects:

> When I worked in the shipyards during the early part of World War II, the Kaiser Corporation was bringing black workers from the rural South to California. Many were just out of farm life and we were teaching them to hold

> plumb bobs and read rules. I was committed to black integration. In fact, we had something called the Shipyard Workers Committee against Discrimination and I was active in that. I was part of that cadre of young white liberal/radicals touched by black experience, excited by it. I didn't just go to a black nightclub in the Fillmore District [in San Francisco] to get kicks; I helped black youngsters get into the union and learn the trade. When they started the NAACP in San Francisco in 1942 or 1943, I was on the committee that drafted the constitution for the branch.[6]

As an extension of his advocacy for black workers Green successfully ran in July 1943 for recording secretary of Local 1149 on a platform that questioned the subservience of incumbent George Sanfacon to the UBCJA International. Green was eligible to run because the standard, four-year, carpenter's apprenticeship program had been reduced to nine months in order to boost the number of journeymen shipbuilders for war-time production. As a journeyman, Green left Western Pipe and Steel and went to work for one of the largest yards in the Bay, Moore Dry Dock in Oakland. It was there that he gained worker support for his defeat of Sanfacon. Reflecting on this period, and connecting it to his sustained relationship with the UBCJA, he said, "I can be opposed to Hutcheson and McCarren [the current UBCJA president], but I'll still be active in my union and in helping the local."[7] Green always expressed pride in his venture into union leadership, but unfortunately world events quickly drew him onto another battlefront—World War II.

* * *

In the three years before the war Green's life, of course, did not consist only of blueprints and union halls. Green saw his shipwright years as fostering self-confidence that spilled into other aspects of his life. He associated growing competence as a craftsman with his first successful experiences asking women out, an articulation of working-class identity and gendered roles. Late in 1942, a friend from Western Pipe and Steel, Tom Nicolopulus, invited him on a double date. Tom's wife, Sarah, thought her college roommate from UC Berkeley, Louanne Bartlett, would get along well with Green. And get along they did. The two couples starting going out regularly to the lively bars and clubs of North Beach and Fillmore and south of Market. "I was getting interested in ethnic music then." Green recalled. "We'd go hear Greek *rebetika* bands or Mexican music. Jack's in the Fillmore was a favorite. . . . We heard Bob Wills playing for the Okie war workers . . . went to Venus Club at Third and Townsend almost every Saturday night if we weren't going to a blues club."[8]

Green kept a small apartment in San Francisco's Telegraph Hill, a bohemian enclave home to two of his favorite night spots, the Iron Pot and the Black Cat. Of the general cultural milieu of the time he said, "SF was filled with guys who had been in the Spanish Civil War, merchant seaman, longshoreman that wrote poetry, shipwrights that were Scottish revolutionaries, Greek refugees that had jumped ship illegally." Antifascism was a pervasive political current, and it infused the arts. Kenneth Rexroth threw the hip parties Green sometimes attended; he had read one of Rexroth's articles in *The Nation*, the cover of which featured an industrial worker with a book of poetry in his pocket. It was quintessential Popular Front imagery that foreshadowed the Beat Generation of the future. San Francisco was fertile ground.

"Soldier, now soldier, won't you marry me, before the fight comes on?" goes a traditional southern song, a sentiment that captures the early years of World War II. Tens of thousands of young couples married before young men left for service, among them Archie Green and Louanne Bartlett. She, as Green liked to note, was "from an old W.A.S.P. family. Josiah Bartlett signed the Declaration of Independence." Having grown up in southern California, Louanne Bartlett had come to the Bay Area for college and graduated from UC Berkeley a year earlier than Green. Her interest in social work took her to the San Joaquin Valley to assist the children of migrants from Oklahoma. She found Green's garrulous nature exciting: "He talked a lot, and I liked it . . . he connected me to the larger world of events out there."[9] Although it was not common for a woman like Louanne Bartlett to date a Jewish man, her secular family ultimately supported their union even though her father did air some initial protest. After Green returned from naval training camp on the East Coast he was briefly stationed at a dry dock in San Diego. Louanne made the trip south, and, with only a small gathering of family members the two married on July 19, 1944. Shortly after, Green was relocated to a base in Albany, California, and in January 1945 he shipped out. Louanne remained living in a San Francisco apartment on Telegraph Hill. She awaited the birth of their first child.

* * *

Unlike Bay Area shipwrights whose skilled labor was urgently needed to increase wartime fleet production, Green, as the newly elected secretary of Local 1149, was not exempt from service. The eligibility did not alarm him. "I was Jewish and anti-Nazi," he said. "When time came to serve, I quit my job. I was glad that I had the choice to volunteer for the navy before getting enlisted in the army. I took it for granted that Roosevelt was right on the war."[10] In January 1944, he shipped out of Albany, California, for naval training near Norfolk, Virginia, and then was stationed in San Diego.

Green was assigned to the navy's Third Fleet under Adm. William Halsey. He was part of a ship repair unit as a carpenter's mate third class. For the remainder of 1944 and the first half of 1945 he was based on the island of Samar in the Philippines. It was northeast of the Leyte Gulf, scene of the war's largest naval battle just months before Green's ship arrived. The Allies prevailed in their attempt to push Japan back from controlling islands they had previously occupied in Southeast Asia. Because Green arrived in the wake of this success, the Samar assignment was rather uneventful. Green spent his days instructing other sailors in rudimentary ship maintenance and repair. That changed dramatically in July 1945. One morning ,when gathered on deck for daily orders, Green and four other sailors were told to ready their bags. They would be leaving to join a new unit in less than twenty-four hours.

"You knew," Green said, "when you were leaving a relatively safe place and were then issued a gun that you were heading for a place of danger. We sailed north and west from the Philippines, tracing the stars."[11] Over time, Green and his comrades pieced together that they were heading for the coast of China. Their mission would fit into Gen. Joseph Stilwell's plan to land on the coast and march west, dividing Japanese ground forces. The strategy was never tested. On August 6, 1945, the Allies dropped the first atomic bomb on Hiroshima. Green's ship was at sea, on route to China when news came of the bomb and Japan's surrender. "My shipmates and I were glad," he recalled. "Obviously, the war was over. We wouldn't need to use our carbines. If there were any guys on our crew who thought that atomic energy was evil I didn't know them. Who knew that tens of thousands died at Hiroshima and Nagasaki? I didn't know of any of this. We only thought of it in terms of: our dangerous assignment was over. We were glad the war was over. We weren't aware of the extent of devastation."[12]

Shortly after the bombings Green's boat arrived in Shanghai, sailed up the Huangpu River, and docked close to the city's Hongkou District where Green would encounter a brutal aspect of war. Shanghai had a large Jewish population going back to the late nineteenth century when thousands of Jewish families fled east from czarist pogroms. Since February 1943, in a square-mile area, between sixteen and twenty thousand of them had been imprisoned under Japanese proclamation.[13] It was a concentration camp in the eastern theater of war. The Hongkou Ghetto did not have gas chambers and Nazi-patrolled barbed-wire fences, but Green described the arrival of U.S. forces there as being "like liberating Auschwitz." Thousands of Jews were found, emaciated, sick, and exhausted. "The first thing we did was go back to our galleys and take out all the big cans of food. We opened the cans with our blades. Men and women were reaching in, grabbing for the food with their hands, cutting their hands on the blades." These scenes of desperation and triumph remained vivid for Green.

For several months he and his shipmates remained stationed at a ship repair base in Shanghai. They worked on small boats, maintained dry docks, and occasionally ventured inland to construction sites at U.S. bases. Green described Shanghai as "fully international" with "colonies of immigrants from all European countries." It was eye-opening for him to meet people from all over the world and engage in the heady political discussions of the day. The ship was organized so only a portion of its sailors could be in Shanghai at any given time, but Green and his best friend, Paul Sedlock, frequently climbed down "Jacob's ladder" on the starboard side of the ship and hired small sampans for a clandestine trip to shore. "Paul and I set a record. We went out fourteen nights in a row until we were practically dead. So much to do there in Shanghai. There were English, Russian, and French propaganda clubs—drinks and food, movies with subtitles, lectures. It wasn't a secret that they [foreign agents] were recruiting and trying to indoctrinate you. In Shanghai, everything belonged to someone—every paper, every club shop belonged to some national."[14] Despite the circumstances of war and his yearning for home Green fondly remembered these "sampan liberties" as some of the greatest adventures of his life.

In December 1945, Green sailed home, arriving in Portland, Oregon, and continuing south to San Francisco. Anxiously awaiting his arrival, Louanne Green held their first son, David, born October 18, 1945, warmly wrapped in her arms. Like millions of other veterans Green now faced the daunting challenge of assimilating back into postwar life. For Green that meant adding to their family and launching into an entirely new kind of political project—organizing fellow veterans.

* * *

More than a half-century after World War II it is challenging to sort through decades of cold war propaganda for a nuanced picture of how veterans felt after the war. Memorial narratives such as Tom Brokaw's *The Greatest Generation* can leave an impression that veterans were warmly welcomed by all civilians and that soldiers, for their part, maintained an upbeat, consensus appraisal of the American political system and social structure.[15] Neither of these caricatures is accurate. Immediately after the war there were many indications, both from the government and popular media, of widespread concern about whether veterans could be successfully integrated back into mainstream society. Memories of World War I's "Lost Generation" were still fresh, and the movies of the era also gave expression to popular anxiety over their ability to resume a normal, productive life. Would veterans be hyper-aggressive or socially stifled by a sharp existential anomie? In addition, the manner in which the war economy finally put an end to the unemployment and instability of the Great Depression raised fears about how the millions who returned could possibly find good jobs. For these reasons and more, the veteran, as Robert Saxe identifies, was seen as both a "threat and hero."[16] Saxe argues, however, that the cultural space available for competing portrayals of veterans narrowed over time; by 1950 the cold war social pressures of anticommunism and domestic consumption had created a homogenized and sanitized image of them as productive workers and patriotic citizens.[17]

In addition to altering how veterans were culturally represented, the cold war had a significant impact on how they could represent themselves. Massive government surveys indicated that the main concerns of many were establishing families and securing stable employment.[18] Those priorities aligned with mainstream civilian expectations and were supported politically by the American Legion and Veterans of Foreign Wars. Both politically conservative organizations dated back to World War I and aspired to significant growth with the influx of World War II veterans. The American Legion especially saw itself as taking up their core concerns. It was, for example, instrumental in the creation and passage of the GI Bill. But for many political and cultural reasons these established veterans' organizations did not seem attractive, appropriate, or politically promising to all who returned.

Before the war was over a new veterans' organization emerged that hoped to give voice to those critical of traditional veterans' groups and who, in general, maintained that the particular experiences of World War II required a new organization. The American Veterans Committee (AVC) emerged in 1943 out of informal correspondence between veterans who had all previously attended the University of California, Los Angeles (UCLA).[19] Gilbert Harrison, previously the editor of UCLA's student newspaper and active in student government, inspired the letter writing and encouraged its formalization. In March 1943, the first *AVC Bulletin* was printed and disbursed to a hundred veterans. The bulletin closed with one of the organization's newly established mottoes: "To achieve a more democratic and prosperous America in a more stable world."[20] By July 1944, under the direction of veteran Charles Bolté, the AVC had formed a national planning committee and was circulating a statement of intent to assist with recruiting members. The mission statement conveyed the AVC's belief that military victory would not be sufficient to achieve the overarching goals of the war. Veterans were called to return from fighting on the battlefield and begin doing so at home for economic equality, civil rights, and international peace.

Before holding its first national convention in 1946 the AVC built its membership to nearly fifty thousand through the establishment of local chapters around the country. Among the recruits was Archie Green, who heard of the organization through contacts at UCLA. Once active in student government there, he had worked with Harrison and had great respect for him. "Upon my return from China I jet propelled myself into AVC and have been involved ever since," Green wrote in 1948.[21] During his first year of volunteer organizing, 1946, he fit in his AVC advocacy around various Veterans Administration day jobs. To pay the bills he did "reconversion work" involved in changing cruise ships that had been converted to military use back to their commercial form. When reconversion work subsided, Green became a training officer in a VA apprenticeship training program.

As for AVC organizing, Green's initial task was to establish a new chapter in San Francisco's Mission District where he and his family lived. He began by holding small outreach events for veterans and the public at large that addressed their most pressing issues: affordable housing, healthcare, and employment. On June 11, 1946, he organized "The Klu Klux Klan—California's New Menace."[22] Other events expressing the progressive and internationalist spirit of the AVC highlighted postwar political conditions in countries such as Japan and Greece. The first major campaign of the Mission Chapter was calling on U.S. senators to support the Office of Price Administration. One outreach strategy Green helped implement was to have Jerry Heilbron, a former combat pilot, fly over San Francisco and drop thousands of AVC leaflets over working-class neighborhoods. "Surrender? Surrender? Surrender? Are you whipped? Will you surrender? SAVE THE O.P.A." they urged. It was an animating spirit of the national AVC: The Armed Forces had prevailed in the war and now it was time for progressive veterans to build a mass movement. Their motto, "Citizens First, Veterans Second," stressed that the movement had the best interests for all Americans.

At the height of its efforts in 1947 the AVC had nearly 125,000 members, and its leaders in Washington testified regularly before congressional committees on matters imperative to veterans' lives. The organization distinguished itself from traditional veterans' organizations in style, procedure, and political principle. As much as possible, the AVC encouraged grass-roots, participatory organizing, which ran counter to the culture of hierarchical leadership in the other veterans' organizations as well as the military itself. The AVC was the only national veterans' group to require all chapters to be fully integrated and politically nonpartisan. Legion chapters, in contrast, frequently denied membership to Japanese Americans and African Americans. Solidly pro-labor, the AVC fought against the anti-labor Taft-Hartley Act and supported waves of postwar worker strikes. The AVC maintained that veterans, like all workers, needed good union jobs. As Robert Saxe emphasizes, "Similar to its stance on civil rights, the AVC's pro-labor policies put it in conflict with consensus norms in postwar America that frowned on social conflict in the face of the expanding cold war."[23]

The AVC provided an excellent outlet for Green to express his political convictions as well as a testing ground for developing his skills as an organizer. He was antiracist, pro-labor, a supporter of strong government involvement in postwar economic regulation, and committed to a liberal, internationalist foreign policy. The outreach and caucusing skills he had earlier forged in the American Student Union, the Young Democrats, and more recently as Local 1149's recording secretary were all useful in postwar organizing, and by 1947 he had turned to full-time work for the AVC. He helped establish dozens of Bay Area chapters with his close friend Timothy Leary, later to become a central figure in the counter-culture. Green became regional vice chair of the AVC on the West Coast and then in 1948 the West Coast regional chair on the AVC's National Planning Committee.

All of that work required great personal sacrifice. As Green exclaimed in an October 13, 1947, letter to national chair Chat Patterson, "I have much faith in AVC, but no cash. I have been unemployed since I lost my VA job. We're expecting a baby in a few weeks and must meet our medical bills."[24] He then requested reimbursement for AVC office rent and purchasing an airplane ticket in order to uphold his responsibilities as regional representative at the next national convention in Milwaukee. Nearly a year later Green shed light on how he navigated the fiscal squeeze: "Much of my AVC activity has been subsidized in the form of personal loans by two friends, neither of whom are vets and both of whom think I'd be better off twenty-six thousand miles from the AVC."[25] The benefactors are unknown, but it is reasonable to speculate on the political reservations they held about the AVC.

From its earliest days as a formal veterans' organization the AVC faced anti-Communist red-baiting in the media and Congress. Critics claimed that the AVC leadership was communist and that the organization was trying to convert veterans into an "army of radicals" threatening the foundation of

American political values.[26] Contrary to these accusations, early AVC leaders were squarely New Deal liberals whose political initiatives reflected a reformist sensibility.[27] In AVC bulletins from 1946, Gilbert Harrison stressed that although the organization believed in the inclusion of all political perspectives, its platform was definitively nonpartisan.[28] All members had to pledge loyalty to the U.S. Constitution.

There is no question that communist and socialist veterans were members of the AVC. Some radical veterans of the day aimed to "bore within" traditional veterans' organizations like the Legion and influence their politics, but for many others the AVC represented a welcome, tolerant atmosphere in which they could be open about their left political positions. The organization was trying to carve out a political space that would become increasingly difficult to maintain within the rising conservative, paranoid climate of McCarthyism. The AVC aspired to uphold free speech and ideological pluralism as part of a progressive, patriotic political project. As its short history illustrates, however, the organization could not survive how the cold war political climate intensified infighting and fractionalization of the American left.

One reason that Green pleaded with Patterson to fund his trip to the 1947 national convention in Milwaukee was because of an alarming intensification of political splintering within AVC membership during that year. Everyone knew that the convention would bring a defining political showdown between three emergent factions. The largest, the Independent Progressives, included the incumbent leadership and promoted a liberal, social-democratic political line. To its left was the Unity caucus, which many members viewed as a front for the Communist Party. Finally, the Build AVC group aspired to sustain organizational coherence by curtailing both the increasing anticommunism of the Independent Progressives and the CP-affiliated positions of Unity. Build AVC tried to maintain a position promoted by the National Planning Committee as late as March 1947: resist any top-down political litmus test for membership in the AVC. As one National Planning Committee document stated, "We abhor both the objectives and tactics of the American Communist Party. We likewise abhor proposals designed to preserve our democracy by muzzling groups which seek to destroy it."[29] Between March and June of 1947—the months leading up to the Milwaukee convention—widespread acceptance of such a position dissolved. As was also the case in the national labor movement, pressure was building rapidly on progressive organizations to showcase intolerance for communist ideas and Communist Party members. The Independent Progressives prevailed in Milwaukee, signifying a victory for the anti-Communist position within the

AVC. The newly elected leadership felt strongly that the organization's only option was to openly and unequivocally distance itself from communists.

As a member of Build AVC, Green disagreed. He maintained the anticommunism he developed in college and on the docks before the war, but personal beliefs did not overshadow his commitment to the principle of political freedom and pluralism. He felt that if the AVC caved in to the witch hunt of McCarthyism it would no longer be a political home for progressive veterans and represent an alternative to the reactionary politics of the American Legion and the Veterans of Foreign War. Green was right. By 1948 the AVC's membership had fallen from its height of nearly 125,000 to twenty thousand.[30] It would officially remain an organization until 2001, but it never regained significant national political influence after 1949. Green stopped organizing for the AVC in 1950 and returned to the trades in order to support a growing family. Shipbuilding along the San Francisco waterfront had declined after World War II, so he went "uptown of the Embarcadero" and found a wide range of building jobs throughout the 1950s.

The story of the AVC, as well as Green's particular political path within it, has importance on multiple levels. On a positive note, the AVC, while influential for only a short time, represented an important moment in political organizing for veterans—a moment where those who best understood the cost of war questioned its purpose and mobilized to change a world that persistently resorts to it. Less encouragingly, the AVC offers a window into how difficult it was for progressives to fare within the suffocating political climate of the cold war. It also reveals the tendency of leftists to turn upon one another, in unproductive infighting, when larger political trends tilt conservative. For those who came to know Archie Green only in his elder years it might be easy to cast him as a fervent participant in that tradition of infighting. When discussing the legacy of the Popular Front or the Green Party's approach to national electoral contests he could fume sectarian smoke like the best of dragons. But these moments belied a larger commitment that was inspiringly manifest during his years organizing for the AVC. In 1947, during the contentious, fractionalizing, national AVC convention, another San Francisco veteran saw this quality in Green. Norman Leonard accompanied him to Milwaukee and, after lamenting pervasive and stifling infighting at the convention, he noted that chapter members should celebrate "the unanimous election as West Coast Regional Chairman of Archie Green, who did not let himself become involved in these ideological fights, [who] showed that California and the whole West Coast can be unified around a man who steers clear of these matters and who exhibits a primary concern for the building and strengthening of AVC as a veterans organization."[31] As Leonard recognized, Green revered pluralism as foundational for the practice of democracy. He was also a political pragmatist who played not so much to win but to advance. Green knew the necessity of working across differences to achieve shared objectives. This was one of the secrets to how he got so much done over so many years, whether recruiting for the AVC, criss-crossing the congressional aisle to lobby for the American Folklife Act, or corralling highly variegated support for the Fund for Labor Culture and History.

Baby Archie with his older sister, Judy, in Winnipeg around 1918. (Green Family Collection)

(Above) Archie with his father, Samuel, and grandfather during one of the grandfather's occasional visits to California from Winnipeg. (Green Family Collection)

(Facing) Lunchbox under his arm, Green buoyantly strides through downtown San Francisco on his way to the shipyards around 1942. (Green Family Collection)

SHAW

(Above) Louanne Bartlett and Archie Green on a weekend visit to San Francisco's Sigmund Stern Grove around 1941. (Green Family Collection)

(Facing above) In the early 1960s, while working at the University of Illinois, Green would venture out during summer breaks to find and record old-time musicians. Here, he stands next to Dorsey Dixon and his mule in East Rockingham, N.C., in 1962. On this trip Gene Earle and Green recorded Dixon's *Babies in the Mill* (Testament Records, T-3301). (Southern Folklife Collection, Wilson Library, The University of North Carolina at Chapel Hill)

(Facing below) With the "Banjo King of the Carolinas," Dock Walsh, in 1962 during the recording of *Carolina Tar Heels* (Folk-Legacy Records, Inc. FSA-24). (Southern Folklife Collection, Wilson Library, The University of North Carolina at Chapel Hill)

(Above) As his public lectures and prolific writing made evident, Green was a voracious reader. Here, he is in his office at the University of Illinois in August 1972, just before he moved to Washington, D.C., to take up full-time legislative advocacy. (Carl Fleischhauer)

(Facing above) The Green family, Urbana, Ill., 1963; left to right, Derek, Louanne, David, Debra, and Archie. (Green Family Collection)

(Facing below) At the Smithsonian Folklife Festival in 1969, Green's good friend Hazel Dickens sang "Black Lung" for the first time in public. Left to right: Maybelle Carter, Dock Boggs, Dickens, Merle Travis, and Green. (Photograph by Diana Davies, courtesy of the Ralph Rinzler Folklife Archives and Collections, Smithsonian Institution)

(Above) Green and folklorist Bill Wiggins, who holds a copy of Green's *Only a Miner,* in a House of Representatives hearing room just before the Subcommittee on Library and Memorials of the Committee on House Administration hears testimony regarding the American Folklife Preservation Act, May 10, 1974. (Carl Fleischhauer)

(Facing above) With the successful passage of the American Folklife Preservation Act behind him, Green was invited to address the White House Labor Day picnic in 1980. The holiday, President Jimmy Carter's last in office, was marked by the U.S. Postal Service unveiling a 15 cent stamp dedicated to "Organized Labor: Proud and Free." A portion of the stamp appears at Green's right. (Green Family Collection)

(Facing below) Green interviewed retired pile butts in 1990 for his book *Wobblies, Pile Butts, and Other Heroes.* (William Myers)

(Above) For more than half a century the Greens welcomed thousands of visitors to their San Francisco home on Casilli Street. Archie, excited, would peer out his window as he awaited the guests. (William Myers)

(Facing above) In 2002 Green worked with Tim Kelley of the San Francisco Landmarks Board to mount a plaque in commemoration of the violent struggle that occurred between police and workers at the Garcia and Maggini Warehouse during the 1934 General Strike. The public plaque has helped restore memory about the nature of the historic strike and the exact location at 128 King Street where it unfolded. Green wears his traditional "Lundeberg Stetson" and a classic "Logger Poetry" shirt. (Courtesy of Michael Munoz, photographer unknown)

(Facing below) During the last decade of his life Green organized a series of "Laborlore Conversations" that brought together workers, scholars, students, and community members who shared a passion for labor culture. Laborlore Conversation III was held in the Ironworkers Hall in Benicia, Calif., in the fall of 2006. From left to right, Elli Matus, John Robinson, Green, Robert Cantwell, and Chris Strachwitz. (William Myers)

THE GARCIA & MAGGINI WAREHOUSE
LOGGER POETRY

Green relaxes in his kitchen,
October 25, 2008. (Michael Rauner)

Part 3 A Decent Philosophy

Culture, Politics, and American Folk Revivalism

Please remember that there were (and are) many alternative paths to the one you walked.

—Archie Green to Pete Seeger, April 19, 1965

On June 20, 1956, Green wrote his first letter to Pete Seeger. For more than ten years Green had been seriously collecting early hillbilly and "race records" (folk and blues), and he requested specific information about the origin of several songs Seeger had recorded. His interest in discography growing, Green wrote hundreds of such letters in the 1950s and 1960s to musicians, record executives, scholars, and collectors. And they replied—effusively. That is what the few dozen die-hard enthusiasts of early-recorded American music did; they corresponded constantly in search of song variations and historical clues to the meaning of lyrics and the musicians who wrote them.

What distinguishes this initial 1956 letter to Seeger is Green's succinct portrayal of who he was and what his ambitions as a collector were. "By way of introduction," Green wrote, "may I state that I put in my apprenticeship on the San Francisco waterfront, and served as secretary of the Shipwrights, Joiners, and Boatbuilders Union before entering the Navy. I am currently employed as a carpenter in building construction. Books and records are my hobby. The challenge I have set for myself is to compile a descriptive checklist of American Labor and Work Songs on Records. If it is at all possible I want to draw from the fields of folk, country and western, pop, blues and other musical forms to tell the stories of workers and their industries. I have begun with coal miners and stevedores, and hope to go on to lumberjacks, needle trades, textiles, etc."[1]

Green then explained that he has been "searching for a theme to integrate [his] trade union experience and [folklore] studies." He suggested to Seeger that this could lie in the study of "industrial folksongs," a phrase he credited to folklorist A. L. Lloyd.

Nine years later, in 1965, Green no longer worked as a union carpenter in San Francisco. His determination to develop a new kind of folklore scholarship combined with a series of auspicious life twists to land him work as a librarian and part-time English teacher at the University of Illinois. From there Green again corresponded with Seeger. On April 19, he wrote, "I am eager to set down my personal growth in the labor-radical movement as it correlated with my interest in folksong."[2] The letter indicates that Green had continued developing his interest in industrial folksongs since first writing to Seeger in 1956 and, most important, reveals that he had grown increasingly aware that the left, anti-Communist politics of 1940s labor movements had shaped his particular approach to folksong scholarship. By 1965 Green viewed labor song studies both as a way to integrate his specific life experiences and integrate many disciplines of study, including ballad scholarship, labor history, and a nascent kind of media-based cultural studies. To that point, such disciplines had been isolated from one another.

In a broad sense, Part 3 examines the converging historical, personal, and intellectual dimensions of Green's search "to integrate [his] trade union experience and studies" through research into industrial work songs. I offer an analysis of how Green's political life history "correlated" with his folk-song scholarship, or, to put it in the form of a specific question, How did Green's left anticommunism combine with his particular aesthetic ideology to produce convictions about vernacular music and cultural pluralism? Within this question, a constellation of more specific questions and themes organizes this section, many of which have to do with the nature and legacy of the cultural politics and aesthetics of the Popular Front in the United States.

Nine years separate the two letters to Seeger. In that time, 1956–65, not only had Green's and his family's lives changed significantly but the nation as a whole had also undergone profound political and cultural transformation. The suffocating blanket of McCarthyism had been lifted. The modern civil rights struggle was in full stride. Parties of the Old Left had given way to chants of the New. A national craze for folk song had swept the nation, placing Joan Baez on the cover of *Time* and turning the Kingston Trio and Bob Dylan into household names. Green's passion for folksong study was no longer the mark of a dedicated underground eccentric. Dozens of folk labels had sprung up, millions of records were selling, and tens of thousands of folk aficionados relished the pages of *Sing Out!*

Sing Out! was the most popular folk music magazine of the day, and for years Seeger consistently pressed Green to contribute an article. He hedged, however, mostly by ignoring the requests, which baffled and frustrated Seeger. In 1963 Seeger asserted that Green must be *"scared* to do an article for SING OUT magazine."[3] Green did not return his letter. In 1965 Seeger prodded further:

> Did something in [*Sing Out*] insult you so that you vowed to never write for it? Did you promise your mother never to write for it?
> Do you disapprove of its policies, all of them?
> Do you disapprove of its personnel, all of them?
> Do you feel its readers are unimportant, all of them?[4]

Finally, in a letter of April 19, 1965, Green explained his reticence, defended his politics, and pushed back at the banjo toting icon of the folk revival:

> Seriously, Pete, I would suggest that you use different language when you pose such questions to prospective contributors. It is not your function to imply that others are scared or lack courage. There have been many places and times in my life when I have been afraid: sand bars in the Pacific, docks on the San Francisco waterfront, building trades union meetings, high-rise jobs. Yet I have come through these experiences with a fairly undamaged psyche and, I hope, a *decent philosophy*.
>
> Because I do not share all of your values, does not mean that I am "scared" to write for *Sing Out*. Please remember that there were (and are) many alternative paths to the one you walked. I have always admired you for your singing out for freedom, and for your skill in using the concert stage as an educational forum, but I have also been concerned at not hearing you speak out for freedom all over the world.[5]

This concluding reference is to the Soviet Union. Green, when he wrote of "alternative paths," was implicitly condemning Seeger's connection with the Communist Party, continued silence on the murderous policies of Joseph Stalin, and stylistic approach to folk song.[6]

For the purposes of this section, the most significant line in the April 19 letter comes later when Green commented, "My views of the People's Songs partisans as well as my views of the *Broadside* writers of today ([Phil] Ochs, etc.) are colored by my experience and values in the labor-radical movement."[7] There was, that is, a link between Green's critical views toward the early folk revival of the Popular Front (1936–41) and his critical views toward the subsequent, much larger folk revival between 1958 and 1964.[8] That link, according to Green, was the "experience and values" he accrued in the "labor-radical movement" of the thirties and forties. Part 3, therefore, asks:

- What are the substance and implications of this link between Green's experiences and politics as a worker and his views toward American folk revivalism?
- How did Green's critiques of the Popular Front as a left anti-Communist shipwright and amateur music collector in the thirties and forties relate to his critiques of the sixties' folk revival?
- How did Green's conceptions of American vernacular plurality and political alliance building constitute a critique of Communist-centered understandings of the Popular Front?
- How did Green express this critique through his long-term project to shape laborlore as legitimate interdisciplinary scholarship and his indefatigable advocacy for vernacular folklife and cultural pluralism?[9]

The Seeger-Green correspondence is fascinating in part because Seeger famously exemplifies a living relationship between the Popular Front and the Sixties folk revival. Most of the cultural histories of American folk revivalism acknowledge this.[10] But the vast majority of these cultural histories are, like Seeger, sympathetic to the politics and aesthetics of the Popular Front and sixties' folk revival. Time and time again in my interviews, Green challenged those accounts. Through examining the politics, aesthetic ideology, and experiences of Archie Green I present an alternative assessment of many of the central questions concerning historians of left culture in post-Depression and post–World War II America.

Historians such as Michael Denning and David Roediger have highlighted a need for studies that consider the cultural politics of the Popular Front from the perspective of "non-Communist socialists and independent leftists" who made up the bulk of the American left in the middle decades of the twentieth century.[11] Study of Archie Green's life and work, especially with reference to the place of folk music in the Popular Front, helps fill that void. Green had deep curiosity for how and why the American left, particularly a portion of the Communist Party in New York City, took interest in folk music. His opinions of the merit and legacy of that relationship run counter to nearly all the published historical assessments of the era. I find it fascinating, and more than a bit ironic, that many who write on this topic begin by acknowledging a personal debt to Archie Green but then arrive at conclusions that he would find deeply suspect.[12]

The focus of this part of the book is not the Popular Front itself but rather an exploration of Green's attitudes toward folk revival in that era; how his attitudes developed through his participation in the expansive folk revival of the sixties; and, finally, how to understand his critical perspectives on these topics as being significantly "colored by experience and values in the labor-radical movement." Green raised important questions about the cultural politics and politics of culture during his long, twentieth-century (and twenty-first-century) life. I am convinced of the continued consequence and relevance of his questions but often disagree with his perspectives. What I find most interesting about our differences is how they reflect his formative politicization in the thirties and my formative politicization in the nineties. Cross-generational dialog is important for how it reveals the distinct questions, charged political concerns, and nuanced structures of feeling that congeal and resonate in different historical eras. Part 3 concludes with reflections on aesthetic ideology and the task of conceptualizing the vernacular at the intersection of twenty-first-century local global culture-making.

Chapter 8 Folk Music and the American Communist Party

In the November 21, 1933, edition of the *Daily Worker*, Henry Cowell argued, "One of the great faults in the field of workers music has been that of combining revolutionary lyrics with traditional music—music which can by no means be termed revolutionary."[1] Cowell, a respected modernist composer, was a leading member of the recently formed Composers Collective—a branch of the Pierre Degeyter Club that was affiliated with the Communist Workers Music League. Made up of a couple of dozen composers and music critics, the Composers Collective included notable cultural figures such as Aaron Copland, Earl Robinson, Elie Siegmiester, and Charles Seeger, father of Pete. Sharing avant-garde tastes, their aim was to create "proletarian music" in the image of European workers' choruses that would fuel revolutionary movement building.[2] As Cowell's comments indicate, a primary question for the collective was, What characterizes revolutionary music appropriate for the working classes?[3] This question is just one articulation of a more fundamental topic that Marxist and non-Marxist leftists debated throughout much of the twentieth century, What is revolutionary culture?

In the 1970s, Green began seriously researching the long history of different left responses to this question. His initial intention was to better understand why the Wobblies did not embrace folk music traditions whereas the Communists ultimately did. Contrary to some contemporary stereotypes of Wobblies, Green reminded us, "Most Wobbly songs aren't protest songs, they are songs of affirmation . . . and they were sung to popular melodies and hymns, usually on piano. Wobblies never played guitars."[4] Although Green never got around to writing a book on the history of the left's relationship to folklife, his inquiry led to research of the debates of early Bolsheviks who, like his parents, fled czarist repression after the failed Russian Revolution of

1905. Cities such as Geneva, London, Paris, and Stuttgart constituted what Zenovia Sochor refers to as "the expatriate world of Russian revolutionaries," where exiled Marxists debated "cultural factors in the process of revolutionary transformation."[5] In *Revolution and Culture*, Sochor traces the heated political and philosophical disagreements between V. I. Lenin and Alexander Bogdanov that so intrigued Green. The differences within these debates eventually had profound implications on the political culture in the Soviet Union. Bogdanov, along with Maxim Gorky, placed faith in workers' culture and, to counter Lenin's version of Bolshevism, began worker education schools on Capri (1909) and in Bologna (1910).[6]

In studying these debates Green delighted in finding there were "sophisticated distinctions being made between high culture, popular culture, and vernacular culture," and he sided with Bogdanov in emphasizing cultivation of, not condescension toward, workers' culture. Green liked to point out that during the Russian Revolution, "Anarchist fringes attacked the opera house as a symbol of Czarist decadence, but Lenin and others *liked* the opera, the high culture. They thought this is what the working classes and peasants had to be brought up to appreciate."[7] A direct legacy of these Bolshevik debates on culture and revolution captivated communist circles in New York City and beyond, beginning in the late twenties and through the forties.

Many historians have examined these debates within the CPUSA. Typically, their analyses organize around contrasting the rigidly sectarian cultural politics of the Third Period with the more expansive and organically "American" cultural politics of the Popular Front.[8] In a passage representative of this framework, Richard and JoAnne Reuss describe the "buoyant nationalist tone of the New Deal and antifascist spirit of the Popular Front" as the "ecological opposite" of the "austere 'proletarian' worldview of the preceding Third Period."[9] All the historians I have read agree that aesthetic ideals transformed during these two periods, but opinions vary widely about why the changes occurred and what their legacy has been for the American left. Differing opinions on these cultural questions often reflect more basic disagreements about the nature and impact of the Communist Party in its heyday. Historians less sympathetic or hostile to the CPUSA tend to emphasize that the party's move toward celebrating American folk cultures stems from strategic policy shifts originating in Moscow. R. Serge Denisoff, for example, maintains that the CP's interest in folk music was a result of Bolshevism and Comintern policy, not Marxism in general. Moreover, these cultural policy decisions reflect the vanguardism in Lenin's *What Is to Be Done?* Denisoff observes that influential communists in Moscow and New York shared the attitude that "workers were not capable of creating their own revolutionary consciousness."[10] On matters of style, he notes that no other left tradition of the day shared an interest in folk song.[11] The socialists, Trotskyists, and Wobblies, all influenced by Marxism as well, sang songs based on popular European and/or American melodies that often originated in hymns. Wobblies' songs often parodied those in the Salvation Army's songbook. These movements paid little attention to folk songs, a point Green also frequently stressed.

Green's critique of the CP's use of folk music is one aspect of his larger critique of the Popular Front and operates on two related levels, the political and the aesthetic. As Green wrote to Seeger, "My views of the People's Songs partisans . . . are colored by my experience and values in the labor-radical movement."[12] The heated political struggles of the San Francisco waterfront during the forties allowed Green to develop strong, left anti-Communist positions that were drawn from a combination of Wobbly anarcho-syndicalism, Trotskyist anti-Stalinism, and New Deal pragmatism.

Green's inclination, like that of many Trotskyists, was to view policies and programs of the CPUSA as directly reflective of decisions made in Moscow.[13] Even within the narrow realm of the CP's relation to folk music there is significant evidence to support that perspective, evident in, for example, the lyrical content of songs written by communist-affiliated members of the Almanac Singers between 1940 and 1943. The Almanacs were a small folk collective, including Pete Seeger and Woody Guthrie, that performed topical songs for left-wing and union crowds. Early Almanac songs focused on the antifascist fervor of the day, strongly influenced by the attention to political songs born of the Spanish Civil War. After the Soviets and Nazis signed the Non-Aggression Pact on August 23, 1939, however, the Almanacs dropped their emphasis on antifascism. The infamous "Yanks aren't coming" period of CPUSA policy had begun. The Almanacs' March 1941 release of *Songs for John Doe* featured antiwar themes, but three months later when the Nazis invaded Russia and the pact was nullified the Almanacs began singing to a different tune. Their May 1942 album *Dear Mr. President* called for Americans to reconcile with Russia and passionately support the antifascist war. Support for World War II took an additional turn in 1942 when Earl Browder, president of the CPUSA, declared a "No Strike Pledge." Until that point, a considerable amount of the Almanacs' material celebrated union power. Suddenly, with the No Strike Pledge those songs were deemed inappropriate. A significant portion of the Almanac repertoire was again dropped.[14]

These inconsistencies echoed loudly in Green's critiques of the CP. Such vehement antipathy, so often born of very real, life-and-death struggles connected to political affiliation during the labor battles of the thirties and forties, can obscure and stunt analysis of larger, complicated, and uneven historical events. This is, in part, why Michael Denning invites an examination that goes beyond a "core-periphery model" of American Communist Party history wherein a fixation on party membership so often over-determines cultural and political analysis. Green did not accept Denning's invitation, and we should remember his adamant reasoning: "Don't defend Stalinism!"

Both risks are avoidable. Social movement scholars such as Bruce Nelson and Robin D. G. Kelley, to name just two, model how to write history that creatively and rigorously navigates the proverbial straits of structure and agency.[15] Those are academic terms for a kind of history that tries to understand why people have behaved as they have by investigating the specific, situated character of humans living with unequal kinds of choices (agency) in a daily encounter with a world systematically shaped by conditions larger than themselves (structure). Green was a pioneer of that kind of history. Historians and American studies scholars have not adequately recognized his contributions to integrating cultural studies with working-class history.[16] I have also learned from his limitations and believe that American communists' attention to folk song, as well as the undeniable influence the CP had on the American left's relation to folklife, must be seen within the larger political, economic, and cultural context of the "laboring of American culture in the twentieth century."[17] I place less emphasis than Green on Moscow's influence on American communist's interest in folk song and have a more optimistic appraisal of the long-term impact of Popular Front and sixties' folk revivalism on American culture.

In his outstanding work *When We Were Good*, Robert Cantwell places the American folk revival in several simultaneous historical and cultural frameworks, notably the nineteenth-century performative conventions of minstrelsy and the twentieth-century quest of Americans, largely immigrant, to configure new identities in the context of the Great Depression, World War II, and the cold war.[18] In the 1910s and 1920s, before any of these events, sales of records and phonographs displaced sheet music as the vehicle for marketing songs. Small record companies sprung up by the dozen to record and promote regional, ethnic and racial vernacular music.[19] In 1910, Teddy Roosevelt wrote a preface to John Lomax's groundbreaking *Cowboy Songs and Other Frontier Ballads*. In 1927, Carl Sandburg released his influential *American Songbag*, giving twenty-four categories of those songs. Within a year, the Library of Congress established the Archive of American Folk Song and appointed Robert Winslow Gordon as its head. Gordon, as Ronald Cohen points out, "preferred folk song collecting among waterfront denizens and hoboes to 'stuffy' academic life."[20]

The Communist Party, founded in the United States in 1919, either did not exist or was still extremely marginal when all of these events occurred. When we think of the folk revival of the late thirties we are quick to imagine Woody Guthrie, Pete Seeger, and Alan Lomax, all individuals who had affiliations with communist politics. But why not imagine Harry Smith piling up records in his Seattle living room?[21] The revival had many origins beyond the parameters of CP influence, and the American communists who were important in the revival had connections to those origins. It was the 1929 stock market crash that created new conditions for the emergence of a national folk revival and the expansion of Communist Party membership into a middle-class base. These two developments had a relationship, but they are not the same thing. Cantwell observes that the "Great Depression added a powerful new economic intensity and a sharp political edge" to long-circulating, nostalgic desires around recreating the "close community of the small town . . . and a sense of direct connection to a traditional collective culture." The depression not only unleashed desperate times but also opened a space, previously caged by the economic strength of the twenties and intense corporate-state repression of the politically radical, where dreams of social justice could emerge to "repair the dreadful racial, economic, and cultural rifts tearing the social fabric apart."[22] Pete Seeger recalls that when he was a teenager, "around 1932–3–4, [he] suddenly found out what unemployment could do to people. The whole country was arguing. People got so mad they thought of radical solutions."[23] Those with long-held radical beliefs, so often working-class immigrants and migrant blacks, had suffered under the antilabor climate, xenophobia, and ascendant racist-nativism of the twenties, and the politics of embracing folk music, which was perceived as so authentically American, should be seen within those historical social pressures.

Several books, including Archie Green's seminal *Only a Miner*, tell the story of how Communist Party organizers from New York City traveled to Gastonia, North Carolina, in 1929 and Harlan County, Kentucky, in 1931 to support and, in some cases, direct militant union organizing in textile factories and coal mines.[24] It is in these years that New York communists and other "fellow travelers" made contact with some radical Appalachian musicians—most famously Ella May Wiggins, Jim Garland, and Aunt Molly Jackson.[25] Green perceptively sheds light on this cultural convergence, noting that "Piedmont mill villages and Cumberland mine camps became meeting grounds for the ideologies of Andrew Jackson and Karl Marx, Abraham Lincoln and Mikhail Bakunin. Few of the mill hands or coal miners were able to synthesize traditional and modern values into lasting literature, but some managed to compose folk-like songs which fused timeworn melodies with strange, revolutionary lyrics."[26] The image of a meeting ground appropriately conjures the influence these groups had on one another. The Communist organizers "were teaching 'Solidarity Forever' in West Virginia in 1931, [and] in return moved 'The Death of Mother Jones' into urban circles."[27] Such events offer questions, To what degree was folk music and its revival seen as a vehicle for CP advancement and to what degree did folk musicians and revivalists see the CP as a vehicle for spreading their art?

In the year Green describes, 1931, the novelist Theodore Dreiser gathered an investigative committee that included Sherwood Anderson and John Dos Passos and went to Harlan with the hope of bringing media attention to workers' struggles. The National Committee for the Defense of Political Prisoners held open public hearings where miners and their family members were invited to testify on their lives at work and at home. In this context, New York City leftists heard some of these "strange, revolutionary lyrics" that Green mentioned. Aunt Molly Jackson, a midwife, ballad singer, unionist, and daughter, sister, and wife of coal miners, testified before the Dreiser committee on infant mortality and malnutrition. In closing her testimony she mesmerized the large crowd with an emotionally wrenching performance of her song "Ragged Hungry Blues":

> I'm sad and weary, I've got these hungry ragged blues;
> Not a penny in my pocket to buy one thing I need to use.
> I woke up this morning with the worst blues I ever had in my life;
> Not a bite to cook for breakfast; poor coal miner's wife. . . .
> This mining town I live in is a dead and lonely place;
> Where pity and starvation are pictured on every face.[28]

News of Aunt Molly Jackson quickly spread through the pages of the *Daily Worker*, and in December 1931 she and her stepbrother Jim Garland returned with Dreiser to New York City. "They sang and spoke to groups of left-wing intellectuals and workers in New York, Cleveland, and elsewhere," and in the process, "many more urban radicals were exposed to indigenous American folk traditions."[29]

The New York City–based Composers Collective is a case in point. Within days of arriving in the Big Apple, Aunt Molly performed her ballads for the largely diehard modernist and avant-garde composers. Reactions varied considerably. The infusion of folk material into radical New York circles against the larger national cultural backdrop intensified debates over which music was appropriate for cultivating revolutionary consciousness. Members of the Composers Collective such as Henry Cowell, who promoted formal choral arrangements as the best expression of the CP's Third Period political and aesthetic goal of creating proletarian music, argued with comrades beginning to claim the merits of "people's music" for emboldening the movement. Margaret Larkin, a left journalist and cowboy singer who wrote for *The New Masses* and *The Nation*, defended Aunt Molly Jackson's songs as "a direct and vigorous expression of large numbers of American workers."[30] Green respected Larkin's insight and advocacy: "She deflated the polemics of doctrinaire Marxists like the *Worker Musician* critic who had attacked American folk melodies as 'immature' and 'arrested' by attributing their debased state in culture to the 'exploitation of the coal barons.' Miss Larkin, well ahead of her peers, was armed with an esthetic which valued the unadorned Appalachian idiom, and which avoided placing Aunt Molly either in a 'folk cellar' or on a revolutionary pedestal."[31]

The last sentence of the quotation hints at the reason Green applauded Larkin while at the same time he frequently attacked journalist Mike Gold, who rigorously defended the legitimacy of folk song as an art form and formulated a relationship between radical politics and folk music. The most widely read communist cultural critic of the Popular Front, Gold tirelessly advocated the poignancy of "Negro folk songs" and the relevance of rural Appalachian material against the critiques of such communist classical composers as Hanns Eisler. According to Charles Seeger, Eisler, well into the forties, would "publicly berate Alan Lomax for foisting those 'damn songs' on the working class."[32] But Gold believed wholeheartedly that folk music would be critical to the success of the communist struggle, and he argued repeatedly in the pages of the *Daily Worker* that the party needed its own Joe Hill—a prognosis Green hated.[33] Why then would Mike Gold, a writer who insisted the "Composers Collective has something to learn from Ray and Lida Auville," early on fiercely defended Aunt Molly Jackson and Sarah Gunning (two of Green's favorite ballad singers), and quite likely brought workers' culture to the attention of tens of thousands, be so despised by Green? The brief answer is that Gold was a communist. But that neglects a deeper, more revealing, level of analysis. When Mike Gold called out "we need our own Joe Hill," it is likely that Green heard a deeply opportunistic attitude that, for him, characterized the Communist Party's relationship to the working class.

There is little doubt that some New York communists saw the discovery of Aunt Molly Jackson as an opportunity. But what kind of opportunity?

Shelly Romalis suggests that different people developed different relationships with the Appalachian transplant. Simultaneously, these people, as did all party members and fellow travelers, maintained uneven relationships with the Communist Party's hierarchy. Dreiser and Dos Passos, for example, "thought Molly was Kentucky herself."[34] These writers "recognized the enormous symbolic power and potential of this bone-weary, aging miner's wife, as spokesperson not only for this specific cause but for larger ideological interests."[35] For folklorists Mary Elizabeth Barnicle and Alan Lomax such interests included the preservation of traditional music. They quickly arranged to record Aunt Molly, Jim Garland, and later, Sarah Gunning.[36] Mike Gold saw in them reincarnations of Joe Hill—new bards to spur on the communist march to working-class triumph.

Romalis argues that whatever one thinks of the communists' interventions in Appalachian labor struggles, it is undeniable that they "captured impressive press curiosity and played a crucial role in representing Harlan and the coal strikes to the outside world."[37] Communist journalism focused on figures like Aunt Molly and Jim Garland, but the exploited miners became a national symbol of the battle between workers and bosses in postdepression America. The folksingers symbolized a kind of authentic American nationalism that could assist the Communist Party in its ongoing challenge of deflecting attacks on members as "radical foreigners" and "outside agitators." Communists such as Gold, who embraced folk music, are best viewed against the backdrop of the larger reactionary social pressures of the twenties. Fierce union-busting, immigrant deportations, and ascendant white nativism formed the backdrop for CPUSA president Earl Browder's efforts to reshape the party as thoroughly American during the Popular Front. "We are," he proclaimed in 1935, "the Americans and communism is the Americanism of the twentieth century."

The most thorough investigation into the relationship between the CPUSA and folk song is Richard and JoAnne Reuss's *American Folk Music and Left-Wing Politics, 1927–1957*. They, like most other authors on the topic, recognize the impact members of the Communist Party had on spreading a national interest in folk song. Their work is unique, however, in extensively documenting that this impact was not the result of initiatives emanating from party leadership but rather an outcome of a small group of rank-and-file members committed to advocating folk song, often in conflict with party authorities. Some worked at labor movement schools in the South, notably Highlander Folk School and Commonwealth Labor College, where pedagogical visions encouraged fusing southern Christian singing traditions with movement-building.[38] Teachers and students often brought folk songs, and a more general attention to folklife, into their future union struggles to build the CIO and later the civil rights movement .

A small group of communists in New York City contributed significantly to building the relationship, both real and perceived, of the left to American folk song. The Reusses suggest that the trend began in 1925, well before the Popular Front, when foreign-language federations were dissolved in an early turn toward "Americanizing" the party. It is in the context of the Third Period (1928–35) that the debates over what constituted revolutionary "proletarian art" became charged. "Well before [Maxim] Gorky started removing the stigma from folk music . . . in his talk to the Writer's Conference in 1934, the American [Composers Collective] had begun changing its own position on the subject."[39] The links communist field organizers made to folk artists in Gastonia and Harlan were critical to that shift. Finally, and perhaps most revealing, JoAnne Reuss's interviews with Irwin Silber confirm that party members and leaders held quite different opinions of folk music.

Silber, born of working-class Jewish parents, grew up on the Lower East Side of Manhattan. Although he was eight years younger than Green, the men's political formations shared similarities, including active participation in the vibrant student politics of the American Student Union. Silber was drawn into the Young Communist League and officially joined the party on his eighteen birthday, in October 1943, whereas Green's short-term experience in the YCL caused him to turn away from the party. In his subsequent political career Silber ranged from being a counselor at a "radical summer camp, to Folksay founder, to American Communist Party section leader, to director of People's Songs and its successor, People's Artists." Perhaps he was most famous for editing *Sing Out!* between 1951 and 1968. It was to that publication that Seeger continually asked Green to contribute. Although Silber never had the public visibility of a performer like Pete Seeger, the Reusses conclude, "Of all the left-wing folk song enthusiasts active in the movement, Silber was the most political."[40] He was, that is, driven by political conviction and seriously involved in the Communist Party. Silber's reflections on the question of how and why the official party developed an association with folk song are therefore invaluable. As he told JoAnne Reuss in December 1998, "The impression that the Communist Party sat around and figured what to do with folk music. Bullshit! The Communist Party didn't know what to do with folk music. . . . Anything they [the leadership and most party members] did consisted of a series of reactions to it, to the extent they even thought about it. . . . Although a number of us in the leadership of People's Songs and People's Artists were members of the Communist Party, the Party itself played almost no role in determining [People's Songs and People's Artists] policies and activities."[41]

The Reusses conclude, "While those in the party club worked to shape a common radical sociopolitical outlook that they felt appropriate for their work in People's Songs and People's Artists, their efforts were mostly ignored by the rest of the communist superstructure."[42] On one hand, Silber's comments and the Reusses' conclusions support Green's portrayal of the CP as hierarchical with party leadership unresponsive to rank-and-file concerns. On the other hand, rank-and-file members had a significant amount of autonomy in the day-to-day shaping of their communist-affiliated organizations, which Green never conceded.[43] That is especially true when it came to matters of aesthetics and culture, a fact that can just as reasonably be interpreted as CP leaders not considering folk music to be a political issue they needed to prioritize. It is ironic that while party leadership expressed next to no faith in members' abilities to create culturally influential and organizationally efficacious art without strict ideological guidance, many members, through initiatives of their own, promoted the importance and power of folk song. In doing so they catalyzed what has been the most lasting influence of the Communist Party on American culture.

Green's assessment of that legacy is complicated and to some degree contradictory. In addition to his critique of the inconsistency of CP policy with respect to the relation between the party and folk music he had yet more to say on the issue, which involved Margaret Larkin. By not placing Aunt Molly in a "folk cellar," Green believed Larkin resisted long-time paternalistic assumptions, most famously articulated in Cecil Sharp's 1915 study of Appalachian ballads, that whites in the region had deeply isolated, almost timeless, cultural forms.[44] That perspective connects the romantic, utopian, and elitist attitudes that northerners assumed about poor, rural whites.[45] Larkin's use of the term *revolutionary pedestal* is in reference to Green's critique of folk revivalists, including but not limited to communists, who frequently projected revolutionary purity on the most oppressed segments of the working classes. Folk artists such as Aunt Molly, Lead Belly, and Woody Guthrie who emerged from these communities became reified symbols of cultural revolution. As the Reusses put it, "Folk traditions assumed an ideological significance far beyond anything intrinsically present in the actual lore itself," and this tendency came out of and contributed to the "radical romanticization of folklore in the noble savage tradition, which in one form or another dated back to Herder and the Grimms."[46] Green's critique of the

CP's romanticization of folk should be seen as linked with skepticism about the Popular Front and his sensibility as a folklorist.

Green contested the two most common characterizations of the Popular Front: that the CP spearheaded an unprecedented coalitional politics on the left and that transformative networks proliferated among radical artists, intellectuals, and industrial workers. When asked about the Communist Party's policy during the Popular Front of working with other socialist and liberal groups to defeat fascism, he satirized the CP's line by calling out, "Let us all work together to fight fascism *according to our platform*."[47] In other words, he did not experience a change from the strict sectarianism of the Third Period and insisted that the Popular Front was basically like other periods in party history. If you did not follow the official line, you were out. As for whether there was a profound shift in the culture of workers during this era, Green insisted he did not see it. He contested Michael Denning's thesis that an extensive "laboring of American culture" occurred in the late thirties and early forties and pointed to his Carpenters' Local 1149 as exemplary. "During the beginning of the war," he maintained, "my local was ten thousand strong. It was representative of the industrial unions that made up the Age of CIO, but I went to all the meetings. I never once heard workers singing labor songs."[48] In support, the Reusses point out that "even during the CIO's most militant days, relatively few workers attended union meetings, much less sang labor or topical songs, except during strikes; Pete Seeger's optimistic estimate is 3 percent."[49] That is a sobering assessment, especially coming from Seeger, who at the time was traveling the country and performing in union halls. Still, it is difficult to agree with the extent to which Green refutes Denning's portrayal of the era.[50]

Movements during the age of the CIO forged a significant laboring of American culture, and Archie Green was a superb example of that transformation. Between 1945 and 1959, years he spent living, working, and parenting in San Francisco, Green used his spare time to cultivate his hobby: collecting records and other artifacts and ephemera of workers' culture. On November 17, 1957, the Bay Area Building Trades newspaper *Organized Labor* ran a cover story, "Brother Archie Green: S.F. Carpenter Helps Preserve Labor's History and Lore." The reporter, Harold Rossman, celebrated Green as a labor historian without the "high sounding academic titles *or* the backing of rich universities" who directed all his spare time and money toward enriching labor's conception of itself and enhancing society's conception of workers. Linking history, art, and workday culture to a broadened vision of solidarity, Green embodied the spirit of Denning's "laboring of American culture." He was a product of a Popular Front sensibility in ways he would never admit because he associated the Popular Front with the Communist Party. It is ironic that I am presenting Green's life as a way of challenging and expanding the narrow views of the Popular Front and its relationship to the CP.

Long before receiving any formal training as a folklorist, Green educated himself through going to libraries, attending professional conferences, corresponding with scholars, and engaging in rigorous shop-floor ethnography. Like other folklorists sensitive to the epistemological politics of the discipline, he knew about tendencies to romanticize folk groups, whether coal miners or indigenous tribes. As one of Green's great predecessors and mentors in the field of public-sector folklore, Benjamin Botkin, wrote in 1944, "In one respect it is necessary to distinguish between folklore as we find it and folklore as we believe it ought to be. Folklore as we find it perpetuates human ignorance, perversity, and depravity along with human wisdom and goodness."[51] Green agreed with this framework for approaching folklife. He emphasized, for example, how communist-affiliated groups such as the Almanac Singers and People's Songs considered songs as political weapons based on an ideological view of folk songs as progressive.[52] These groups, in some sense, avoided conservative or politically reactionary elements of folklore by writing their own topical lyrics set to traditional forms.[53] Green did not initially become interested in folk songs because of having opinions about their political implications. He did so because he liked to hear them on the radio in the late twenties. He saw political significance in folk song, but the significance was of a different order and his views developed over many decades, products of his folklorist orientation.

Chapter 9 Moments in the Making of a Laborlorist

In the forties and fifties, when rainy San Francisco days cancelled work at building sites, Green frequently headed for a library. One day, when it was sunny, he asked his foreman whether he could have the day off to go to Stanford University for a meeting. The foreman asked, "What kind of meeting?" "The Modern Language Association," Green replied. Part amused, part baffled, the foreman approved the trip. Green wanted to hear a presentation on William Faulkner and meet Charles Seeger, the well-known ethnomusicologist who was keynoting the conference. A few years later, still a carpenter, Green traveled to Santa Monica to moderate a panel at the American Folklore Society's annual meeting. Green read voraciously during any free moment. Louanne Green recalls that in this period of his life he spent countless hours intensely thinking about how ideas fit together, how a particular historical event or cultural phenomenon fit within larger regional, national, and global contexts. His intellectual mentors included Louie Adamic, Carey McWilliams, Horace Kallen, and his new friend, Peter Tamony.

A homegrown intellectual and jazz enthusiast, Tamony founded the Hot Music Society of San Francisco, and Green met him at a society-sponsored concert. Tamony lived with his sister in a Mission District townhouse filled with books and cardboard file boxes in which he sorted thousands of clippings he had snipped of words used in different ways. He was obsessed with etymology and slang, publishing frequently in newspapers and language journals, including a series of articles in Ralph Gleason's short-lived *Jazz* magazine on the words *jazz, bop, jive*, and *swing*. Similarly, in a 1963 *Western Folklore* article, Tamony detailed the many meanings of the word *hootenanny* for folk revivalists. His use of etymology to open political and cultural history deeply impressed Green. The men shared an interest in workplace language, and Tamony encouraged Green's pursuit of occupational folklife and suggested he begin his own study on the origins of *hillbilly*.[1] Tamony's friendship and mentorship was an important thread in the tapestry of influences that shaped and inspired Green's meticulous detection in researching workers' cultural expressions from the forties until his death.[2]

Not long after meeting Tamony, Green was introduced to John Neuhaus by a friendly San Francisco librarian who recognized their shared interest in work songs. Neuhaus was a long-time "doubleheader," holding union cards in Lodge 68 of the International Association of Machinists and the Industrial Union 520 of the Industrial Workers of the World (IWW). Featured in Joyce Kornbluh's *Rebel Voices*, Neuhaus passionately researched Wobbly song history and regularly performed from the huge repertoire he had collected. Quite naturally, he and Green became very close friends. In a tribute to Neuhaus, Green highlighted his playful mastery of workers' slang as well as the creative way Neuhaus "integrated and synthesized his experiences" as a worker and untrained folklorist.[3] Their close friendship made Neuhaus's untimely death in 1958 especially tragic. Weeks before dying he gave Green a small metal machinist's tool box holding twenty-six of the twenty-nine IWW "Little Red Songbooks" published to that date. Neuhaus asked that Green carry on his effort to publish a comprehensive catalogue of Wobbly songs and their history. The release of *The Big Red Songbook* in 2007 marked a fifty-year journey to fulfill that commitment.[4] It is from friends like Peter Tamony and John Neuhaus that Green learned invaluable research habits and the worth of having keen scholarly instincts for musical and textual analysis. Perhaps most valuable, he witnessed firsthand in the lives of Tamony and Neuhaus exemplary models of how creative and insightful intellectual work can flourish outside the academy.

According to Green, by 1957 he was seriously involved in record collecting and had begun compiling a coal-mine discography. Aside from frequenting Jack's Cellar, a tiny record shop in San Francisco's Western Addition, Green found most of what he wanted through mail-order catalogs. He also developed close relationships with many other serious collectors by corresponding with them. "At that time," he claimed, "there were only ten or twelve serious collectors in the whole country, and I knew about ten of them."[5] Some, such as Wayland Hand, George Korson, and D. K. Wilgus, were professional folklorists, but many in this small group, including Bob Pinson, Fred Hoeptner, and Eugene Earle, pursued old-time music scholarship after work or in retirement.[6] Green corresponded regularly with all of them, and the content of those voluminous letters makes for an interesting study on the development of labor song scholarship in the twentieth century.

John Greenway's 1953 publication of *American Songs of Protest* marks an important moment in Green's life as well as for the field of folk-song scholarship. Greenway raised challenging questions about folk-song categorization and the nature of "the folk." Along with the work of George Korson, Greenway was making important new links between social movements and their songs. *American Songs of Protest*, for example, is the first academic book to research Aunt Molly Jackson and Woody Guthrie, but, as the author conceded, the repressive climate of McCarthyism limited the degree to which he openly explored connections between folk singers and the Communist Party.[7] When Green's friend Bob Burke, a librarian at the Berkeley Bancroft, told him about Greenway's book, he immediately went down to the San Francisco Mechanics' Institute Library to find it. Reading *American Songs of Protest* in 1954 was, he recalled, "as close as I would come to a seminal, life changing moment; the first time in my life that I felt I knew more than the author. I had always until then been a neophyte."[8] Green liked the book, but its shortcomings tapped a nerve. "I had lived trade unionism," he said. "I knew unions that sang, but my shipwrights union had never heard a song between 1941 and that day [in 1954]. This notion that unions are always on the march and singing, that's bullshit." Green immediately wrote to Greenway in Denver, and the Greens gave a party in his honor when he visited San Francisco in 1955. Like so many scholars Green contacted, Greenway responded with generosity to his inquiries and encouraged Green to pursue folk-song studies more formally. Toward that end , Greenway informed him that Aunt Molly Jackson was living outside Sacramento. It was riveting news. Green contacted Jackson and shortly after initiated eight visits, during which he conducted his first field recordings and interviews.[9]

Green's contact with other collectors and musicians extended internationally. In 1956 Eugene Earle told him about a young man in Australia, John Edwards, who had amassed a significant collection of early American folk and blues music. Only in his twenties, Edwards was publishing important contributions to folk scholarship and discography and had formed an epistolary relationship with dozens of American hillbilly artists, including Buell Kazee and members of the Carter Family. Edwards worked in Sydney as a clerk in the Government Transport Office and, like many of Green's contacts, pursued music scholarship after hours. The Edwards-Green correspondence abounds in specific details about songs and records and consistently ventures into questions now considered the domain of cultural studies. In an April 2, 1957, letter Edwards explained his interest in expanding conceptions of folk music: "I wanted to prove to my own satisfaction that the music of artists such as [the Carter Family, Bradley Kincaid, Jimmie Rodgers, and other big names] WAS important and of lasting value as folk music."[10] Four months later in a follow-up letter Edwards continued that line of thinking: "In recent times, I have given much thought to the purist attitude toward hillbilly. There are a world of ideas and arguments which could and should be developed to the full. The purists maintain that when a member of the folk became so sophisticated as to sing into the microphone of a record company talent-scout, the results were a definite departure from the folk idiom, but I can't entirely agree. . . . Do the purists sincerely believe Tanner produced at that session an inferior or watered-down version of the music he'd played probably for years previously without thought of recognition? Did he consciously strive to produce an 'act'?"[11]

Their correspondence also reveals that they both were thinking practically about how to channel song scholarship into professional life. Green encouraged Edwards to move to the United States and take up study under Wayland Hand, D. K. Wilgus, or Kenneth Goldstein. He would not, however, live to take that opportunity; he was killed in a traffic accident on December 24, 1960. In the event that something tragic would happen to him, Edwards had prepared a note in the top drawer of his desk specifying that "Gene Earle . . . be given full freedom to take over . . . my collection" and that "all materials be used for the furtherance of serious study, appreciation, and preservation of genuine country or hillbilly music."[12] The story of how Eugene Earle, Archie Green, and some two dozen other collectors transformed Edwards's wish and collection into the John Edwards Memorial Foundation is one of the most important chapters in American old-time music scholarship.[13]

Green, however, did have an opportunity to develop his years of study and collecting into a professional career as a folklorist. The transition began in 1959 when Bernard Karsh, a professor of sociology from University of Illinois, met Green in San Francisco. The meeting had been arranged by Green's friend Bill Friedland, a Detroit autoworker and folk-song performer who had turned to an academic career in industrial sociology. Karsh was impressed by Green's intellect as well as his sizeable collection of books and records. Shortly after the meeting he called Green from Illinois and offered him a job in the library of the Institute of Labor and Industrial Relations. The offer presented a significant logistical and existential dilemma. Although his family was rooted in San Francisco and his identity was rooted in the trades, he could not deny Karsh's assessment that his ambitions as a union official were politically unrealistic in the cold war environment.

Green agreed to a one-year training program as a librarian and left for Urbana. Louanne and their three children—David, fourteen, Derek, twelve, and Debra, seven—remained in San Francisco. Green found the work and town uninspiring, and separation from his family was depressing. He returned home after the year and hoped to work in the library of San Francisco State University. When that did not work out he resumed uptown carpentry. It was not long, however, before another offer from Urbana challenged his plans. Martin Wagner, director of the Institute of Labor and Industrial Relations, offered an assistant professorship in English and a half-time job in the ILIR library. "I'd rather be a shipwright in San Francisco than a professor in Urbana," was Green's reply.[14] Wagner, however, persisted. He would not take no for an answer. It was the only time in Green's life where someone worked to convince him that a new direction was critical, and in the late summer of 1960 the Green family moved to Urbana. They rented out their home on Caselli Street, and Green began his transition from worker-intellectual to professional folklorist. His path would continue to be anything but conventional.

During his first year as a professor Green exhibited a level of productivity that would become standard for decades to come. His handful of publications from 1960 drew heavily from work that he had begun while still a San Francisco carpenter. The university's resources and work hours enabled him to formalize and polish these inquiries, which included a rigorous combination of discography and labor history in "The Death of Mother Jones"; a tribute to his Wobbly friend John Neuhaus published in the *Journal of American Folklore*; and his first etymological study, "*Dutchman*: An On-the-Job Etymology" for *American Speech*.[15] In all his work he was very much present as a worker. In many instances he mentions lore encountered at a worksite, in others he discusses the culture and history learned through correspondence with workers like James Farrance, "coal digger," who told Green how he sung of Mother Jones: "I sang ['The Death of Mother Jones'] at union mass meetings when we was on strike. The miners went wild over it."[16]

It is not surprising, therefore, that later in life Green rarely identified himself as a teacher and seldom discussed the years he spent instructing at multiple universities. His comment to Wagner about preferring to be a shipwright more than a professor in part reflects alienation from university campuses, even after earning a Ph.D. at age fifty-two in the University of Pennsylvania's prestigious Folklore Program. What stimulated and engaged him in Urbana was the Campus Folksong Club. Shortly after arriving in the Midwest, a collector friend invited him to be an emcee, along with Studs Terkel, at the initial Chicago Folk Festival in winter of 1961. Showcasing such traditional performers as Elizabeth Cotten, Roscoe Holcomb, and Frank Proffitt, attendees and critics alike celebrated the gathering. Several University of Illinois students attended, and they asked Green to become faculty sponsor of their new Folksong Club. For the next six years he would use it and its popular newsletter, *Autoharp*, to further develop his interests in vernacular music.

At the height of its popularity the Campus Folksong Club counted nearly five hundred members, but, like most student organizations, a small core group sustained its daily life. In addition to planning campus concerts for performers ranging from Glenn Orhlin to Lester Flatt and Earl Scruggs, from the Stoneman Family to the New Lost City Ramblers, members would tune their guitars and banjos and break out songbooks at weekly folk sings. As one former club member, Bob Sayers, stressed, "For many of us, the Folksong Club *was* our social life." By "us" Sayers meant not just students who had a passion for traditional songs but also those who tended to occupy a moderate political and cultural position. "The folkies," Sayers claimed, "had a kind of romantic left wing politics; it wasn't the politics of people on the barricades. We weren't part of the hippie scene completely either. We were 'wholesome' in a strange way—a subset of people different from the hippies and the real politicos."[17] It was the mid-sixties, and such social differences were amplifying. With sons David and Derek serving in Vietnam, Green, as club moderator refrained, according to Sayers, from much political discussion. That reticence was likely a combination of his general distaste for ideological imposition and an internal struggle between supporting his sons and having an anti-imperialist philosophy.

When it came to opinions about folk music, however, Green, to say the least, was far more forthcoming. In the height of the sixties' folk revival, when college "folkniks" were much more likely to listen to Joan Baez and Pete Seeger than Buelle Kazee and Glenn Orhlin, Green consistently promoted the importance of traditional rural performers. When enthusiasts were quick to turn to West Virginia or the Piedmont for discovering folk sounds, Green led the club in producing records like *Green Fields of Illinois*, a collection of recordings from artists in rural Illinois that included a forty-page booklet on lyrics, source history, and artists' biographies.[18] Green occasionally tolerated student wishes for hosting "citybilly" performers, sometimes a pragmatic decision financially, but in general the club focused on what Green increasingly called "vernacular music" of traditional regional origin. That, in large part, was a result of Green's aesthetic ideology.[19]

Chapter 10 Vernacular Music and Cultural Pluralism

When *New York Times* cultural critic Robert Shelton attended the 1961 Chicago Folk Festival, he observed tensions over what focus, form, and future the festival should pursue. "Some questions remain unresolved around the festival's future direction," he wrote in his review of the gathering. "Should, as Archie Green, University of Illinois folklorist, suggested, the program stress the Chicago tradition of the industrial city, of immigrant songs, the labor movement and other indigenous heritages? Should it, as the delegation of thirty from the University of Michigan feels, put less emphasis on history and more on the 'here and now' of folk song and on its talented young purveyors?"[1] Shelton's questions not only point to vying conceptions of the sixties' folk revival but also reflect larger, long-time debates around cultural conservation, national identity, and artistic authenticity in Western civilization. If the concern of midwestern folk music enthusiasts in the early sixties was whether the promotion of urban folk interpreters like Pete Seeger and Phil Ochs would come at the neglect of folk originators like Frank Proffitt and Elizabeth Cotton, European cultural critics for some two hundred years had been questioning the threat of mass culture to "pure" cultural traditions. In *Folk Songs* (1778), Johann Gottfried Herder searched for discreet categories that would help him establish critical differences between nationally authentic and affirming folk songs and some of their so-called debased spin-offs. His distinctions rested on tenuously constructed dichotomies made between the agrarian and the urban, the preindustrial, and the industrial, and, ultimately, folk and rabble. "People," Herder wrote, "does not mean the rabble in the streets, which never sings or creates but rather screams and mutilates true folk songs."[2]

The period of the Popular Front in the United States saw another negotiation of this long-time debate, and, as in Herder's time, the stakes were linked with imagining new kinds of nationalism. In a 1993 essay on the history of when and how "vernacular" was first used to describe particular musical idioms, Green traced the phrase to critical discussions of Marc Blitzstein's 1937 Popular Front musical *The Cradle Will Rock* (1937).[3] Blitzstein was a member of the Communist Party–affiliated Composers Collective. Like other collective members he was influenced by the radical German modernists Bertolt Brecht, Hanns Eisler, and Kurt Weill. In *The Cradle Will Rock*, Blitzstein aimed to create a "proletarian opera" that departed from the narrative structures and conventions of dialog and singing associated with traditional musical theater. His story, set in the allegorical Steeltown, America, draws dramatic resource from the CIO's successful 1936 union organizing campaign at U.S. Steel. Blitzstein not only looked to represent the American worker in new ways but also experimented with staging that would creatively engage working-class audiences.[4] According to his friend and fellow composer Aaron Copland, *The Cradle Will Rock* established Blitzstein as "the first American composer to invent a vernacular musical idiom that sounded convincing when heard from the lips of the man-in-the-street. The taxi driver, the panhandler, the corner druggist were given voice for the first time in the context of serious musical drama."[5]

Green disagreed with Copland and other sympathetic critics who characterized Blitzstein's work as capturing vernacular idiom. He asked, "Why didn't Blitzstein—who wanted his music to serve the working class and who accepted Communist Party goals in cultural politics—seek out the varied folk songs known to workers in Pittsburgh, Bethlehem, Youngstown, Gary, or Birmingham? Conceived during the glow of CIO victories at U.S. Steel, *The Cradle* was literally in rehearsal when 'Little Steel' broke labor's seven-state organizational strike (June, 1937). These advances and defeats pulsed in *The Cradle*; why no echo of traditional music from hearth and forge?"[6] Michael Denning's examination of the musical also refers to this contradiction: "The roots of *The Cradle Will Rock* did not lie in a particular steel strike, nor in the accordion-driven Polish and Slavic polkas that dominated the musical culture of the Midwestern steel towns. Rather, its roots lay in the American and European musical avant-gardes of the early 1930s."[7] But Green went further than Denning by examining the implications of this contradiction. "Was it sufficient," he asked, "for the composer to vernacularize a text without a real desire to use folk music? In returning to Copland's formulation that Blitzstein invented a 'vernacular musical idiom,' I ask, what did the phrase mean? . . . It is highly ironic that Blitzstein's turn to vernacularity excluded the real voices of laborers and washerwomen."[8] Green was yet again referring to larger criticisms of the Popular Front's cultural politics, notably the blurred distinctions between originators and interpreters of folk styles. Green went on to note, however, that at the same time some critics were labeling *The Cradle Will Rock* as "American vernacular," another collective member, Charles Seeger, had begun to use that term in a much more specific way for music created by regionally specific folk communities.[9] Seeger's definition would serve ethnomusicologists for decades and closely approximate Green's perspective.

Returning to Robert Shelton's 1961 article on the Chicago Folk Festival, we find Green presented as an outspoken proponent for traditional, regionally rooted music. Shelton's characterization was absolutely right. As Green's 1993 article "Vernacular Music" attests, he had extremely strong feelings on the topic. The degree to which he approved of Merle Travis or Hazel Dickens was matched by the degree he abhorred the sounds of Woody Guthrie, Pete Seeger, Bob Dylan, and Bruce Springsteen as well as any number of contemporary folk interpreters and community-based labor choruses that regularly belt out "Solidarity Forever" at small labor events across the country. As folklorist and radio host Nick Spitzer warns, "The question of the authentic is a hard one with Archie."[10] To understand how and why Green distributed criticism requires some history on how various sectors of the left have related to folk music and also a sense of Green's aesthetic ideology.

Green's first exposure to folk music was in his childhood home. In their Boyle Heights kitchen, Green remembers his mother, Rose, singing Yiddish and Ukrainian songs from the Old Country. The after-school culture program at the local Workmen's Circle also included singing a range of European folk songs. In the mid-twenties, when Samuel and Rose Green purchased their first radio, young Archie was fond of listening to early country and western swing shows such as the *Blue Monday Jamboree*. The earliest songs he remembered enjoying were Vernon Dalhart's "Wreck of the Old '97," Carl Sprague's "Bury Me Not on the Lone Prairie," and Haywire Mac's "Big Rock Candy Mountain." Green reflected on his childhood love for country and western radio in a number of his writings. "Long before I could identify any musical genre, I liked radio cowboy fare. Harry 'Haywire Mac' McClintock stands out as the earliest star I associate with a given performing style. In short, broadcasts firmed my notion of authenticity before Hollywood introduced singing cowboys via film soundtrack."[11] In another passage illustrative of the qualitative nature of Green's notion of authenticity he observed, "To this day I cannot explain in rational terms Harry 'Haywire Mac' McClintock's hold on my childhood imagination, but I still recall with pleasure his repertoire and manner."[12]

Well before he connected with the political left, therefore, and well before middle-class singers such as Seeger began singing traditional folk material, Green had acquired a taste for a particular southern sound that he experienced as authentic. When Green, as a library volunteer at his elementary school, stumbled across John Lomax's *Cowboy Songs*, he did so years before he encountered the Young Communist League or the Almanac Singers. Lomax's book signified for Green that the songs he was hearing on the radio were as special as he felt they were; they could be studied, compared, and categorized.

In terms of seeing a larger context for Green's early interest in southern music, Robert Cantwell best articulates the lure and power American folk and blues has had on first-generation, working-class individuals. He notes of another folk enthusiast, "Folk music had given Helen Schneyer the 'sense of yesteryear' so perennially compelling to the sons and daughters of immigrant parents seeking to gain psychic possession of their adoptive culture."[13] Green had similar existential needs. They were evident in his early fervor for the Boy Scouts and, as a high school and college student, his engaged excitement for the expansive visions of the CIO and New Deal. Green's love for country, blues, and old-time music was part of becoming an American.

Green began seriously collecting records after returning from the Pacific Front. By the time he put down his carpenter's toolbox in 1959 and stepped up to the lecture podiums at the University of Illinois he had thorough knowledge of traditional folk performers and a well-developed philosophy about their significance to American cultural democracy. Green's student Bob Sayers recalled that the young, urban, middle-class folk interpreters who were gaining huge popular attention in the early sixties were of little interest to Green: "These people didn't mean anything to him in terms of his view of the world."[14] Green encouraged Folksong Club members to pursue traditional performers. When summer break came he would join other collectors from the JEMF on road trips to the Appalachians in search of obscure performers who, in some cases, had not been recorded in more than thirty years. He did not relate, Sayers added, "to these musicians in the way most of us do—the aesthetic way—for him [it was] the historical context that matter[ed] most." Sayers was right about the discovery of one passing reference to a coal strike, in an otherwise unknown song, elevating its performer, in Green's eyes, to great significance, but while his passion for regional history was undeniable, so, too, was his genuine love for the old-time sound.

In the wake of the late-thirties' folk revival, performers and enthusiasts like Pete Seeger and Irwin Silber promoted the term *people's songs* as a way of pushing past heated debates over what constituted an authentic folk song.

Could a young Harvard dropout like Seeger be a folksinger, or was that mantle reserved for the poor, marginalized, and regionally bound? "People's songs" was meant to dissolve such dichotomies and, very much in the spirit of the Popular Front, articulate a common relation between those who sang folk songs and those who, by virtue of origin, were folksingers.[15] Green never used the term for three reasons: It emerged from communist-affiliated folk circles; it flattened a categorical distinction he wanted to maintain; and the sounds of most of its interpreters made him cringe. Alternatively referring to their work as "pabulum" or "Mickey Mouse music," Green felt that the vast majority from early Seeger to contemporary Anne Feeney were "like a miller that takes good whole grain and then pounds it into white flour—gutless, vitamin-less flour."[16] It is not that Green lacked sympathy for the progressive politics associated with this interpretive tradition. In large part he agreed with the antiwar, pro-union, environmental ethic they favored. Green emphatically stressed, however, that any good to society conveyed through such lyrics was far outweighed by the negative consequences of a pop-oriented style. The pabulum style, from his perspective, produced cultural homogeneity:

> When the Weavers and Pete Seeger were singing, "The Banks of Marble" and "Roll the Union On" . . . that was bullshit. The value of folk song for me then and now, if you formulate a strong interest in tradition, is that even though you were singing murder ballads and blues in bawdy tradition . . . that would alert students to the role of particular groups in a plural society. Remember, I have said Mike Seeger in the Ramblers has been more radical than Pete Seeger singing songs of the Popular Front. I know my view is not accepted, but it has served me for many years. Here's my basic philosophic assumption: the Weavers, that preceded the Kingston trio, by pabulumizing music and making one folk music style available for all Americans . . . well that was good for middle-class kids at UC Santa Cruz, but it was no damn good for kids in the barrio, or kids in the slums, or kids in the Appalachian villages. What I want is kids in Appalachia to explore Appalachianality, and black kids to explore Negritude, and Hispanic kids to explore Chicanoismo, and that can only be done in a plural society goddam it. I'll stick with that philosophy 'til my dying day. And if it bothers Pete Seeger, so be it. If it bothers Bob Dylan, or Joan Baez, or Bruce Springsteen, so be it.[17]

It is ironic that Pete Seeger and his comrades in the early folk revival explicitly saw their work as contesting pop culture uniformity. The members of the Almanac Singers and later People's Songs were convinced that the social realism of folk music was an effective and urgently needed affront to what

Seeger called "the heavy hand of entertainment monopoly."[18] Furthermore, as many historians of the early folk revival note, members of left folk circles believed that their advocacy and performance of folk material would educate Americans to their folk heritage and, ultimately, empower marginalized communities against commercial cultural monism. Green did not see that happening, and he registered disapproval by avoiding the terms *folk song* and *folksinger*. By the mid-sixties, these terms, he believed, were void of substance. Green preferred the phrase *vernacular music*. Despite his view that critics such as Aaron Copland misapplied the term, it provided for Green the ability to reference traditional, regionally specific and rooted music.

It would be easy to dismiss Green's opinions as a matter of personal taste, and, on a deeper level, a projection of aesthetic essentialism. I asked him many times, "Doesn't your specific use of the term *vernacular music* fall apart when we closely trace, in terms of style and history, the constituent features of a given song?" Were his views another version of the long history of folklorists romanticizing the folk, another version of Herder's invocation of the "people"? Green appreciated these critical questions and was aware of how recent generations of anthropologists and folklorists have significantly discredited the idea of "authentic culture." Furthermore, he made important contributions to cultural critiques within the humanities and social sciences that have problematized, through historical work, traditional discourses around cultural essentialism. His book *Only a Miner*, for example, helped open room for what are now cultural studies and media studies. Its case studies of commercially recorded coal-mining songs defy traditional views of workers' culture as distinct and discreet from elite and popular culture. The entire book exemplifies how Green perceptively understood the mutually informing, socially produced categories of high, low, and middle culture. Similarly, his understanding of how culture (laborlore) was produced in urban industrial sites debunked long-lived assumptions that folklore only emerges in the rural pastoral. Green's conception of the vernacular was not simply a matter of taste, it was also a matter of political project.

John Storey's insights on cultural analysis and cultural production provide a framework for thinking about Green's critiques of folk revivalism and his privileging of the vernacular. In his incisive *Inventing Popular Culture* Storey argues for why we should see aesthetic evaluations as connected to political values:

> The fundamental problem with [analytical] approaches which privilege the aesthetic, regardless of how "democratic" their intent, is that they always lead to cultural objects and practices being separated in terms of their textual

> properties. To think, therefore, in terms of aesthetic value is to think outside the material and historical concerns of cultural studies; inevitably it leads to an argument that sees cultural practices which are defined as art as existing in some magical way outside historical and social contingencies, that is, as transcending the social and the historical, whereas cultural practices which are defined as non-art are embedded in the historical and social and can be explained in terms of this embeddedness. Although I recognize that evaluation is a core practice in the making of culture, I refuse to limit this to questions of purely aesthetic value, worrying over whether or not something is good or bad in some mythical and mystical universal sense, rather than say, *good for this, bad for that*, etc.[19]

Green's passion for vernacular music may have begun with a personal taste for the strained mountain call of a lone ballad singer or the western twang of Haywire Mac, but his lifelong promotion of the vernacular was about unwavering belief in the importance of cultural diversity for building a democratic world. The vernacular as an aesthetic, to view Green's beliefs within Storey's framework, is good for cultural pluralism. More precisely, it is a category Green maintained for the purpose of building certain kinds of institutional power and creating a society of different, more just, social relations.

Green understood the dialectical relationship between aesthetic relations and social relations of power. From this perspective his defense of the vernacular is best seen as a strategic essentialism used to advance his many inspiring projects.[20] From the Campus Folksong Club and JEMF to the establishment of the American Folklife Center, those projects shared a goal of deepening democracy. Nick Spitzer has shared a complementary assessment that speaks to the traditional music to which Green was first exposed and the way he linked the traditional with social justice: "Archie's vision of the authentic does go back to people within a particular culture stream, people within more intimate community settings, people who are the sources of the symbolic forms he most valued. For Archie the original context and sources of styles that were codified in his lifetime were the ones that are most authentic. And I think Archie's view was that social justice, in part, is the reason you make decisions for inclusion of people in the financing of public agencies or the public airwaves. You make choices to include those who don't have access to a type of commodification that makes them more appealing to a broader audience."[21]

Green's operative conception of the vernacular was a strategic essentialism; he fully understood the philosophical and historical dead end of immutably constructing certain cultural practices as "authentic," "pure," and thoroughly "traditional." As Green said of early attempts to define "hillbilly,"

"The intellectual problem is that there never was a pure period because the so-called pure period that we defined was itself a synthesis out of earlier forms. In tracing this kind of a process, it's like peeling an onion, you take off each layer and you try to come to the core and you find the core is nothing but a layer rolled up in itself. It's endless peeling."[22] If that is the case, a quandary remains: How could Green critique so strongly the adaptations popular and commercial folk interpreters have made to musical traditions from which they learned? How could he consistently blast as pabulum the music of Pete Seeger, Bob Dylan, Joe Glazer, Anne Feeney, and hordes of other folk interpreters? The best answer lies in Green's perspective that, to borrow Storey's words, "Aesthetic relations . . . mimic and help to reproduce social relations of power."[23] Green winced at the typical rah-rah, upbeat arrangements of contemporary labor choirs, but his more fundamental and paramount concern was that the marginalization of certain regional and ethnic cultural forms reflects continued economic and political marginality of those regions and ethnicities. Cultural pluralism and its link to freedom, democracy, and equality were Green's primary battlefront.

These foundational social goals are best advanced through critiquing and creating alternatives to the mainstream systems of cultural production and distribution that leave so many unheard and so few heard everywhere. This is a battle waged more on the grounds of power and politics and less around questions of aesthetic merits and differences. Green admirably fought such battles, but the music Seeger, Dylan, Baez and company have created is hardly pabulum. The popular success of cultural adaptations (e.g., early Dylan) often, paradoxically, leads to discoveries and popular revitalizations of older cultural forms, a circulation that challenges Green's assumptions and projections around the contemporary spiral into cultural uniformity. I would talk with Green, for example, about how the Charleston was a current dance craze in my favorite San Francisco bar and how the best dancers, dressed to a tee in driver caps and flapper dresses, often learned new moves by watching YouTube videos excerpted from rare film shorts of the twenties. I also described, after it became too overwhelming for him to get around in the huge crowds of Golden Gate Park in his last years, how some hundred thousand people came out to hear his friends Hazel Dickens, Doc Watson, Earl Scruggs, and others in the Hardly Strictly Bluegrass Festival in 2007. Many undoubtedly were there to hear major artists such as Gillian Welch and Steve Earle, but just as many were there to hear all the artists. A handful of enthusiastic college students arrived early at the 2008 festival and staked out front-row spots to see Emmylou Harris. During their long wait for her, however, they also enjoyed old-time artists Curly Steckler and Earl Scruggs. Such spiraling, circuitous journeys to the traditional definitely made sense to Green. He said as much in the early seventies, when, thinking about the influence of Carl Sandburg's writing on folk revivalists, he observed, "Carl Sandburg is best known to folklore students for his popular anthology *American Songbag* (1927); this book helped tens of thousands of new reader/listeners to cross the threshold which led 'back to' traditional folk song."[24]

My conversations with Green on authenticity were at times argumentative, but the arguments were not intractable. They constituted a cross-generational exchange wherein Green recognized that I traversed the partially new and shifting landscapes of the culturally vernacular. I, in turn, realized that Green had accomplished vital political work through a more than "decent philosophy" of how cultural pluralism and tradition vitalize democracy. As he said to Pete Seeger in 1965, "There were (and are) many alternative paths" to walk in the world.

Part 4 "Always on Stolen Time"

Folklore, Labor History, and Cultural Studies

Imaginatively, we reach under
the melting pot to retard its flame.

—Archie Green, on the work
of public folklorists

In 1967 the Smithsonian sponsored its first American Folklife Festival on the expansive public green of the National Mall. The brainchild of folk music field collector and performer Ralph Rinzler, the festival reflected how a new generation of folklorists was reconceptualizing the academic discipline in relation to the public sector.[1] Rinzler, who had worked for the Newport Folk Festival, "effectively lobbied S. Dillon Ripley, the secretary of the Smithsonian, to take traditional artifacts out of their cases and reveal the people and the cultural dynamism that lay behind the static dioramas and exhibits."[2] Showcasing craft demonstration, decorative art, traditional music and dance, the new festival succeeded, on the one hand, in exhibiting traditional cultural forms as living, contemporary practices. On the other hand, its emphasis on preindustrial forms of cultural expression reinforced a limited conception of folklife as always antiquarian and backward-looking. The emphasis troubled Green—one of Rinzler's close friends. The men met through their mutual involvement in folk music programming during the early 1960s and shared instincts and skills for public presentation. Unlike Rinzler, however, Green came to folklife through twenty years as a union shipwright and carpenter. In the late 1960s, as Rinzler developed the Smithsonian Folklife Festival, Green was parlaying his unique life history as a trade unionist and amateur folklorist into doctoral work that would forge an unprecedented scholarly integration of labor history, folklore, and cultural studies.[3] It is in that context that he and Rinzler began to discuss how the Folklife Festival could highlight the skills and cultural expressions of contemporary craft and industrial workers.

By 1971 Green had persuaded Rinzler to add a new thematic section to the festival. They called it "Working Americans," and Green became a behind-the-scenes coordinator of the program. That July, in the humid heat of Washington, D.C., thousands of people interacted with glass blowers, meat cutters, sheep shearers, and metal workers as they publicly demonstrated their skills just beyond the steps of the nation's Capitol. By the third day of the festival, nine ironworkers had given the Mall a bold new visual centerpiece. Their towering, two-story, steel I-beam frame emerged as a kind of alternative national monument honoring the history, culture, skills, and sacrifices of the workers who had built America.[4] Two days into the construction, the *Washington Post* ran an article on how unexpected and captivating it was to see a dozen union "hardhats" displaying their daring skill against the backdrop of the Washington Monument.[5] While the *Post* focused on the entertainment quality of the craftsmanship, my interest is in how the Working Americans exhibit—with its innovative assertion of workers' culture into quintessential public space and public imagination—provided a symbolic opening ceremony for the next forty years of Archie Green's inventive scholarly and public-sector work.

The Working Americans exhibit at the Smithsonian's 1971 Folklife Festival constitutes a milestone for labor-oriented public history in the United States and offers a means of analyzing how Green's development of laborlore made an important contribution to fundamental shifts in the disciplines of folklore, labor history, and American cultural studies between the late 1960s and early 1980s. Green's deeply interdisciplinary scholarship challenged labor history to be more attentive to workers' culture. It inspired cultural studies to ground research in workers' history, and it pushed ethnography to be more aware of political conditions and implications. Just as Green's work behind the scenes to expand the scope of the Smithsonian Folklife Festival was under-recognized and underappreciated, so, too, have been his transformative contributions in the humanities and social sciences.

To get at this range of interventions, Part 4 examines Green's development of laborlore as an interdisciplinary cultural studies practice aimed at illuminating the rich, expressive traditions of working people.

I have four objectives in this section. First, there is a benefit to making a comparative examination of the incredible range of projects Green undertook. Dozens of interviews with students, friends, and colleagues reveal that most think of Green's work in relation to what they know best. Folklorists honor his public-sector work, labor historians know his occupational lore, music scholars best appreciate his discographies and liner notes, ironworkers revere his trade union commitment and fervor for local, public history; and Appalachian scholars draw from his complex regional sensibility. There are also the linguists, visual theorists, museum curators, material culture scholars, and, of course, Wobblies. This section theorizes connections between Green's varied projects and sheds light on the core commitments that motivated his scholarly and public-sector work.

Second, the social, political, and cultural history discussed in previous chapters allows better understanding of the relationship between Green's life experiences and his intellectual, political, and civic projects. His syndicalist ideals uneasily combined with New Deal political pragmatism to form a unifying thread in his life and work. These two resources, like the Popular Front social movements of which they were part and parcel, have contradictory, antagonist elements. Green's laborlore can be seen as a continued negotiation of their different social visions. The Popular Front undeniably constituted an explosion of workers' social and political power, yet, according to Green, it gave birth to cultural forms, political discourses, and institutions that in the second half of the twentieth century strangled workers' advancement and weakened American democracy.

The third objective of this chapter is to highlight how Green prefigured, and in some cases directly figured into, profound disciplinary shifts in folklore, labor studies, and American cultural studies, beginning in the late 1950s. This inquiry simultaneously offers a better critical appreciation of Green's work and a renewed examination of the political stakes and analytical practices that constitute these groundbreaking forms of knowledge production. Green's work has too often been omitted from prevailing historiographies of new labor history and American cultural studies. To include his laborlore in these historiographies, however, expands the discussion of what the scope and significance of new labor history and American cultural studies has been and can be.[6]

Finally, this section's examination of laborlore as an interdisciplinary cultural studies practice culminates with an interpretation of its pedagogical grounding and consequence. Green's work may best be understood as a twofold political education project toward deepening democracy. Drawing from the tradition of critical pedagogy (radical educational theory and practice), I describe laborlore as a pedagogy of culture and a culture of pedagogy. The U.S. labor movement, as no shortage of organizers and labor studies scholars have noted, needs to expand and revitalize its commitment to the political education of workers if it is to reverse the decline in its strength. Laborlore, through its epistemological and political foundations, creatively serves that organizing effort.

Chapter 11 Alternative Popular Front Imaginary

Public sector folklorists like Archie were doing the dialogical ethnography thing well before the "cultural turn" . . . which came to anthropology and other social sciences via James Clifford and others.

—Nick Spitzer

In the late 1950s, while still a union carpenter in San Francisco, Archie Green coined the term *laborlore* to refer to a broad range of culturally expressive practices within trade unions, among them clothing styles, songs, shop-floor stories and jokes, posters, work rituals, and strike chants. Over the next twenty years he expanded that definition to more broadly include the work traditions and cultural practices of all workers.[1] A concept he initially used only in personal correspondences, *laborlore* first appears publicly in print in Green's 1960 tribute to his close friend and mentor John Neuhaus, the San Francisco machinist and long-time Wobbly who had given Green his collection of IWW songbooks.[2] Five years later, while working as a librarian at University of Illinois Institute of Labor and Industrial Relations, Green published his first attempt to theoretically outline the concerns of laborlore. Beginning with a critique of labor studies, his article "American Labor Lore: Its Meaning and Uses" reveals how expansively Green thought about the disciplinary horizons for studying workers. "Seemingly, no American labor specialist in the present decade," he proposed, "is ready to attack the question of the Industrial Revolution's impact on rural life; no scholar has squared a union against Robert Redfield's formulation of 'The Folk Society'; few students care to grip the slippery question of whether working class culture is folk or popular, sylvan or urban, peasant or bourgeois, naive or technological. The simple task of following unemployed Kentucky miners north to observe changes in their traditions in response to new circumstances is beyond the scope of present-day labor study centers. No academic institutes offer courses in industrial lore; no labor song bibliography contains anything comparable to the studies of proletarian novels."[3] Even that brief quotation, by virtue of the questions it raises, makes evident that Green's interest in workers' history, culture, and consciousness engaged—as well as indicted—a wide range of social science and humanities scholarship. His battlefield was not just labor scholarship. By 1965 he was already challenging folklore, history, sociology, cultural anthropology, musicology, and literary studies.

The refreshing, cross-disciplinary nature of Green's laborlore questions owed their development to his upbringing in working-class Boyle Heights, work camp experiences with the CCC, years of work on bustling San Francisco shipyards, and passionate study of vernacular music in postwar America. Green's curiosities and concerns were products of a personal history as much as an era. Coming into his political and intellectual identity during the age of the CIO, Green began wrestling with questions he would not publicly articulate until decades later when he began to publish scholarship. The time lapse, a kind of "long fetch," is critical in understanding Green's life as a worker-intellectual and how his writing has been received.[4] Green was fifty-two in 1969 when he earned his Ph.D. from University of Pennsylvania's Department of Folklore and Folklife. He also had a family and thirty years of trade union experience. That unusual life trajectory helps in understanding why folklorist Debora Kodish describes Green as "post-disciplinary-pre-disciplinary."[5] His intellectual life was predominantly shaped on the worksite, and that made a difference in the questions he posed and how he engaged with scholarly traditions.[6]

Green was a quintessential outsider to the academy, not only because of the origins of his scholarship but also because he was never comfortable once positioned within academic life. It is significant that he resigned immediately after earning tenure at University of Illinois. The Greens' youngest child, Debra, had decided not to go to college, so Green felt financially able to move to Washington, D.C., and begin voluntarily lobbying on behalf of the American Folklife Preservation Act. Even more relevant to this argument is the amount of scholarship he completed after "retirement" in his late sixties and then in his seventies, eighties, and nineties. In 1982, after several years teaching at University of Texas at Austin, the Greens returned to San Francisco to retire in the original house they purchased in 1950. From then on, working from a desk in its sunny living room, and with regular bus trips to libraries around the Bay Area, Green published more than sixty articles, ten chapters in academic anthologies, the collectively edited *Big Red Songbook*, and five more books of his own. His enormous productivity late in life can obscure the fact that in terms of his foundational intellectual concerns he was a product of the historical events of the thirties and forties.

To view Green and his laborlore work as emerging out of the energies of the Popular Front during the age of the CIO recasts him as a member of an earlier, broadly conceived circle of public intellectuals. Again, recasting is required in part because Green's voluminous productivity late in his long life can obscure the earlier association. Recall that Green was born in 1917, two years after Alan Lomax and Américo Paredes, a year after C. Wright Mills, and two years before Pete Seeger. Green was also born before Louis Althusser (1918) and Raymond Williams (1921) and some years before E. P. Thompson (1924) and Herbert Gutman (1928). It is a chronology that reveals the patterns between the fundamental questions of laborlore and the constellation of concerns taken up by this seminal group of twentieth century intellectuals, all of whom, because they did the bulk of their work in midlife, had lasting impact on activist thinkers coming of age in the New Left.

The foundational concern for this group of intellectuals was understanding how the working class changed in light of major world events: World War I, the Bolshevik Revolution, state repression of radicalism in the 1920s, the Great Depression, the general strikes of 1934, the birth of the CIO, the rise of fascism, World War II, the reconfiguration of capital through the New Deal and the war, and the rise of modern mass cultural industries. Laborlore fits into a reconceptualization of the working class insofar as it begins from the premise that workers are makers of culture not passive recipients. Green experienced firsthand that cultural agency in the 1940s and set out to document it. He found direction in the gritty social history and investigative reporting of Louis Adamic and Carey McWilliams; the state-sponsored documentation of work culture spearheaded by Benjamin Botkin in the WPA; and, more intimately and directly, the immigrant shipwrights of San Francisco who displayed culture, politics, and historical consciousness on a daily basis. In this climate, rethinking the worker was also about rethinking what it meant to be an intellectual and developing new theories about processes of cultural production.

Green dedicated *Only a Miner: Studies in Recorded Coal Mining Songs* to his father, Samuel, "for whom the skills of hand and head are one."[7] That simple and revealing honorific shatters a dichotomy rooted in the philosophical thought of Greek antiquity and persistent in both the liberal and socialist lineages of the Enlightenment—there are those who do manual work and those who do mental work. In contrast, Green's conception of laborlore, reflecting the integration of his father's life and the blossoming of new social types in the age of the CIO, proposed seeing workers as a type of intellectual.[8] Manual labor requires and informs mental labor. Green's friend Peter Rachleff addressed those beliefs: "Archie was a practitioner of the kinds of theories C. L. R. James was promoting. Workers are intellectuals. They understand what they are doing. Guys like Archie and Stan [Weir] would emphasize that to begin talking with workers, ask them to tell you a funny story. Workers' power lies in knowledge—that's what syndicalists believe."[9]

As Rachleff understands, that perspective resonated in the heated debates of the thirties and forties as progressives questioned the social function of intellectuals in relation to workers' movements, the transforming nature of university life, the bureaucratization of the state and unions, and the implications of the mass media on democracy and social justice.[10] Green's forging of laborlore should be seen as one sustained vector of that cultural-political milieu. Indeed his long life history—the choices, commitments, and sacrifices he made—signaled an important fight for the lives of workers and public intellectuals against conservative forces in the second half of the twentieth century. McCarthyism and the cold war did much to foreclose on the lives of labor intellectuals and gut progressive labor. The project of laborlore was and is a defense against that assault. In this fight, Green drew inspiration from a cast of Popular Front predecessors, much in the way Studs Terkel, Myles Horton, Howard Zinn, and even the younger Bill Moyers did as well.

Just as left intellectuals in the thirties and forties discussed the repercussions of the birth of mass media and the modern cultural industries, Green rigorously took up modern popular culture—its technologies, discourses, and marketing forms—in his laborlore work. *Only a Miner* laid groundwork for that analysis. Whereas earlier work on coal-mining songs by George Korson hinged on sustained suspicion of the influence of outside culture on miners, whether communists in the National Miners Union or popular radio, Green's book is explicitly about how folk and popular culture processes intermingle.[11] Songs become social texts that reveal changes in industrial processes, union struggle, worker migration, and how people negotiate conflicting social values and multiple identities. "It is my feeling," Green writes, "that in ballad scholarship the known song itself is but the visible portion of a largely hidden iceberg."[12] His case study of Merle Travis's huge mid-fifties hits "Dark as a Dungeon" and "Sixteen Tons" illustrates that the iceberg includes personal history, regional history, and the larger social and political-economic conditions within which they are embedded. With the advent of mass-circulated LPs and television, for example, song study for Green had to include analysis of the marketing strategies and cross-media distribution forms that had begun to characterize the cultural industry. His analysis therefore extended to the fledging history of Capitol Records, its experiments with new forms of packaging material for radio, and the meteoric rise of performer and NBC television host Tennessee Ernie Ford, who successfully covered Travis's songs.

Green's laborlore, with its dialectical approach to tracing how folk culture and popular culture cross-pollinate in the long history of songs, performers, and marketing, challenges the better-known left cultural theories of the era developed by writers like Theodore Adorno, James T. Farrell, and Dwight MacDonald.[13] Because Green aligned with their left anticommunism and shared their derision for the cultural initiatives of the Popular Front, it might be easy to lump them together as cultural critics. But Green did not view popular culture, as these critics were inclined to do, as always artistically debased and socially repressive. He disliked the performance style of popular folk interpreters such as the Almanac Singers, but his critique was not rooted in intractable suspicion for commodity form, new media technologies, and the emergent mass distribution channels of popular culture, as it was for the other critics.[14] Consider, for example, a passage near the end of *Only a Miner*: "From the perspective of staid folklorists who view the entertainment media as destructive of traditional folkways, television is a monstrous instrument. From the perspective of other folklorists, this medium may prove to be an effective source for future lore."[15] It is a subtle but fundamental insight into Green as a cultural theorist: he recognized that the cultural meaning and status of a song or any other human artifact is never predetermined and never permanently fixed.[16]

As a manifestation of his keen ethnographic sensibility, Green saw how humans constantly reinterpret and appropriate cultural objects in their own fashion in different contexts. Robert McCarl has described how such cultural perspectives informed Green's work: "*Only a Miner* operates on several levels at once—work cultures of mining communities yes, but more than this. He was also tracking how the miners' cultural materials were creeping into popular culture and, in a certain way, through sanitized versions that dulled down the ideology that was involved in the creation. Take Merle Travis' 'Sixteen Tons.' It becomes a big hit for Tennessee Ernie Ford, but look at the oppositional weight in the origins of that song. Archie pulled out these complex historical processes. He anticipated how mass culture can draw from but also turn back on working people."[17] These insights would later becomes central to the field of cultural studies.

Green viewed mass media culture industries as having many different consequences, positive and negative, antithetical and contradictory. That perspective paralleled his attitude toward another major concern of left intellectuals during the age of the CIO, the bureaucratization of the state. On one hand, his attraction to syndicalism made him skeptical of the increasing concentration of government power and the extension of its regulatory function in more facets of everyday life. On the other hand, Green celebrated the pragmatic coalitional politics of the New Deal and was swept up in enthusiasm for the AFL and CIO's expansion during the thirties and forties. Such pragmatism, especially revealed through his optimism for organization-building, defined Green far more than the classic syndicalist ideal of scorning electoral politics and state reformism. Julie Ardery is correct when she says of Green, "What's particular to Archie is that he was politicized in a time, the New Deal, when there was such tremendous hope for what organizations could do. He seized upon the power in organizations: labor organizations, civic organizations, community organizations."[18]

In fact, when Denning argues that the "real story" of the cultural front in the age of the CIO is "the story of modern forms of political struggle within state agencies and cultural institutions" that might as well serve as a prologue to the fifty years of initiatives in which Green participated to transform federal government agencies, academic associations, and trade union culture.[19]

The Dean of Public Folklore

Folklore, to borrow a favorite cultural studies trope, is a discipline at the borderlands. It has distinctly premodern, modern, and postmodern features; it lies uneasily between the humanities and social sciences; and it challenges distinctions between scholarship and advocacy. These dualities reveal folklore's capaciousness as much as its tensions, contradictions, and limitations. They also suggest why Archie Green felt drawn to folklore's pursuits and practitioners. He was a borderland character and had the entangled sense of marginality, hybridity, and freedom that suggests. More than by any other professional label, Green was known as a folklorist, and more than any other community (with the possible exception of his local carpenters' union), folklorists have revered and honored him. He made enemies as well. Green pushed and pulled at the discipline, and, as is usually the case, that made some unhappy. An older cousin of cultural anthropology, folklore's disciplinary origins are implicated in modernity's nation-state projects. Nationalism has always drawn from and depended on folklore to bolster romantic origin myths and define as natural and eternal a relationship between a specific body of land (state) and a specific human community (nation). Nationalism, therefore, simultaneously looks backward and forward. It is nostalgic in the way it helps construct the past and bolster traditions against the often dizzying winds of modernization and cosmopolitanism. It is forward-looking in the sense that it can serve particular visions of the future—imagined social destinies.[20]

Especially since the early seventies some folklorists and anthropologists have critically and historically taken up how folklore has, from its beginning, been defined through contested politics of culture.[21] The phrase "contested politics of culture" highlights the way the discipline has always taken shape through spoken and unspoken struggles around what counts as authentic culture in any given social historical context. Archie Green was at the forefront of taking up that constellation of issues. Well before many in the field, he gave critical thought to long-time assumptions of culture and knowledge inherent in folklore. With laborlore's concern for cultural practices within industrial workspaces, he stretched disciplinary assumptions about the relationship between tradition and modernity. Similarly, his emphasis on public, worker-centered projects sparked healthy debate about the relationship between folklorists and the designated folk. Because he rarely wrote formal theoretical pieces, Green is not usually thought of in this light, but both the nature of his laborlore research and his public orientation deeply challenged assumptions within folklore as a discipline.

At the first Working Americans exhibit on the National Mall in 1971, Green convinced Rinzler to expand his conception of who constituted "the folk," and his relationship to ironworkers was explicitly one of advocacy. He did not entirely dismiss the category of the traditional, but he was at a borderland, revering tradition yet seeing it in new places and reifying the authentic yet stretching its horizons. As he wrote in 1978:

> As a scholar I have long accepted limited views of folk society and traditional behavior. Similarly, I have felt at ease with conventional methods in research. As a citizen I have wanted to see marginal or overlooked persons, including industrial workers, achieve their "place in the sun." I continue to be partial to people labeled "folk" and treasure their lore. In examining the twin roles of study and action, I know also that scholarly conduct does affect the identity and esteem of the subjects of my research. Accordingly, I am not immune from responsibility beyond the academy. Hence, the kinds of questions asked here about bus drivers, boat builders, airline pilots, and television anchor women, are not only conceptual, but are also civic and moral in nature. Scholarly choices of field or method do have consequence in the larger society. It seems

> to me that our sensitivity is heightened and our reports strengthened if we can articulate and face openly the dilemmas posed by the cliché, "scholarship *versus* activism."
>
> This attempt to make palpable a contradiction in my own thought, as well as attention in this paper to past definitions and early writings, springs from a hope that some folklorists in the future will resolve or bypass such ambivalence. Ideally, less torn than their predecessors, they will manage to explicate old lore in new industrial settings as well as seek fresh patterns in work-oriented expression.[22]

This passage embodies and prefigures several ideas central to critical shifts in folklore studies between the late sixties and the eighties, changes catalyzed by folklore's encounter with feminist theory, poststructuralism, and postmodernism. These shifts, alternately referred to as "the reflexive turn," "the postmodern turn," or "the cultural turn," transformed not just folklore but many other social science and humanities disciplines. Over and over, Green placed himself in what he wrote; invariably, readers learned why he knew about his topic, why he cared about it, and how he proposed to work through it. It is a distinctly feminist practice. Green's writing exhibits heightened awareness of how social location relates to knowledge production, whether in terms of personal, political, and aesthetic investment in subject matter or of sharing openly what he could not see and did not yet know. He was, as these qualities of his scholarship indicate, attuned to the fundamentally social nature of knowledge and serious about how he took up the ethical imperatives of being an ethnographer and public intellectual.

These characteristics as principles and as writing techniques grew out of his history as an avid old-time music discographer and consummate etymologist. A discographer and etymologist, as Green's personal correspondence indicates, always depends on others for clues, leads, and feedback. Discography and etymology are collective disciplines. One of Green's earliest published essays, "*Dutchman:* An On-the-Job Etymology," is proof of his commitment to an open process. "Perhaps," he concludes, "a curious reader would like to present his own etymology for *dutchman*. Of particular value would be trade journal or workingmen press usages of the term in the days of early German immigration into the United States."[23] These qualities also indicate, in the anti-Stalinist tradition, his aversion to dogma and intolerant certitude. Green purposively left open many of his inquires, and his open partisanship was not so much a critique of scholarly objectivity as of the objectivity-subjectivity binary and the power relations so often masked by claims of disinterested inquiry. As Green once maintained, "Cultural conservationists cannot escape political action, whether testifying on local zoning laws or articulating outrage at the sight of oil-drenched otters in the Prince William Sound or oil-drenched cormorants in the Persian Gulf. . . . We train to explicate artistry in all its settings, to probe metaphor's limits. We seek to preserve fiddle tune and guitar run, barn sign and scrimshaw token. But day to day news pours into parlor, den, or office about social inferno, new horrors confronting people and environments."[24]

For all these reasons Green's public folklore should be viewed as an innovative extension of long-time struggles within the discipline to push beyond the more conservative, literary, and academic aspects of folklore studies toward new kinds of fieldwork and new forms of public presentation. Horace Kallen, Robert Winslow Gordon, B. A. Botkin, and Constance Rourke, folklorists and pragmatic philosophers of the Progressive Era and Popular Front who argued for the central role of pluralistic cultural life to egalitarian democracy, were, for Green, models of how folklore scholars could take principled, public stands to support oppressed and marginalized people and the cultures they fostered.[25] Botkin, who spearheaded folk documentation within the New Deal's Federal Writers Project, was an exemplary predecessor whose recognition of "industrial folklore" paved the way for Green's laborlore studies. Botkin's advocacy of the social and political significance of documenting former slaves, industrial workers, and new immigrants telling their own histories inspired Green to emphasize in his own work the importance of what culture means to the very people who create it.

For decades Botkin defended the legitimacy of "applied folklore" against academics such as like Richard Dorson of Indiana University who maintained that it "debased the coin of scholarship."[26] Green directly entered this debate in the decade that he lobbied in favor of the American Folklife Preservation Act. The bill, after several rounds of defeat, eventually passed unanimously in 1976, opening the door for the creation of the American Folklife Center within the Library of Congress.[27] Senate hearing records reveal Green and Dorson in an impassioned exchange over the appropriate purpose and practice of professional folklore. Dorson asserted that a folklorist does not serve humanity "by tying in his research and his scholarship with social causes," and then Green rebutted, "The price for so-called objectivity is often sterility." "What is the commitment of a scholar as a citizen?" he asked the senate committee. "At what point does his conscience impel him into some form of action?"[28] Green never used Botkin's term *applied folklore* because he felt it incorrectly indicated that academic scholarship is "unapplied" in a falsely objective sense. Instead, he used *public folklore* or *public-sector folklore*, terms embraced by an emergent generation of folklorists in the seventies. One of them, Robert McCarl, recalled of Green, "You can't work in public folklore for any amount of time with local communities without a real in-depth negotiation with what you are doing and why you are doing this, but many people in the academy can persist without this, they have enjoyed a sense of remove. Archie Green has always called them on it."[29]

One way to understand the difference between Dorson's and Green's views of folklore is that Dorson worked vigilantly to defend and build the legitimacy of folklore within the academy and focused his advocacy on university deans and presidents, scholarly associations, and disciplinary journals. Green struggled in these sites, too, but he devoted the bulk of his work to persuading government agencies and the trade union movement of folklore's worth. He was compelled to battle on different fronts than Dorson, but by no means did he limit his advocacy to senate hearings or annual meetings of the American Folklore Society.

In 1975 at the University of Texas at Austin, Green designed and taught the first course on "Folklore and the Public Sector" with the enthusiastic support of his new colleagues Roger Abrahams and Américo Paredes. The twenty-seven-page course syllabus displays his profound understanding of political, intellectual, and cultural history in the United States. The course moved chronologically from colonial America to the present but was organized thematically "against a backdrop of polarities: high vs. low esthetics, native vs. foreign origins, melting pot vs. pluralistic commitments, commercial vs. community settings, [and] public vs. private modes."[30] Nick Spitzer is but one of many innovative practicing public folklorists inspired through Green's course. A graduate student at the time, he recalls it being a moment when folklore "was feeling the pressure of sociolinguistics and hard-nosed symbolic anthropologists to go in a theoretical direction. . . . They were always adding 'istics' to folklore to draw this out: folkloristics—a more formalist science of the communicative aspects of culture we were dealing with." Although Green respected those changes and drew from the growing body of theory, "He didn't see [folkloristics] as an end. He saw it totally as a means. He always saw that what is much more important is the people, their art, its meaning *to them*, and its meaning *to all of us, as people*."[31]

A decade after concluding his lobbying and teaching Green wrote, "Coming to the academy after seasoning in a bicultural family and after learning a waterfront trade, I could help articulate a legislative agenda for folklife."[32] He not only often honored predecessors like Kallen and Botkin but also, correctly, noted that none of his predecessors had pursued the idea of translating cultural pluralism into federal law.[33] "The American Folklife Preservation Act," observes Sandra Gross Bressler, "is the only piece of Congressional legislation that signifies a national commitment to cultural diversity."[34] In the wake of the law's passage, federal and state funding for folklife research and presentation has grown significantly.[35] Students of folklore have increasingly pursued ethnographic fieldwork and as a consequence have been well positioned to make substantial contributions to debates about the politics of culture throughout the humanities and social sciences since the eighties. More important, these public folklorists have facilitated innumerable community projects that examine and celebrate cultural pluralism and people's history.[36]

As a discographer, laborlorist, and public-sector innovator, Archie Green's impact on the field of folklore and the related field of public history was profound, but his interdisciplinary sensibility and imaginative civic orientation requires looking beyond folklore to better understand the nature and extent of his intellectual and activist contributions.

Chapter 12 New Labor History and American Cultural Studies

Archie was there before any of us were, when there was no such thing as Appalachian studies.

—David Whisnant

In 1959, when Bernard Karsh recruited Green for a job in the Labor and Industrial Relations Library at the University of Illinois, it was on the strength of his knowledge of labor history and worker culture. Once in Urbana, Green efficiently handled his library duties and devoted much energy and time to directing the hugely popular Student Folksong Club. This combination of employment and personal interest gave Green, for the first half of the sixties, a unique platform from which to conduct research into the connection between labor song and labor history. During school breaks he would frequently join other aficionados of old-time music such as Ed Kahn and Norm Cohen on lengthy road trips in hope of locating obscure hillbilly musicians, who in some cases had not recorded or performed in decades. Drawing from such research, Green began his lifelong practice of prolific publishing. In the early sixties he wrote articles for regional magazines, essays for academic journals, and a steady number of liner notes for the burgeoning folk record industry. By 1966, through seminal articles like "The Death of Mother Jones" and "Hillbilly Music: Source and Symbol," Green had made a name for himself in the American Folklore Society and larger folk revival circles. The initial conference presentation and subsequent publishing of his paper "Hillbilly Music: Source and Symbol" was particularly significant in firmly establishing hillbilly music as a fecund and academically legitimate area of study for folklorists. Encouraged by this influence, Green decided to enter University of Pennsylvania's doctoral program in folklore in order to deepen his studies and lend authority to his scholarly contributions. Taking a leave of absence from Illinois, Green began doctoral work under the supervision of MacEdward Leach, one of the few ballad scholars at the time who encouraged his unorthodox historical work.[1]

Green's dissertation on recorded coal-mining songs became the groundbreaking book *Only a Miner*, which the University of Illinois Press published in 1972 as the inaugural study in its now-extensive Music in American Life series. Green recognized that *Only a Miner* advanced, through scope of inquiry and methodology, beyond traditional disciplinary boundaries. "Many scholars," he asserted, "place no importance on the intimate relationship of the disciplines of folklore and history. But even folklorists (like [George] Korson) and historians (like [Philip] Foner) who clearly understand the relationship find it difficult to blend disciplinary skills." As a corrective, Green proposed an "integrated historical-folkloric technique—one that assumes . . . that folk composers and formal historians both cope with narrative art [and that] not only [is] the folk ballad a historical document but that the historian is also a special kind of singer of tales."[2]

In *Only a Miner*, song study becomes a portal into the complex intersections of technological development, worker migration, Appalachian history, social movement study, artist biography, record industry history, shifting race and gender relations, prison history, and the formation of working-class identities. The book, which is representative of Green's larger laborlore project, expresses and foreshadows many of the intellectual and political commitments of two emergent and related scholarly transformations of the day: the rise of new labor history and the impact of cultural studies–ethnic studies on American studies.

In a 1965 article written with an uncharacteristically theoretical focus, Green posed questions that were ahead of their time: "Does a [scholar] station himself at the furnace hearth, the personnel office, or the juke joint? Are our commitments strong enough to push us to steel not only where it is shaped physically, but also where the expressive life of its workers is shaped? It is entirely possible that future research in industrial culture will belong more to labor historians, industrial sociologists, or ethnic studies specialists than to folklorists."[3] Such questions illustrate the disciplinary shift that would come to be known as writing "history from below" or, in academic parlance, new labor history.[4]

New labor history's emphasis on workers' identity, culture, and struggles emerged as a response to the limitations of the Wisconsin School or Commons School of labor history. In the first half of the twentieth century labor studies was practiced as a subset of economics, and the leading proponent was John R. Commons at University of Wisconsin-Madison. Green's favorite professors at UC Berkeley, Paul Taylor and Ira Cross, identified with the Wisconsin School, which focused on labor's institutional history through studies of unions, union leadership, and major labor strikes. These studies looked favorably upon trade unionism insofar as they saw it as a stabilizing factor for capitalism's continuation. Whereas Wobblies and Marxists had long seen inherent antagonism in the worker/employer relationship, the Wisconsin School believed in the possibility of a broad worker-employer consensus, and its labor scholarship reflected that political commitment.

By the late fifties and early sixties a number of young U.S.-based scholars, the best known of whom being Herbert Gutman and David Montgomery, began developing other approaches to labor history. Deeply influenced by E. P. Thompson, Christopher Hill, and other British Marxist historians, they took up labor studies from the disciplinary perspective of social history, using the analytical tools of historians. In itself, this was a generative break from the questions and methods of economic history. Their early work moved the core concerns of the field away from institutional labor history toward working-class history, a shift reflective of how their radical readings of capitalism differed from the liberal views of the Wisconsin School.[5] A generation of student activists from the New Left poured into graduate schools in the late sixties and early seventies, further propelling scholarly interest in uncovering workers' struggles and cultures. Often emerging from passionate engagement in the civil rights, anti–Vietnam War, and women's movements, the students developed new perspectives on the working class, the development of oppositional cultures, and the dynamics of social change.

Central to these shifts was an expanded conception of where one could find "the worker" and, by extension, an expanded conception of what kinds of social-historical materials could be looked at to illuminate worker identity, culture, consciousness, and struggle. In this respect, history from below challenged both Marxist and liberal assumptions about the working class. New labor historians saw that politics dwells in, congeals around, and emanates from places and identities unmapped and undetermined by economic modes and relations of production. Transcripts of union meetings might still be significant, but they were no longer sufficient. The politics of the everyday, to use a popular and revealing phrase, started to become an important historical concern.

It is no wonder that new labor history began to draw heavily from folklore studies. With their long history of ethnographic fieldwork, folklorists have meticulously been documenting the speech, rituals, songs, jokes, fashions, and visual art of people living their everyday lives in everyday contexts at work, at home, and in public. Yet despite the centrality of folklife to the intellectual and political vision of history from below, folklorists have been inadequately recognized in the commonly circulated origin stories of new labor history. The absence of Archie Green from standard historiographies of the discipline is a case in point.[6] In 1965, when Green encouraged labor historians to look beyond the parameters of the work place and examine the fuller cultural life of workers, he had not yet heard of E. P. Thompson, Herbert Gutman, or David Montgomery. It was in the next ten years that their work would become widely available and influential, the same years in which *Only a Miner* began to circulate.[7] Green's book was never reviewed by a labor history journal, nor was it mentioned in the United Mine Workers periodical. Almost immediately, however, it became a revered founding document for the nascent field of Appalachian studies.[8]

The central issue is not that one more name should be added to the list of founding (white) fathers of new labor history. It is more consequential that the epistemological and methodological transformation of history from below—a transformation born of complex, far-reaching, and often revolutionary social forces—has over time been reduced and disciplined into a short list of a handful of writers within the academy. Remembering other influential tributaries in the origin story of new labor history can make a difference for how we understand labor history's current horizon of concerns and their political consequences. Bringing Green and others into historical view is less about altering the past and more about rejuvenating and decalcifying current historical work.

As Robin D. G. Kelley's *Race Rebels* makes clear, W. E. B. Du Bois and C. L. R. James have also been insufficiently recognized as paramount to making the analytic interdisciplinary connections through which new labor history found life. Kelley explains, for example, how their absence might account for the overly white and Eurocentric focus of the first wave of new labor historians.[9] Similarly, David Roediger points out that the work of George Rawick and Alexander Saxton should be essential in viewing the forces that turned labor history toward workers' culture.[10] Rawick drew from African American slave studies in *The American Slave: A Composite Autobiography*, and Saxton wrote many novels before embarking on his landmark *Rise and Fall of the White Republic*. Rethinking new labor history should be done in light of all these intellectuals, not just Green.

Green's vision of laborlore challenges the trend of new labor history to ask questions and focus on sources that define the kind of history it originally set out to contest. In general, the Wisconsin School labor history confined itself to institutional histories of unions and the famous men who led them. There was little room for worker experience, worker subjectivity, and worker folklife. Likewise, little attention was given to women, workers of color and immigrants who have often labored under the most exploitive conditions. Green helped address these shortcomings through laborlore's focus on cultural and worker subjectivity, but not all new labor historians have embraced his concerns. As Roediger observes, "You would think that Archie's studies about language—his word studies of fink, wobbly, scab, etc.—would be really interesting to labor historians. But this gets entangled in the minds of some labor historians with what they regard as an attack on materialism by the linguistic turn and cultural studies. Their idea that language studies always and inevitably take you away from material life, work, and oppression and gets you talking in an ethereal realm that never gets you back to class relationships. That's just flat wrong. That's not what Archie does at all."[11]

A central development in new labor history is that when labor scholars began serious consideration of questions of workers' culture they were challenged to think in new ways about the roles and places of workers' voices. These concerns necessitated fresh research methods and encouraged a democratization of the processes of history-making. The disciplinary transformations were not only about new subjects and hidden histories but also about allowing workers to speak for themselves. Archie Green helped direct the democratization process, not only because he embodied a link between labor history, folklore, oral history, and cultural studies but also because he forged inroads for workers' culture in public history. Green's initiation of the Working Americans exhibit in 1971 and his indefatigable commitment to the establishment of the American Folklife Center (1976) should be acknowledged as politically and historically related to other radically democratic projects of the era, including Alice and Staughton Lynd's publication of *Rank and File: Personal Histories by Working-Class Organizers* in 1981 and Herbert Gutman's American Social History Project at CUNY in the same year.[12] It was Green's experience as a worker, his syndicalist-rooted commitment to the dignity and intelligence of working people, that combined with his skills as an ethnographer and folk festival impresario to makes these interventions imaginable and manifest.

* * *

The disciplinary transformations in folklore and labor history in the late sixties and seventies were related. Scholars who led these shifts were inspired by the same political, cultural, and intellectual climate that catalyzed the birth of ethnic studies, feminist studies, cultural studies, and significant changes in the organizing questions of American studies. Embedded in these new developments was also the energy to initiate urban studies, regional studies, community studies, and a host of other inventive disciplinary formations that drew together in new ways history, sociology, anthropology, literary studies, linguistics, musicology, visual theory, political theory, and critical pedagogy. It would be overwhelming to trace the specific political, professional, and intellectual lineages that constituted these transformations, yet many of their concerns are part of Green's writing. That is partially explained by his early exposure to, and long-time contemplation of, how cultural meaning travels across time and space through different systems of symbolic order.

Green had a great capacity for seeing how a cultural artifact, whether blues song, retirement ritual, or popular work hat, shifts in meaning when performed and interpreted in different places and times by communities other than those that created it. Nowhere is that skill more apparent than in his brilliant account of the rise and fall of the "cosmic cowboy" in Austin's psychedelic country rock music scene of the seventies. "Austin's Cosmic Cowboys: Words in Collision" draws on his long-time practice of exhibiting how word study can reveal profound social change but takes that research approach to new frontiers. Green traces how the figure of the cowboy has undergone a virtually unimaginable reconfiguration in social meaning, from national mythic hero to a deviant antihero on the fringe of society. Tuxedoed icons of the Grand Ole Opry have been displaced by swaggering outlaw spirits such as Kris Kristofferson. While the study is rooted in his firsthand investigation of Austin's clubs and recording studios, a full reckoning with the cultural forces at play necessitates a sweeping social history of the American cowboy alongside a cogent reading of the mix of tensions and transgressions defining race, class, geography, and technology in the sixties and seventies. The essay's opening and closing lines set and capture the stakes: "Having reached the eighties, we are conscious that much of the new vocabulary of the sixties and seventies, psychedelic or apocalyptic, is already dated. The very technology which extends language into space through computerized rocket travel also renders many neologisms obsolete before they take hold widely. . . . Sensitive to cosmetic portraits and plastic packaging, I am chiefly concerned about our fragmented polity, about Americans in collision with each other. Is there any way to pull our society together into a sane future if disparate cultural expressions cannot be respected and shared?"[13]

The expansive quality of Green's thinking and activist interventions were in no small part a product of coming of age in an era when substantial intellectual work took place outside the academy. Many who inspired and, in some cases, personally mentored Green were journalists (Louis Adamic and Carey McWilliams), workers (Benny Carwardine and John Neuhaus), musicians (Sarah Ogan Gunning and Hazel Dickens), and eccentric, free-range intellectuals (Peter Tamony, George Korson, and John Edwards). Even the professional academics from whom Green learned (Horace Kallen, B. A. Botkin, and Wayland Hand) had strong connections to the public sector and social movements.[14] As Michael Denning, Robin D. G. Kelley, George Lipsitz, and David Roediger emphasize and exemplify, it makes a difference intellectually and politically to have footing in multiple communities. The differences are manifest at the level of analysis (what we pay attention to interpreting) and the level of accountability between knowledge production and community life (what kinds of knowledge are created for whom).

When I traveled around the United States interviewing dozens of people who worked with, studied under, and befriended Green, I heard time and time again reflections that revealed the differences social roots and routes had made in his work. Many in that extensive community recognized how his unique experiences registered in the questions he raised, material he saw worthy of analysis, connections he theorized, and civic interventions he imagined and organized. There were patterns in the commentaries, some obvious such as his role in founding the American Folklife Center and others subtle. One example of the latter is the question of Green's influence on American cultural studies. I believe, with others, that Green should be seen as a major figure in the development of cultural studies in the United States. The claim, however, is hard to pursue and gauge for two related reasons. First, Green's writing takes up many kinds of questions and, as a result, figures into a wide range of disciplines. Second, cultural studies has taken shape as a set of concerns and methodologies in different ways across the humanities and social sciences at various times from the fifties to the present. The turn to culture in the new labor history of the late sixties was quite different from the "cultural turn" or "linguistic turn," as it is often described, which saw the rise of poststructuralism and postmodernism in the eighties.[15] Although they are related, "cultural studies" in this volume refers to the earlier, broader movement to prioritize cultural analysis at the level of everyday life practices in the humanities and social sciences. These two attributes—the breadth of Green's work and the multiplicity of what we can consider cultural studies—help reveal the nature of each other. We learn something of Green when we view laborlore as an interdisciplinary cultural studies practice, and we learn something of cultural studies when we consider the questions, methods, and interventions of Archie Green's many projects.

In 1998 Brian Finnegan, a graduate student studying with American studies professor John Vlach, wrote a provocative article taking up the question of Green's relationship to cultural studies. Playing off the title of Green's first book, Finnegan's "Only a Folklorist, or Cult Stud?" proposes that Green, and other folklorists such as Roger Abrahams, offer "a parallel history of cultural studies in the United States."[16] By constructing a "parallel history," Finnegan seeks to establish Green's writing alongside the standard origin story of cultural studies as emerging from Birmingham, England, through the work of Raymond Williams and Dennis Hoggart. He also demonstrates that Green's work prefigured many central insights associated with later key cultural studies thinkers such as Julia Kristeva, Jean Baudrillard, and James Clifford. Indicative of the academic trends at the time, Finnegan maintains that Green's examinations of work songs and commercial graphic art contain insights that later cultural studies theorists would describe as "intertextuality," "the precession of the simulacra," and "hybridity."[17] Finnegan's analysis complements my earlier discussion of how Green's interests relate with those of other thinkers who came of age during the era of the Popular Front in the late thirties and forties. Questions of commodification, representation, and new subjectivities concerned both Popular Front intellectuals and post-sixties cultural studies intellectuals. Remarkably, Green was born early enough—and lived long enough—to participate in the discourses of both eras.

One way to track that continuum is through the sixty-eight consecutive articles Green wrote in his nearly twenty-year series, "Commercial Music Graphics," for the *JEMF Quarterly*. The *Quarterly* is widely considered as essential to the establishment of blues, folk, and country music scholarship, and its long-time editor Norm Cohen describes Green's "Graphics" series as "perhaps its most significant contribution to music scholarship."[18] "Graphics" offer a glimpse of how and why Green should be viewed as an influential cultural studies thinker. Early in the series, Green stated his objective: "to follow country music history to the present through its visual representations."[19] He began a critical analysis of images from twenties' and thirties' album covers, record label catalogs, and magazine advertising, as a way of "understanding how hillbilly music became a discrete commercial idiom."[20] Over the years, Green expanded his visual readings to movie posters, popular fiction, ethnographic films, museum exhibits, easel paintings, and lithographs. As he said in his twelfth "Graphics" article, "At its simplest level, a piece of graphic design can announce, advertise, or sell music; at a complex level it can make a significant statement about the context in which music is received and understood in society."[21] Similarly, in his concluding article, "Graphics #68," he observed, "By turning to case studies of individual songs (including attention to catalogs, brochures, and similar sales material) I could situate each song in a wide setting of social history and literary landscape."[22]

Concern for social context challenged Green to think deeply about how social norms, tensions, and contradictions are negotiated through visual images in the commercial market. To better understand the implications of the symbolic world, he pushed himself to "see music" and "hear art."[23] Time and time again from 1967 to 1985 he discussed race, class, and gender formation in relation to the visual and in relation to commercial markets, questions pursued by many contemporary cultural studies scholars. Green recognized that to get at the meaning of any cultural object it is necessary to go to those who received it and examine the cultural context and material conditions within which they made meaning of the object, whether song, poster, dance step, or popular joke.[24]

Interpreting a late-twenties' brochure for "Old Time Edison Disc Records," Green noted, "The visual feature . . . that especially interests me is the cover drawing of 'happy darkies' dancing to banjo music in front of a southern home. It is no great mark of sophistication in 1971 to comment on racial stereotypes (plantation life / minstrel show / coon song) in American art. A question from the perspective of today is: Why was a drawing of Negroes used in the 1920s to illustrate music by white performers directed at a white rural-derived audience?"[25] That complicated question reveals as much about how Green perceived the transmission of meaning across social divisions as it indicates how the skills of folklore assisted him in forming such questions.

In one sense, folklore's long tradition of thinking through particularity, cultural variation and transmission, regionalism, and ethnography prepared Green and other folklorists to think through social difference, situated-knowledge, the subaltern, reflexivity, diaspora, and local and global cultural processes in ways that have become fundamental to cultural studies since the eighties.[26] The "Graphics" essays consistently illustrate how Green took up such issues within and between many different time periods. Take, for example, his comments on a 1962 concert poster of J. E. Mainer and the Crazy Mountaineers from Galax, Virginia. Green had learned that Mainer, a white performer, had ceased using the poster and no longer performed the act it promoted after passage of the Civil Rights Act in 1964. "Surely," he wrote, "in the 1970s we are ready to discuss the Afro-American minstrel show as it lingered for more than a century in white rural drama and country music. . . . It is my belief that, less than ten years ago [1965], J. E. Mainer was still presenting to rural folk audiences a skit based on the folklore of slavery. Ironically, he gave up this form at the precise time when popular culture superstars were able to use (and be used by) the giant music-entertainment medium to reach uncounted millions of Americans with 'hip' rock forms of Sambo and Liza."[27] Just as Green's attention to the lore of industrial workers challenged stereotypical conceptions of folklorists as only antiquarians, here the "Graphics" series read contemporary culture with an eye to how the past endures in the present. "Hearing the visual" and "seeing the music" historically, Green viewed seventies' rock stars as drawing performative conventions from a long history of minstrel staging.

The "Graphics" series effectively illustrates what Debora Kodish respects about Green's work: "One of the enduring lessons from Archie is to do work that's good, and to do work that is useful. He used theory, but when you look at his work, he also has solid information everywhere."[28] While Green engaged many of the discussions central to cultural studies, he never wrote in a way that was accessible only to academics in the field. This practice was a matter of principle. Reflecting on the political imperative of cultural conservationists, Green wrote, "We measure growth by framing cultural-conservation discourse in the largest settings at our command. To take the high road in our strategies implies willingness to question internal language, to stand back from catch words of our respective professions (*invented tradition, pristine park, old-time music community, impact assessment, holistic reach*). In using plain speech to communicate with others inside and outside our professions, we undergird analysis, advance action, and step into coalitions."[29] These commitments stem from Green's primary loyalty to work that bridged contemplative practice with public action.

As with his contributions to folklore and labor history, considering Green's work from the perspective of cultural studies again reveals collective public orientation. The "Graphics" series, as a long-term anchor for the *Quarterly*, expressed the mission of the John Edwards Memorial Foundation. "We set as our task to serve not only the academic community," said JEMF founding member Ed Kahn, "but also to try to integrate record collectors, discographers, fans, performers, and representatives from the music industry into our work. We wanted representation not only from the United States, but from around the world."[30] That Green was a strong force in shaping this participatory, educational, and organizational vision comes as no surprise given how he channeled the principles of laborlore into a wide range of intellectual and public sector projects that ranged from the Working Americans exhibit in 1971, to *Only a Miner*, to the American Folklife Preservation Act.

Chapter 13 Laborlore

A Pedagogy of the Working Class

Archie is best seen as a principled public intellectual.

—Debora Kodish, founder of the Philadelphia Folklore Project

We have seen that during the age of the CIO, when Green's political convictions were formed, he was attracted to both the revolutionary tradition of anarcho-syndicalism and the pragmatic, reformist agenda of New Deal liberalism. There are significant and irreconcilable differences between these social visions but both provided room and resource for Green's multifaceted laborlore project. Whether expressed through his books, public history projects, or federal legislation, laborlore grows from a principled respect for working people. Green assiduously collected, presented, and interpreted workers' culture because he believed that honoring workers is essential to building a democratic, pluralist society. Grounded in that conviction, he was much more likely, in the later part of his life, to discuss politics in terms of a struggle between cultural monism and pluralism—tendencies that can cut across different political-economic orders whether socialist dictatorship, corporate liberalism, or Islamic theocracy—than to defend the abstractions of socialism, anarchism, liberalism, or any other political form. Thus Robert Cantwell can accurately portray Green's work as a sustained "conversation on the politics of culture."[1] Green was oriented to politics through culture, and, for him, culture exerted definitive political power. "I think attention to particular cultures goes with pluralism," he observed. "Monism goes with pop culture. When I emphasize that Britney Spears and Bruce Springsteen and Pete Seeger end up in the same functional category, I'm not talking about their ideology. It is their *style* that is going to rule over their ideology. The ideology of the songs will be forgotten, but the style will prevail."[2] For Green, the ascendance and proliferation of a pop homogeneous style was pluralism's poison.

Laborlore, as a form of investigating and honoring workers' diverse cultures, was Green's strategy for advancing pluralism. It is important to know, however, that in his final years, he considered whether that strategy might have been a complete failure. "Even if my position is well defined, it has not been achieved," he admitted. "In terms of Washington, D.C., or Sacramento, the labor movement does not support cultural work. In trade union education today, the cultural dimension is downplayed. The emphasis is on grievance procedures and basic service unionism." Despite voluminous books, exhibitions, and a Living Legend Award from the Library of Congress in 2007, Green in pessimistic moments would say, "I consider myself an abject failure: no one in trade unionism has taken up cultural work."[3] His day-to-day, year-after-year life choices defied this pessimism. Up until his death he loyally paid carpenter's union dues; continued to advise scores of folklorists, labor historians, and trade unionists all over the country; and advanced dozens of initiatives through his Fund for Labor Culture and History—all activities that illustrate his idealism, hope, and tenacity, along with, admittedly, his stubbornness.

So what can be said of laborlore's accomplishments? To care about Green's life-long work and the democratic, pluralist society it promoted it is useful to view laborlore as a twofold political education project that builds a pedagogy of culture and a culture of pedagogy.[4] From his earliest attempts within his own union local to teach worker history and folklore in the fifties through to his final days of leadership of the Fund for Labor History and Culture, Green developed a specific pedagogy of culture. At the same time, his efforts to spread that form of cultural literacy and knowledge took shape through sustained commitment to creating a culture of pedagogy. This culture consists of a huge informal community of educators—what Julie Ardery calls Green's "invisible university"—as well as a collection of progressive institutions and a spectrum of educational initiatives. The challenge for those who identify with Green's vision is to build upon both dimensions of his laborlore work.

To view laborlore as a pedagogy of culture is to place Green's work in a lineage of left social theorists, many of them Marxist and anarchist, who have believed culture should play a central role in organizing working-class social power. From Alexander Bogdanov and Antonio Gramsci to C. L. R. James, Paulo Freire, and Myles Horton, many writers have sought to understand and engage with the political implications of worker culture.[5] They have asked,

What qualifies as worker culture? Is worker culture conservative or progressive? and, What place does worker culture have in social movement building? These questions raise many others. Worker culture, like the workers from which it emanates, covers the entire political spectrum. Workers produce culture whether they are anarcho-syndicalists or right-wing conservatives. Only a contextualized examination of a specific cultural practice can begin to approach its social meaning and its political implications. In terms of the question of political education, laborlore implicitly instructs against carrying predetermined notions of worker identity and culture. Instead, as an ethnographic practice and sensibility it challenges us to start with questions, not answers. At its best, laborlore begins with open examination of workers' culture and provides research tools to gather relevant information and present that information to workers and nonworkers alike. This is laborlore as a pedagogy of culture—a set of tools for learning and teaching about workers' culture toward the aim of deepening democracy and fostering egalitarianism.

Laborlore proposes that workers are a type of intellectual. This perspective links it to a tradition of critical pedagogy strongly influenced by Gramsci, Freire, and Horton among others. The humanist tradition holds that all people, by virtue of their continued and necessary effort to interpret their worlds and give meaning to their lives, function as intellectuals. Green's attention to how this constant meaning-making process can be accessed through folklife has important implications for worker organizing. Laborlore as a pedagogy of culture, in a way akin to Gramsci's notion of "common sense," helps us understand the political and cultural assumptions around which workers' identities form. This, of course, is a complicated meeting place of attitudes on class, race, gender, sexuality, family, religion, nation, and media. Such complexity is precisely where discussions in labor movement education need to take place; laborlore can assist in this task because of its concern and skill for discerning the expressive qualities of worker folklife.

In a condensed, revealing expression of how Green viewed the relationship of politics and culture, he told me, "As long as the labor movement keeps listening to the Solidarity Singers, it doesn't have a chance." "Solidarity Singers" refers to any one of dozens of volunteer community choirs around the country that get together to sing the most popular traditional labor songs such as "Solidarity Forever" and "The Preacher and the Slave."[6] These choirs often sing at union conventions, May Day gatherings, or workers' rallies, and their presence often stands in for, or is projected as representing, workers' culture and history. Green's point was not that the choirs are ill-intentioned or should cease but that the contemporary labor movement should understand that it could find much-needed strength through examining and celebrating more diverse cultural practices. Rather than gather into nostalgic choirs it should take up expressive practices that reflect the dynamic cultural pluralism within its own rank and file. Such a move would represent a shift in how workers' education is commonly approached, and, by extension, a transformation in understanding how political education relates to the larger objective of building working-class solidarity.

Green never claimed that culture is the only key to building labor movement strength. He did not promote laborlore as a panacea or alternative to other kinds of essential movement-building strategies such as nurturing new leadership, litigation against employer illegalities, caucus-building, winning good contracts, and direct action on the shop floor. Instead, he believed all such efforts are served by deeper attention to worker culture. Viewed as a pedagogy of worker culture, laborlore critiques organizing strategies that do not see how politics and culture complement one another in movement-building.[7] Laborlore implies that movement-building is most effective when rooted in the politics of the everyday lives of workers, a realm so deeply cultural and so deeply entangled with folklife.[8]

Whether in the form of the Campus Folksong Club, the Smithsonian's Working Americans exhibit, or the Folklife Preservation Act, Green approached his work on folklife with the sense and sensibilities of a movement organizer. At every turn he looked for ways to enlarge and better network communities of workers, scholars, activists, and politicians who shared concern for folklife. As he reveals in "Raven, Mallard, and Spotted Owl—Totems for Coalition," the instinct was rooted in personal and social history: "To my mind, the term *cultural conservation community* recalls a program from Franklin Delano Roosevelt's day, the Civilian Conservation Corps, an appropriate analogy for the mobilization of effort. In the years ahead an appropriate name will emerge to characterize the joint efforts of those concerned with cultural conservation. We need a coalition, perhaps a clearninghouse/lobby/editorial chamber. We agree that efforts to preserve cultural material must include its presentation. We have not yet charted a formal organization with a constitution, bylaws, officers, and dues, but we anticipate a future alliance."[9]

A consummate matchmaker and organization-builder, Green always thought about how projects advance through the strength and facility of the right collection of partisans. He had, as Robert Cantwell has noted, a gregarious knack for "turning perfect strangers into cultural informants at a moment's notice."[10] Then there was his tenacious capacity for working a crowd. So many in his community witnessed time and time again how he energized social gatherings. He would work his way through meetings making new matches and then move on to renew others. This sense of movement-building through networking is as much about the efficacy of teamwork as it is Green's deep pragmatic belief in the social nature of all knowledge. Building this "invisible university," at times not so invisible, is what gives his laborlore project a culture of pedagogy—linking people who have a shared interest in learning and teaching about workers' culture and history.

To understand what made Archie Green tick, it is essential to see how continually driven and inspired he was to learn, teach, and, most important, create situations in which others could learn and teach. This is the "principled public intellectual" Debora Kodish has described. This was the worker-intellectual, teacher, and organizer, always scoping out fresh ways to bring together contemplation and action. "One example illuminates the ties of study, criticism, and action," he wrote of his years lobbying for the folklife bill. "During Washington lobbying years, I viewed Senate and House office buildings as an extended seminar room. Occasionally I strayed from the Hill to talk in arts and humanities agencies. Visiting Nancy Hanks at the National Endowment for the Arts, I shared thoughts about art itself: contrasts between New Deal murals and the abstract expressionism of her era; unseen links in the seeming oppositions between avant-garde and folk art; community norms in evaluating folk artists."[11] In a similar vein, but this time with an emphasis on workers' empowerment, Green's assessment of the Smithsonian Folklife Festival illustrates his quest to build a culture of pedagogy. "One of the purposes of the Festival of American Folklife is to permit the broad public to observe craftsmen at work and to talk with them face to face about working experience. A by-product of this interaction is that the Festival's craft participants become conscious of their roles as teachers. Naturally mechanics on all urban construction sites know that sidewalk superintendents enjoy gawking at work in progress. Only infrequently do construction men converse with street watchers. The Festival setting, however, provides an excellent platform from which carpenters can describe their adventures to countless supers."[12]

Green's drive to create spaces where the public could learn from workers and about workers found its fullest and final expression through his creation of the Fund for Labor Culture and History (FLCH). A nonprofit educational organization established in 2000, the FLCH has been raising money to fund a wide range of educational projects that in one form or another broaden public understanding and appreciation for labor. Since 2000, for example, the organization has subsidized the publication of numerous books on workers' craft and culture such as John Robinson's *Spanning the Strait: Building the Alfred Zampa Memorial Bridge* and Nolan Porterfield's edited volume *Exploring Roots Music: Twenty Years of the* JEMF Quarterly. It has also supported the making of labor films such as Maria Brooks's *Shipping Out* and *Pilebutt: Working under the Hammer*. Seeking to share labor's many voices in a multiplicity of mediums, the FLCH also worked with Stephen Wade to create a series of brief work tales for broadcast on National Public Radio.

Reflecting Green's belief that the physical sites where workers have labored and struggled must be remembered, many FLCH projects have focused on the public preservation of locations and equipment important to labor's past. In 2003, for example, a bronze plaque was mounted outside the former Garcia and Maggini Warehouse on San Francisco's Embarcadero in honor of the workers who fought and died in the 1934 maritime strike. In 2005, the fund supported the International Brotherhood of Electrical Workers effort to mark, also through a public plaque, the first commercial electric power station in the United States. One of the most ambitious long-term projects of the FLCH has been its commitment to "Save the Copra Crane," the last remaining piece of machinery on the San Francisco waterfront to be hand operated by cargo-hauling longshoreman. Seeing how this industrial artifact on Pier 84 symbolized a defining era in San Francisco's history, Green set out in 1995 to coordinate retired longshoremen in a Copra Crane Labor Landmark Association. Over time, the association recognized the importance of working with community environmental groups that had long sought to transform Islais Creek, site of the Copra Crane, into a restored and public green space. Collectively they have designed plans for the Islais Creek Waterfront Parkway that integrate ecological sustainability, cultural heritage, and community recreation. The idea is that the Copra Crane will be the centerpiece of a Pier 84 educational center, where retired dockworkers could inform visitors about the sounds, scenes, and stories of the historic worksite. At the time of this writing the crane remains preserved, but efforts to create the larger parkway face continued obstacles.[13]

Hoping to inspire new generations of laborlorists, the FLCH provides two scholarships for graduate students who wish to pursue projects in workers' culture and history. The first scholarship, the Archie Green Occupational Folklife Graduate Fellowship, was established in 1994, years before FLCH formally became an organization, and is administered by the folklore program at the University of North Carolina at Chapel Hill. Since 1995 more than $100,000 in graduate student fellowships have been awarded to twenty-five UNC graduate students across the disciplines of folklore, history, anthropology, and journalism. To this date, the scholarships have vitally funded eight dissertations and seventeen master's theses in work culture and history. In 2008, in honor of Jack Henning, a California labor leader, the FLCH awarded its first Jack Henning Scholarship in Labor Culture and History. The recipient, Alex Johnston, completed a graduate degree in social documentation at University of California, Santa Cruz, by creating *Way Down in the Hole*, a riveting film on the brutal Colorado coalfield wars of the early twentieth century.

By far the most unique and defining project of the FLCH has been its annual commitment to hosting what Green dubbed Laborlore Conversations. First held in 2004, the one-day conversations bring together trade unionists, academic labor historians, occupational folklorists, archivists, anthropologists, graduate students, and assorted community members. The diverse and democratic character of the event, its fundamental accomplishment, was generated and sustained for years through Green's charisma. The cross-cultural demographic of the conversations have been reinforced by his insistence that each year the host location alternate between a union hall and a university. Past locations include the Piledriver's Hall in Oakland, California, the Library of Congress, and University of North Carolina, Chapel Hill. The conversations have been free, open to all, and, historically, provide breakfast, lunch, and dinner to participants. The fund underwrites presenters' travel and board expenses, a generous and unorthodox practice significantly responsible for diversifying the kinds of people who can share their experiences.

For all these reasons, the annual laborlore conversations exemplify how Green's life work was in essence a synergistic building of a pedagogy of culture and a culture of pedagogy. Unlike most academic conferences, laborlore conversations are held in one large room.[14] Green relished the fact that all participants would engage with each other in the same space—an important community-building function. The conversations are typically organized around three thematic panels with three to five presenters on each. Sessions are spaced throughout the day and culminate in lively vernacular music performances, whether Appalachian balladeers, East Texas zydeco, or Mexican *cumbia*. At any given conversation you might hear a former pile driver and union organizer such as Mike Munoz sharing how the illustrations of radical artist Giacomo Patri dramatically shaped his working-class politics. Or, in 2006, at the Ironworkers Hall of Benicia, California, Suzanne Povse, a helicopter mechanic from Philadelphia, poignantly shared her experience as a woman laborer in the male-dominated metal trades. Two years later, at Laborlore Conversation V, graduate student Jeff Currie presented his research on how young generations of the Lumbee Indians in North Carolina have taken to expressing their pride as skilled sheetrockers through inventive rap songs. Conversations traditionally conclude with scholars such as Nick Spitzer or Robert Cantwell connecting and counterposing ideas from the day with generative questions and reflections. Through these kinds of presentations and the dialog they catalyze, participants grow in their capacity to see how work shapes personal and collective lives. Green's Fund for Labor Culture and History, for its part, moves a small step forward in its ambition to help remake the world, a theme appropriate for the conclusion of this study. Archie Green's laborlore projects emanated from a belief in the dignity and intelligence of all workers. From the basis of that belief, Green pursued a fundamental question, a question that comes to us as the ultimate challenge of building upon his legacy, How can we organize society around a principle of respect for all workers?

EPILOGUE

A Conversation with Archie

Nick Spitzer

I first became aware of Archie Green's work in folk music at the University of Pennsylvania's college radio station WXPN in Philadelphia in 1970. I was enthralled by his liner notes on a RCA Carter Family LP collection from 78s, *'Mid the Green Fields of Virginia*. Archie's mix of populism, aesthetic appreciation, and cultural history of the iconic Anglo-Southern music ensemble helped me first understand the value of vernacular arts, humanities, and diversity in American society. His vision of pluralistic democracy embedded in the expression of folk communities encouraged readers and listeners to step beyond their own culture—to appreciate what was in their midst. It revealed the powerful idea that I could share appreciation of a cultural expression and its aesthetic value while recognizing my difference from the social location and political views of its creators and performers. Romance and reality could be mediated by the art of the scholar and the knowledge of the performer.

I met Archie five years later as a graduate student at the University of Texas in Austin while working weekends at the seminal progressive country station KOKE-FM, "Goat Roper Radio." One Saturday night I was playing that same Carter Family and their version of "Give Me the Flowers While I Live," which then segued into the Rolling Stones' dissolute country classic "Dead Flowers." The telephone in the studio rang after the segue. It was Archie, effusively telling me I should sign up for his folk-song class. I told the upbeat voice on the line that I was already enrolled.

We went on to form a strong mentor-student bond that semester—talking ballads and work songs, cosmic cowboys and all-night truck drivers, the disappointments and promise in American cultural life. Archie and I visited Austin clubs, like the Split Rail, a former stagecoach stop where cowboy bluesman Bill Neely held forth along with such Lonestar luminaries as Lubbock singer Joe Ely, fiddler Alvin Crowe, and Texas Playboy Jessie Ashlock. At the venerably hard-nosed Broken Spoke on South Lamar or the newer "hippie country" dancehall at the edge of Hill Country, Soap Creek Saloon, Archie would work the room. Part professor, part cultural lobbyist he had been in Washington, he proffered a string of handshakes, mini-lectures, and the inevitable, "You need to meet _____ " to whomever he was introducing. "He's a good man!" It was a marvel to see the diminutive Green holding forth among tall Texas hipsters and rearguard rednecks in cowboy hats, their attention rapt by Archie's embracing cultural populism. It also didn't hurt that he loved honky-tonk music.

The second semester at the University of Texas, Archie taught Folklore in the Public Sector. It was a breakout moment in folklore studies, a reorientation to a more engaged field of public discourse. He skillfully combined accounts of precursors, ranging from Thomas Jefferson's interest in Native American languages to Ben Botkin's popular folklore, and the resulting conflict with academics, as well as tales of Archie's own decade spent working the halls of Congress to advance what would be eventual passage of the American Folklife Preservation Act in 1976.

I left Austin, aka "Groovers' Paradise," in 1978 for the Old South plantation gone suburban meets industrial Baton Rouge. The mission was to establish the Louisiana state folkorist position and program, so the spring of 1979 we invited Archie to our first state folklife conference. His will to advance consciousness of the significance and value of community-based culture in a state ready to be encouraged was on full display among Cajun cultural activists, Baton Rouge bluesmen, and north Louisiana good ol' boy geographers. We stayed in touch when I moved on to the Smithsonian Institution's Office of Folklife Programs. Archie was always concerned about what he viewed as the Institution's lack of efficacy in local or national cultural programs. He continued to be a constant voice of advice in projects ranging from the Folk Masters concert series at Carnegie Hall to the *American Routes* Fourth of July shows broadcast on NPR from the National Mall.

I recorded an extensive oral history over three days with Archie at home in San Francisco in 1993. He was a humorous and trenchant commentator for the *American Routes* Labor Day program in 1998, the first year we went on the air (http://americanroutes.publicradio.org/archives/show/493/labor-day-with-archie-green).

As the years passed I visited Archie and Louanne in San Francisco too few times. I stayed connected, however, by reading his remarkable *John Edwards Memorial Foundation Quarterly* graphics series, the topics of which ranged from Miguel Covarrubias's mambo dancers to J. Frank Dobie's "cowboy friends." To this day I still teach Archie's essays on vernacular culture—"Hillbilly Music: Source and Symbol" to "Stitching Patchwork in Public"—his many laborlore topical studies and his grand books about working men and women in coal mines, driving piles, crafting tin, or on picket lines. Young students are taken by the intensity, passion and eloquence that rises from the pages.

During Archie's last months in early 2009 we moved closer again. He would regale me during long telephone conversations as I traveled through late winter's humid nights across Louisiana on projects or wherever I was on the road, whether to Nevada or Washington, D.C. Just back from the doctor with worsening news, he said, "I'd be crazy to say I want to die, but everybody has to go." There was frustration leavened with humor in his voice. Archie didn't want to give up his lifelong fight on behalf of folk culture, traditional artists, and their serious inclusion in the modern American polity. If he could live longer for anything it would be that sense of mission. He remained concerned to the end about cultural and economic policies of the then nascent Obama administration, lobbying his Congresswoman, Nancy Pelosi, for a new documentary structure tied to stimulus spending and suggesting I go back to Washington to help effect it.

With his days dwindling, on March 17, 2010, I came to visit for the last time at the modest house on Caselli Street overlooking San Francisco's Mission District. As in years past, Archie and I sat facing one another on well-worn wooden chairs framed by the picture window. In conversation, we seemed to float above the street below, where a stream of visitors and colleagues had long made pilgrimages for an audience, a friendly argument, or provocative advice. Archie's words and ideas came slowly at first, but he warmed to the encounter and lifted all our spirits. For a couple of hours his fatigue and pain receded just enough for him to share dreams of an America to be and memories of life in his city and country. Archie's reflections offer a map for the cultural future of folklorists, Americans, and world citizens.

As sons Derek and David returned from union participation in a weekend St. Patrick's parade and daughter Debra listened in along with Louanne Green, herself infirm in the next room, I recorded our session with the help of Adam Machado. He had been assisting Archie on scholarly writing and social programs for several years, providing youthful energy and the quiet ability to listen deeply. Friends Davia Nelson of the Kitchen Sisters and Arhoolie Records' originator Chris Strachwitz arrived to join us. Archie's deathbed was his final soap box.

* * *

Recorded and edited by Nick Spitzer and transcribed by Alex Annis at 224 Caselli Street, San Francisco, on March 14, 2009.

AG: I have a strong belief in cultural pluralism and in vernacular culture. I believe that our society and the large transcontinental societies of Russia, India, South Africa, China, Brazil . . . any sovereign country that has imposed a pattern of sovereignty on time zones has the ability to send a helicopter from Time Zone A to Time Zone B, and you can continue war. As long as we can fight the war in Afghanistan, that is bad for the world. That is what I believe.

An alternative to a world dominated by a few powers that have worldwide power is cultural pluralism. Is there some form of government that deals with the reality that people are different? Citizens differ in value, differ in language, differ in culture. Sometimes the differences are big. Sometimes they are small. Sometimes they are manifested in something as small as the way you cut or paint your fingernails. Sometimes they are very large. I've puzzled all of my life on what is the appropriate mix of cultural pluralism and vernacular culture.

That is, if you take the Bush/Cheney model it is "one culture fits all." One language, one voice, one religion, one patriotism, one center of American experience. By definition, to my way of thinking, that is bad. That is, you can't have that kind of a model unless a dominant group will exploit a subdominant group. Whether the exploitation comes in the form of a radio license or in newspaper control or political control or economic control, it is still control. How to break that pattern . . . how to diversify power is the big political problem of the day. It becomes compounded because in diverging power out of Washington you also strengthen the hands of the fundamentalists, reactionary groups in American life that as a mantra talk about less government. How you can blend the notion of more government, that is a strong federal power, with the notion of local autonomy and community control is a huge, huge problem for American life.

NS: What would you advocate as a mechanism at the national level to document and encourage vernacular creativity and cultural pluralism? Talk about what you'd like to see in cultural stimulus.

AG: Here's what I would do. I would ignore the cultural programs of the past federal government, namely Library of Congress, Smithsonian, the two Endowments in favor of a current, or a new thing. . . . Americans like new things. I would favor an American Recovery Act in whatever form it takes. I would make the analogy back to the New Deal and the blue eagle. When President Roosevelt was confronted with massive unemployment and resorted to Keynesian economics to stimulate the economy he developed something called the National Recovery Act. Under the NRA, someone designed the blue eagle. Every factory, every shop, every individual was proud of displaying a blue eagle emblem or a blue eagle sign in the window. The blue eagle became the symbol of national recovery. Interestingly enough, the head administrator who is now forgotten was named Hugh "Iron Pants" Johnson. He was a general. That would be like appointing General Colin Powell today.

Instead of appointing an industrialist or an economist or a labor leader to head the recovery program, you would appoint a general, which would symbolize the importance of the task and that the task was above politics. You would need a general who wore iron pants, who was tough enough to tell General Motors, "Detroit is through." Or wield the big stick against industry. Assuming that the president will appoint someone, a general or not, to head the recovery program, I would say the first step is within his administrative power to hire a documentary staff so that from the beginning the jobs are "shovel ready." You would build a component into those jobs of photo documentary. If a bridge is to be constructed, you take a picture of the bridge. If a high-speed railway is to be constructed, you take a picture of the high-speed railway or the right-of-way with the weed patch showing where the right-of-way will run.

Or if a new mill is to be built to run new forms of energy and to break our dependence on Middle Eastern oil, you take a picture of the weed patch and say, "This is the site of Obama's new unit." Given the fact of early documentation, you go on with photography, radio, plays, art exhibits. You have artists doing murals, doing prints. You use every expressive form to convey the excitement of building that is going on. It is very exciting.

In the 1930s *Fortune Magazine* was huge and it grew. It had big pictures and color illustration—photo essays by Margaret Bourke-White. Even though the bourgeois found a value in extolling the strengths of capitalism, it has built its resilience. Now, in addition to that it is very important that the recovery unit not only feed information about the jobs program to the public, but it is highly important that some of the material is fed back to the workers involved. There you have the dual foundation that pictures—say, a wonderful series of pictures taken in the Tennessee Valley Authority—the dams under construction. The pictures not only helped the country understand rural electrification, but the pictures helped workers involved take pride in their work. They were part of a collective enterprise that was helping, not hurting, America.

These people on the photography project, the arts project, the music project, had some awareness of folklore that came to them through two traditions. One was the romantic European tradition out of academic folklore, but the other was the popular notion that came with the Popular Front in the antifascist period.

NS: Why should Americans, writ large, know the culture of work?

AG: The main reason is that through the circumstance of geography and world politics, our country started as an imperial adventure by overseas adventurers from England, Spain, Portugal, Holland, Sweden, France, Germany. They came to what was called the New World, and they had to start building. If they didn't cut trees, if they didn't fashion mud into mortar, if they didn't learn to cut stone and, ultimately, if they didn't learn to beat iron and steel we would have no civilization. We had one preceding the European colonists. The red men had a pretty advanced form of life but not superior to the European invasion. The invaders, plus the assistance of African American slaves, ultimately dominated the country and the continents beyond in the world.

The story of America from one level has been the story of work. . . . Cutting down—some of our first timber exports were from Maine as early as 1620 where we cut huge pine trees and shipped them to England to be masts for ships. The lumber, then in a unit, holding strength was more valuable than lumber cut up for homes. I've told you the story of sawyers, but you also want to know the story of timber fellers and timber exporters. Ultimately, because we were isolated from Europe by three thousand miles we gradually established a textile industry and other trades, the canals and railroads. We have been building initially a nation-state and then a world-state.

If that story isn't adventurous, if it doesn't catch the imagination of listeners, behind American myths you have the story of American work. The cowboy has been mythologized, but at one level the cowboy was a super market employee. The cowboy was a brother and sister to the stacker boy and stacker girl who put the products on the supermarket shelf every day that the cowboy helped bring cattle to the market. Every mythical occupation, every romantic occupation represents a form of work that was needed in society for other people to be happy or other people to exchange their labor power for products that would make them happy.

You had workers in Hollywood. You had workers on the radio. You had workers in whorehouses, but the total of all work together is, I think, the most adventurous story in America. It is exemplified by one of our four or five great novels: *Moby Dick*. What the hell is *Moby Dick* about if it is not about man seeking oil products for lamps? All of that work on the Yankee whaler—and the folklorists are off in the corner studying scrimshaw and they wonder why they are so backwards. Scrimshaw is interesting, but scrimshaw was something that whalers did in their leisure time to cut the monotony and the stench building.

"I've been working on the railroad all the live long day . . . oh Dinah blow your horn."

Sidewalk superintendents are eternally fascinated. I used to walk down Constitution Avenue and Independence Avenue in Washington. I remember when the FBI Building was under construction. I'd stand there and look up at the high steel and see these guys maneuvering on a steel beam, and I used to think of them as ballet dancers. They were clunk-clunking along, lumping along, awkward in their overalls, but they were as delicate and as graceful as any ballet dancer at the Metropolitan. Of course I felt that someone in the National Endowment for the Arts ought to be paying attention to the dances of the ironworkers. The rod busters. . . .

NS: You have followed the songs surrounding work, that express work, that time work. Why is the song about work and the work song important?

AG: Well songs are poems and plays—important for encapsulating emotion. In a few stanzas, either a work song or a ballad, you can capture or encapsulate some of that spirit. You come to, "I've Been Working on the Railway," or the "Wreck of the Old 97," or "Which Side Are You On," or songs of that nature. The singer has the ability to project the meaning and the trauma of all of this work experience in a few minutes. It is a very turn-on experience. Whether it is a Peter Seeger, or a Bruce Springsteen, or Utah Phillips, or Merle Travis, they know it. They know they have that power. They sing about Okies, or Arkies, or Wobblies, or lumber workers, or railroad workers. When Johnny Cash used to have the ability to sing a current country and western song like "Jackson," but if you ask him to shut his eyes and sing a song that sounded as if his father were singing about an early Arkansas episode he could do it. He had that capacity to go back in time. That was part of his power.

NS: What is the importance of cultural continuity for Americans at the community level? Whatever their community may be—African Americans, southerner, cowboy, modern computer worker—what is the importance of continuity of culture?

AG: That is easy because the importance is that discontinuity is disruptive of life. If life goes too fast—too many computers, too many airplane flights, too much modernity—many individual people, many citizens cannot accommodate. Even though we live in a computer age, the number of people that cannot be reached by their computer is immense because the number of people born in every generation who cannot cope with previous conditions or with change is great. It is absolutely necessary for a society to spend some of this resource on museums, on archives, on old forms of instrumentation that convey old sounds, old styles in a familiar voice. You can't—if you are working in radio—you can't work on the assumption that everyone listens to the radio.

NS: In an ideal world, what would America look like if culture, creativity were honored? What would be your idealized vision of a future of America?

AG: In an ideal America everyone—every group no matter how small—would have access to the radio, to the presses, to the cameras. That concentration would not be in the hands of Manhattan, or the hands of Washington, or the hands of Hollywood but a group of Laotian farmers or Serbo-Croatian bartenders. The tiniest cultural group would have as much access to the means of dissemination as the next group. If you try to flesh out cultural pluralism you have to give people access to the tools. Politically we would devise a system to de-sovereignize a nation or all nations; to decolonize all nations, to empower local groups, to perform their cultural acts, to listen to the cultural acts, to take pleasure in their cultural acts . . . that might be the ideal.

NS: What has been great for you in your lifetime working and living in San Francisco?

AG: I think I've been fortunate. I came here in 1937 when I went to the University of California. It has been home since. San Francisco, for me, has been a cosmopolitan mixture of black, white, Latino, Oriental. San Francisco has also been a progressive city. Advanced in race relations, advanced in intellectual thought. In *The Nation* magazine or *New Republic* there was an article after World War II about the worker on the docks in San Francisco who was seen as a longshoreman. He had a hook in one hand—a longshore hook with bales of cargo—but he had a poetry book in his other hand. Whether it was Jack Kerouac or Kenneth Rexroth, who wrote the article. They had a good cover. That was an ideal that attracted me to San Francisco. I tried to make my contribution.

NS: You mention labor and you mention the literary world here. What about music in San Francisco?

AG: Starting about 1941 when I first became a shipwright and I was making $20 a week—that was fifty cents an hour. A journeyman was making forty hours a week a $1 an hour. That was a huge sum of money for someone who hadn't been making anything before. I could buy a suit at Hastings. I could buy records, and I did. One of the first records I bought was Haywire Mac *Cowboy Songs*, "Hallelujah, I'm a Bum," and I also bought a Flamenco record, "Las Niñas de las Piñas" [The Girls of the Pines]. I bought blues at that time. I began buying old Count Basie and Duke Ellington and I also. . . .

NS: This sounds like an *American Routes* program!

AG: Well maybe it was. . . . I also liked hillbilly music. Earlier I had heard on the radio . . . growing up in the West, which I'm glad I didn't grow up in Greenwich Village, but I always thought of country music as western music. Even when we heard Vernon Dalhart singing "Wreck of the Old 97," we thought of that as a cowboy song. Any guy with a guitar and a nasal voice must have been cowboy. I grew up in an immigrant enclave. I didn't grow up on a shit-kicker ranch. I think I accepted that notion of cowboy music all the way through Bob Wills. I remember hearing Bob Wills and liking him very much.

When I went into the navy one of the songs that was popular on the jukebox was "There Will Be Smoke on the Water, on the Land and the Sea." I remember writing back to Louanne to buy that record for me. I think it was 35 cents. I think it was a purple-labeled Okeh. So that the continuity of *American Routes*, as you say, sustained me for a long time.

When I first started going out with Louanne, we used to go to a Greek nightclub down near Third and Townsend that is the railroad station. There were many war workers in town, including Turkish and Greek—there were quite a few Greek merchant seamen. They used to come to the Venus Club, and it had a little pick-up band of a bouzouki, flute, fiddle. That was our hangout. In addition sometimes on Saturday night we'd go to Jack's Record Cellar, and we'd hear Saunders King, and it was preceding that black trio that was popular. . . .

NS: Nat King Cole?

AG: Yeah, Nat King Cole. We could hear a live music of every genre right here in San Francisco. I remember there was a nightclub just where Valencia turned on Market. It had been a German or Viennese beer garden before the war. One night they painted the sign "Western Music Tonight." The old audience died out and the new audience came in. All of the sudden there was shit-kicker music on Market Street. I thought that was great because up until then they had come up the peninsula as far as the Brisbane. I knew that from the beginning, from the first time I heard whining Nashville guitar, I loved it.

NS: So you talk about that music and the music around you. What happened in San Francisco leading up to the 1960s in terms of the folk movement and the emergence of the San Francisco rock world?

AG: We had some things in common with Greenwich Village. That is the folk song revival was pretty much a universal all over the country so when people talked about the California folk scene they were obscure in reference, because did they mean a replication of Greenwich Village as it sounded on the East Coast or was there a West Coast style? So that in San Francisco, we did have some leftists who modeled themselves after The Weavers and The Kingston Trio. They were Lou Gottlieb . . . The Limeliters. They were our version of the revival, but while the Limeliters were going on we also had some people coming in to Berkeley—Chris Strachwitz would be an example—who were marching to a different drum, listening to a different sound. And Chris would invite to the campus Lightnin' Hopkins and Fred McDowell. And he began to infiltrate the folknik audience with great success so that on the Berkeley box [an Arhoolie anthology collection entitled *Hear Me Howling! Blues, Ballads, and Beyond—as Recorded by the San Francisco Bay by Chris Strachwitz in the 1960s*] we may get a pretty good soundscape of that period.

NS: What was the value of the Berkeley Folk Festival and the folk scene here for music in America in general?

AG: The value was that Chris was able to make the blend of . . . or he was able to steer the revival in the direction of tradition. I see Chris as part of a tiny group in America. People like Mike Seeger, Dick Spottswood, Norm Cohen, myself, Ed Kahn, Gene Earle—growing up within the revival but working with it by our affection of traditional music. Our role, wherever it was with whatever records we put out, was to educate the audience away from the dominant popular forms that to this day I despise. I don't like Bob Dylan. I don't like Bruce Springsteen. I don't like . . . but when it comes to Joan Baez I liked her politically but didn't like her aesthetically.

Maybe I ought to tell you my story about Joan Baez. One year, old-time singer Sarah Gunning went back to Newport. I had something to do with that. Sarah came home. We were talking about it.

I said, "Sarah, how did you like or did you meet anyone in Newport?"

"Yeah, I met all the big wheels. I met Joan Baez."

I said, "How did you like Joan?"

Then she said, "She is a nice young lady, but she couldn't sing very well."

It seemed to go against the grain. Sarah, who had this high lonesome sound and an awkward voice and maybe appealed to thirty people and she was putting down this gal who appealed to thirty thousand people.

I said, "Well, describe it."

She said, "Well she knows some of the songs, but she can't sing them."

She didn't say it but . . . "She doesn't appreciate our style." Then she added, "If I could spend a couple of weeks with Joan, I could teach her how to sing."

I thought to myself that was a wonderful story on the difference in style and the difference it represented in American culture. And how hard our task would be from my point of view if I kept pushing vernacular style—especially where I tried to win unions over, would be an impossible task. How to get humans to quit listening to the Popular Front and to start listening to vernacular music I often thought was my most difficult assignment.

NS: What makes San Francisco a special city in America and the world today?

AG: Because it is willing to accept the fact of cultural mix. It is willing to give gays, lesbians and queers and minorities, African American, Latin American, Oriental American, political power. There is a kind of willingness or a tolerance to live together in San Francisco and, hopefully, we can spread that throughout the country. I am concerned that say a county in western North Carolina or eastern Tennessee has the highest percentage of Bush voters of any county in the United States. I'm not worried about San Francisco, but I'm worried about Sullivan County or Jones County and what can be done in those counties to change American life.

NS: Finally . . . what do you want America to be as a cultural community?

AG: We don't need any more cultural imperialism. We don't need any more domination by one race. Once class. One vision. One philosophy. That is why I'm as critical and as hostile to totalitarianism when it comes up in a Marxist form or a Freudian form or a structural form or an academic form. I don't like a big boss telling me what to do in the union. I don't like him on the job. I end up with an anarchist philosophy.

NS: Can an anarchist philosophy sustain American culture?

AG: Probably it can't, but if there has to be a choice at least take the choice of one that satisfies you intellectually.

* * *

Suddenly tiring, Archie ended the conversation. After the audio stopped rolling, with an avuncular kiss goodbye, Archie told me to work only on what I cared about most. Eight days later the man of so many words, ideas, and projects in public folklore and the culture of labor was gone. We continue to hear and be influenced by the voice, passion, humor, and intellect of Archie Green. As we work on, Archie is with us.

Acknowledgments

Archie Green had a great idea: In the main entry of every building, a mounted photograph should portray and name all of the laborers who worked on that building. Just as most buildings, without such an honorary plaque, obscure the social labor of the many workers who produced them, a single author's name on a book jacket conceals the deeply communal nature of the ideas and energy coursing throughout the pages within. This project never would have happened without Archie Green's unwavering, generous commitment to sharing his life and lessons, both bitter and sweet, with me. I also extend deepest appreciation to Louanne Green, Anjelica Palmera, and the entire Green family for their patience, support, and kindness. My parents, Andreé and John Burns, have supported me in every way at every turn; their love is water and wine. My graduate school advisors at the University of California, Santa Cruz—Barbara Epstein, George Lipsitz, David Brundage, and Paul Ortiz—exemplify how to do scholarship that is politically relevant and how to sustain commitment to students as the center of a dedicated teaching practice. I have tremendous respect and gratitude for them as well as the many mentors in Archie's "invisible university" who encouraged and influenced this work, among them William Friedland, Robert McCarl, John Vlach, Paul Buhle, Derek Green, Tom Walker, John Robinson, Robert Cantwell, Julie Ardery, Guha Shankar, Adam Machado, David Taylor, Maria Brooks, Shelly and Coleman Romalis, Ronald Cohen, Harvey Schwartz, Kerry Taylor, Michael Munoz, Norm Cohen, Don Watson, William Sheilds, and Judith McCulloh. As visionary, indefatigable public intellectuals, David Roediger and Nick Spitzer have my highest respect. I deeply appreciate their contributions to this book. Carl Fleischhauer, Michael Rauner, and William Myers generously offered their brilliant photographs. Laurie Matheson and her co-workers at University of Illinois Press believed in my project from the beginning, and Mary Giles provided superb copy editing. My work was intellectually supported by the Bancroft Library (UC Berkeley), the American Folklife Center, the San Francisco Labor Archive, and the excellent Southern Folklife Collection at University of North Carolina, Chapel Hill, home of the Archie Green Papers. A Bancroft Library Dissertation Fellowship funded my initial year of research. Finally, I thank the many friends and families who kept me hiking, dancing, singing, gardening, and dreaming through this disciplined effort: Claire Duplantier and family, Joey and Granny Todd Smith, Matt Spalding, the Rainey-Carlone family, Chris Carlsson, Michael Whitson, Derek Hitchcock, Will Grant, and the entire Source to Sea Community, the Cole family, the Puhvels, all Laurel Manorites, Lathan Spaulding, the Kirk-Lesassier family, James Rowe, Alexis Shotwell, Chris Dixon, Maia Ramnath, Rashaad Shabazz, Greg Caldwell, Alex Johnston, the ALO families, Ailen's Brigade, the Aldrich family, the Subterranean Art House, the Lilac Field, and the extended Burns and Morrisroe families.

Notes

Introduction

1. "Working-Class Hero" is from the album *John Lennon/Plastic Ono Band* (Apple/EMI, 1970).

2. Denning, *The Cultural Front*, xviii.

3. Archie Green to Professor Richard Dorson, Jan. 30, 1962. Richard Dorson file, Archie Green Papers (20002), Southern Folklife Collection, Wilson Library, University of North Carolina, Chapel Hill (hereafter Archie Green Papers, Wilson Library, UNC).

4. "Recognition of Archie Green."

5. Gross Bressler, "Culture and Politics: A Legislative Chronicle of the American Folklife Preservation Act."

6. Buhle and Schulman, eds., *Wobblies*.

7. The term *Old Left*, as used to describe Green's generation of political activists, gained traction in younger, New Left political communities of the 1960s. The term naturally reflects the younger generation's intention of distinguishing and distancing itself from its predecessors. Core differences revolved around issues of leadership, organization, relation to the state, the nature of imperialism, and conceptions of politics and power.

8. Denning, *The Cultural Front*, xiv.

9. In its most specific meaning, the Popular Front refers to an antifascist political strategy adopted at the Seventh Congress of the Communist International in the summer of 1935. In terms of the Communist Party's political platform, the signing of the Hitler-Stalin Pact on August 22, 1939, marked the end of the Popular Front (Parts 1, 2, and 3). The alliance building, which was central to the Popular Front in the United States, entailed important new relationships between cultural work and political work.

10. Denning, *The Cultural Front*, xviii, 5; David Roediger, Foreword, in O'Conner, O'Conner, and Bowler, *Harvey and Jessie*, x.

11. In leading up to the publication of this book, I published an article focusing on Green's contributions to public labor history. Burns, "Going Public," 164–79.

12. Finnegan, "Only a Folklorist," 43–63.

13. Ransby, *Ella Baker and the Black Freedom Movement.*

14. Lipsitz, *A Life in the Struggle*, 242.

15. On the prominence of narrative in New Labor History see Green's *Taking History to Heart*, 9.

16. Portelli, *The Battle of Valle Giula*, 259.

17. Roediger, "Poetry and Working Class History: Sterling Brown, for Example," in *History against Misery*, 52.

18. Burns, "Going Public," addresses this long-term project of Green's.

19. There are many varieties of syndicalism, making it difficult and unproductive to neatly define the term. At its core, as a philosophy of social change, syndicalism asserts that workers (and their workplace) can and should be the primary unit around which society is organized. Syndicalists of many viewpoints therefore share the belief that workers, organized as some form of association or union, should control the means through which a society produces what it needs to survive and flourish. For more on syndicalism in the context of United States labor history it is important to study the Industrial Workers of the World and the Syndicalist League of North America.

20. MARHO (Radical Historians Organization), *Visions of History*, ed. Henry Abelove et al., 153.

21. Kundera, *The Book of Laughter and Forgetting.*

22. Kelley (*Race Rebels*, 10) emphasizes that social movement studies need to ask more questions about why people make the commitments they do.

23. Pete Seeger file, Archie Green Papers, Wilson Library, UNC.

Chapter 1. Family, Revolution, and Emigration

1. For most of this book I will refer to Archie Green by his surname. Because this chapter includes many references to his parents and siblings, however, I will occasionally use his given name.

2. Interviews with Archie Green, Feb. 10, 2006, March 27, 2008.

3. Trotsky, *The History of the Russian Revolution*, 10–15.

4. Lenin, *What Is to Be Done?* Written as a political pamphlet in 1912, *What Is to Be Done?* maps out Lenin's conception of how a revolutionary vanguard party can lead the working classes.

5. I use *Samuel* rather than *Shmuel* to refer to Green's father because that is how Archie referred to him throughout our interviews.

6. Interview with Mitzie Green, Dec. 22, 2006.

7. Interview with Archie Green, Feb. 21, 2006. Given Samuel's combined interests in Jewish cultural nationalism, modern secularism, and socialism, it is surprising

that, according to Archie, he never spoke about the Bund (or Jewish Labor Bund). The Bund, founded in 1897, was a socialist union of Jewish workers that spread across many countries within the Russian Empire.

8. Interview with Archie Green, Feb. 10, 2006.

9. Interview with Archie Green, Feb. 21, 2006.

10. Trotsky, *The History of the Russian Revolution*, 10–15.

11. Interview with Archie Green, Feb. 10, 2006.

12. Richmond notes in his autobiography, *A Long View from the Left*, that approximately three thousand radicals who had been exiled from Russia after 1905 returned after 1917. Samuel and Rose Green, however, never returned to the Ukraine.

13. Interview with Archie Green, Feb. 21, 2006.

14. Green suggested that some of Rose's siblings spelled the family name *Goosen*, *Guzen*, or *Gosik*.

15. Interview with Archie Green, February 21, 2006.

16. Samuel's brother, William Green, became a newspaper editor in Wenatchee, Washington. According to Archie, William wrote an autobiography, which he published through a local vanity press. I have been unable, however, to locate a copy.

Chapter 2. Boyle Heights in the 1920s

1. Sanchez, "What's Good for Boyle Heights Is Good for the Jews,'" 633–61.

2. Ibid., 635.

3. Ibid.

4. Green remembered living in three different homes in Boyle Heights. The first was two or three blocks from Sheridan Street School where he attended kindergarten. Around 1926–27 the family moved to their second house on Pennsylvania Avenue near St. Louis Avenue, where they had Mexican neighbors and Green first heard *corridos*. While living there, he attended Second Street Elementary School. A year later the family bought a home in the 100 block of Echandia Street.

5. Interview with Archie Green, Feb. 21, 2006.

6. Ibid. In "Encountering Mass Culture," chapter 3 of *Making a New Deal*, Cohen warns against making generalized claims about the extent to which mass culture in the twenties and thirties was taken up by American workers. Instead, she illustrates how only a situated analysis of the ways in which workers related to different production and consumption patterns can begin to get at what meaning a cultural practice or commodity had for various individuals.

7. Ibid.

8. Ibid.

9. Interview with Archie Green, Feb. 10, 2006.

10. Ibid.

11. Ibid.

12. Sacco and Vanzetti were two Italian-born American workers, labor organizers, and anarchists who were tried, convicted, and executed on August 23, 1927, for an

alleged armed robbery and murder of two pay clerks. Their arrest and controversial trial ignited international protest. Significant post-trial evidence suggests their innocence and confirms the perspectives of many historians who argue that the incident marked the tragic height of post–World War I Red Scare political repression and American nativism. Avrich, *Sacco and Vanzetti*; Feuerlicht, *Justice Crucified.*

13. Flynn stresses that many children of her generation were introduced to political organizing through attending meetings with their parents. *Rebel Girl*, 59.

14. Interview with Archie Green, Feb. 21, 2006.

15. Ibid.

16. Books widely considered as founding texts in the field include Frankenberg, *White Women, Race Matters*; Morrison, *Playing in the Dark*; and Roediger, *The Wages of Whiteness.*

17. Interview with Archie Green, March 3, 2006.

18. Sanchez, "'What's Good for Boyle Heights Is Good for the Jews,'" 636.

19. Jacobson, *Whiteness of a Different Color*; Brodkin, *How Jews Became White Folks.*

20. Sanchez, "'What's Good for Boyle Heights Is Good for the Jews,'" 643.

21. Interview with Archie Green, Feb. 10, 2006.

22. Ibid.

23. EPIC refers to Upton Sinclair's proposed End Poverty in California program, the centerpiece of his influential yet ultimately unsuccessful campaign for governor of that state in 1934.

24. Weintraub, *The I.W.W. in California, 1905–1931*, 279.

25. Interview with Archie Green, Feb. 10, 2006.

26. From an unpublished essay by John Vlach, "Always on Stolen Time: The Sources and Rationale for the *Graphic* Series," 8, author's possession. Green said that Granz had started dating Maria Bryant, an African American jazz vocalist and dancer, and the relationship opened many connections to black musicians for Granz.

27. Interview with Archie Green, Feb. 10, 2006.

28. Interview with Mitzie Green, Dec. 22, 2006.

29. Adamic, *Dynamite*; interview with Archie Green, Feb. 21, 2006. Green proudly emphasized that his foundation in reading labor history was not Bimba's popular *History of the American Working Class*—the first Communist Party, Marxist history of the American working class and required reading for YCL members.

Chapter 3. Student Politics and Labor in the Thirties

1. Cohen, *When the Old Left Was Young*, 134, 183.

2. Interview with Archie Green, Feb. 10, 2006.

3. During the Communist Party's Third Period such leftists were referred to as "social fascists." A year later, when the party shifted to a Democratic Front, they, of course, advocated Roosevelt's New Deal.

4. Interview with Archie Green, Feb. 10, 2006.

5. Ibid.
6. Interview with Archie Green, Feb. 21, 2006.
7. Ibid.
8. Cohen, *When the Old Left Was Young*, 134.
9. Ibid., 118.
10. Ibid., 169.
11. Special thanks to Bill Friedland for clarifying these lyrics. In 1952 Friedland, with Joe Glazer, recorded *Ballads for Sectarians* (Labor Arts).
12. Interview with Archie Green, Feb. 21, 2006.
13. Ibid.
14. Ibid.
15. Ibid. Parts 2 and 3 explore Green's anti-Stalinism.
16. Interview with Archie Green, Feb. 21, 2006.
17. Ibid.
18. Ibid.
19. Terkel, *Hard Times*, 396.
20. Cohen, *When the Old Left Was Young*, 263.
21. The full text of Governor Olson's speech is at http://www.californiagovernors.ca.gov/h/documents/inaugural_29.html.
22. Interview with Archie Green, March 3, 2006. By "we" Green was referring to himself and his best friend at Cal, Mitch Kunitani. They had been friends since junior high school in Boyle Heights and after World War II they would reunite as political allies within the American Veterans Committee.
23. Cohen, *When the Old Left Was Young*, 203.
24. Ibid., 191.
25. Denning, *The Cultural Front*, 8. For explanation of central concepts see xvi, 9, and 21.
26. Cohen, *When the Old Left Was Young*, 76.
27. Interview with Archie Green, March 3, 2006.

Part 2. Triangle of Commitments: San Francisco Maritime Politics of the Thirties

1. Boggs, *Living for Change*, 49.

Chapter 4. From Berkeley Stacks to Stake-Side Trucks

1. Anon., "The Trade Union Movement."
2. From correspondence with author, Sept. 5, 2007.
3. Interview with Bill Friedland, Oct. 27, 2006.
4. Oaxley, "Educational Activities in CCC Camp," included in U.S. Civilian Conservation Corps. Miscellaneous Publications 1933–41, SD 143 A296, Main Library, University of California, Berkeley.
5. Interview with Archie Green, Feb. 21, 2006.

6. A motto repeated in many CCC publications. U.S. Civilian Conservation Corp. Miscellaneous Publications 1933–41.

7. Interview with Archie Green, Feb. 21, 2006.

8. Interview with Archie Green, March 3, 2006.

9. Ibid.

10. Ibid.

11. Western Pipe and Steel was located between Oyster Point and Sierra Point just south of Brisbane, Calif.

12. Green, *Harry Lundeberg's Stetson*, 23.

13. For detailed discussion of the 1934 San Francisco General Strike see Nelson, *Workers on the Waterfront*, and Quinn, *The Big Strike*. On the concept of "social warrant" and the "'34 men" see Lipsitz, "Stan Weir: Working-Class Visionary" in Weir, *Singlejack Solidarity*, 346–56.

14. Nelson, *Workers on the Waterfront*, 160–66.

15. Maclean, *The Legend of Red Clydeside*, 1.

16. Interview with Archie Green, March 22, 2006.

17. The most detailed account of Green's work experience on the war-production waterfront is in the interview by Fredric L. Quivik (Nov. 12, 2001) conducted for the Rosie the Riveter Project, Regional Oral History Office of the University of California, Berkeley, Bancroft Library, Labor Archives and Research Center, San Francisco State University.

18. Ripley and McHugh, *John Maclean*, 26.

19. Ibid.

20. Ripley and McHugh examine how prevailing popular and historical memories of John Maclean emphasize his Scottish nationalism. That certainly holds true for the Clydesiders Green knew. Part of Ripley and McHugh's purpose, however, is a more critical assessment—and, ultimately, diminishment—of that role.

21. Hinton, *The First Shop Steward's Movement*.

22. Ibid., 276.

23. Ripley and McHugh, *John Maclean*, 157.

24. Ibid., 135.

25. Ibid., 139.

26. Maclean, *The Legend of Red Clydeside*, 104.

27. Hinton, *The First Shop Steward's Movement*, 123.

28. Palmer, *Organizing the Shipyards, 16.*

29. Ibid., 27.

30. Ibid., 34.

31. Ibid.

32. Author correspondence with Bernard Mergen, July 14 and July 15, 2007; Mergen, "A History of the Industrial Union of Marine and Shipbuilding Workers."

33. Author correspondence with Bernard Mergen, July 15, 2007.

34. Interview with Archie Green, April 14, 2006.

35. Harvey Schwartz interview with Archie Green, Sept. 29, 1997, 15, author's possession.

36. Interview with Archie Green, July 20, 2007. On February 24, 1990, Green met E. P. Thompson for the first and only time. They both presented at "A Conversation of Learned Hands: Maritime Culture 1915–1950" at the Apostleship of the Sea in Brooklyn, N.Y. Green's talk focused on Carwardine's history, and he remembered with pride that Thompson praised the presentation.

37. For Green, cultural sovereignty referred to the nature of a group's capacity to define and maintain its own cultural expression.

Chapter 5. "Brother Slugging Brother": Sailors, Longshoremen, and Legacies of the '34 Strike

1. Lipsitz, *A Rainbow at Midnight.*

2. Goldberg, *The Maritime Story*; Kimeldorf, *Reds or Rackets?*; Markholt, *Maritime Solidarity*; Nelson, *Workers on the Waterfront*; Quinn, *The Big Strike*; Schwartz, *The March Inland.*

3. Record provides the best account of the ideological and pragmatic basis of this feud in "Ideologies and Trade Union Leadership."

4. Nelson, *Workers on the Waterfront*, ch. 6; Kimeldorf, *Reds or Rackets?*

5. Nelson, *Workers on the Waterfront*, 125.

6. Larrowe, *Harry Bridges*; Cherny, "The Making of a Labor Radical."

7. Nelson, *Workers on the Waterfront*, 139.

8. S. Schwartz, *Brotherhood of the Sea.*

9. Nelson, *Workers on the Waterfront*, 152.

10. Ibid., 192.

11. Ibid., ch. 7; Markholdt, *Maritime Solidarity*, chs. 17, 18.

12. Pacific maritime histories agree that Lundeberg's decision to reaffiliate with the AFL was hastened and determined by Bridges's decision to align with the CIO.

13. Nelson, *Workers on the Waterfront*, 192.

14. Ibid., 205.

15. Articles in the ILWU *Dispatcher*, Sept. 21, 1945, Nov. 29, 1946, Oct. 10, 1952.

16. Record, "Ideologies and Trade Union Leadership."

17. Ibid., 58.

18. Ibid., 59.

19. Ibid.

20. Ibid.

21. Ibid., 87, Lundeberg's emphasis.

22. Ibid. Many librarians, labor historians, and former workers hold with a position that I find discouraging: The waterfront was a brutal place, everyone employed thugs and goons, and the Harrys did what was necessary for the survival of their unions.

23. Markholdt, *Maritime Solidarity*, 336.

24. Schwartz, review of *Maritime Solidarity.*

25. Nelson, *Workers on the Waterfront*, 238.

26. Additional examination of Green's left anticommunism focusing on issues of culture and politics in the relationship between the CPUSA and traditional American folk idiom appears in chapter 3.

27. Markholt, *Maritime Solidarity*, 366.

28. Nelson, *Workers on the Waterfront*, 316n39.

29. Ibid., 240, 239–42 (the Shepard Line beef). Other descriptions of the incident appear in Markholt, *Maritime Solidarity*, 359–77, and S. Schwartz, *Brotherhood of the Sea*, 122–25.

30. Markholt, *Maritime Solidarity*, 376.

31. S. Schwartz, *Brotherhood of the Sea*, 123.

32. Nelson, *Workers on the Waterfront*, 241.

33. Ibid., 244.

34. ILWU *Dispatcher*, Oct. 10, 1952.

35. ILWU *Dispatcher*, Nov. 29, 1946 (on Taft); Nov 12, Dec. 10, 1954 (on racism); Sept. 30, 1939 (on lack of union democracy); Sept. 14, Sept. 28, 1956 (on goon squads); and Dec. 7, 1951 (on Mahoney).

Chapter 6. Harry Bridges and Reconsiderations of Communist Party History

1. People rooted in Trotskyist or liberal political perspectives tend to use the term *left anti-Stalinism* as a label for this tradition. My problem with this label is in its sweeping application. To apply the censure *Stalinist* to all Americans who were CP members or fellow travelers detracts from the historical weight of Stalin's grave authoritarianism and murderous crimes and, in so many cases, mischaracterizes the people. Green and others disagree with me on this choice.

2. Preis, *Stalinists on the Waterfront.*

3. Denning points out that the "major CIO unions hostile to the Communists had few West Coast members, and since the Communist Party was smaller, the California Popular Front was less divided internally; one finds fewer denunciations and recriminations among both Communists and non-Communist leftists on the West Coast than in New York" (*The Cultural Front*, 19). From that perspective Green's history sheds needed light on experience of West Coast left anti-Communists.

4. Schwartz, review of *Maritime Solidarity*, 120.

5. Kerry, *Workers, Bosses, and Bureaucrats*, 110.

6. ILWU historian Harvey Schwartz points out that Bridges fought against arbitration in 1934, "but when it served the longshoremen as well as it did, his feelings about arbitration shifted." Interview with Harvey Schwartz, Feb. 28, 2007. Critics of the ILWU and CP emphasize that Communist attitudes toward arbitration shifted in relation to the Comintern's shift of policy between the Third Period and the Popular Front in 1935.

7. Harer, "The Trouble with Harry Bridges," 9.

8. Thomas, "West Coast Longshoremen and the 'Bridges Plan,'" 362.
9. Green and Rosemont were the primary forces behind publication of *The Big Red Songbook* in 2007.
10. Rosemont, *Joe Hill*, 365.
11. Ibid., 366.
12. Allen, *The Port Chicago Mutiny*, xiv.
13. Weir, *Singlejack Solidarity*, 243. When discussing the CP's shifting relationship to African American workers' rights during this period, historians are most likely to bring up the party's changing positions toward plans for the 1941 March on Washington. Lieberman, *"My Song Is My Weapon,"* 7–8; Isserman, *Which Side Were You On?* 118–19, 141–42.
14. Zeiger quoted in Stepan-Norris and Zeitlin, eds., *Left Out*, 84.
15. According to Bill Friedland, some former Trotskyists and Wobblies refer to this phenomenon as a "Stalinist scholarly renaissance." Correspondence with the author, Sept. 2, 2007.
16. Isserman, *Which Side Were You On?*; Kelley, *Hammer and Hoe*; Cochran, *Labor and Communism*; Naison, *Communists in Harlem*; Painter, *The Narrative of Hosea Hudson*. See also Brown, ed., *New Studies in the Politics and Culture of U.S. Communism*; and Quam-Wickham, "Who Controls the Hiring Hall?"
17. Interview with Archie Green, Jan. 17, 2007.
18. Kutler, *The American Inquisition*, 150–51; Schwartz, H., "Harry Bridges and the Scholars," 76.
19. Cherny, "Harry Bridges and the Communist Party."
20. See UDR website, including links to papers at http://depts.washington.edu/ilwu/uniondemocracy2_files/frame.htm.
21. Bill Friedland has pointed out that Stepan-Norris and Zeitlin's *Left Out* falls within a long tradition of sociological examination of democracy in unions. Michel, *Political Parties*; Lipset, *Union Democracy*.
22. Levi et al., "Union Democracy Revisited," 25–26.
23. A discussion of Weir appears in Larrowe, *Harry Bridges*, 364–70, and Weir, *Singlejack Solidarity*, 109, 199.

Chapter 7. Union Service and Organizing World War II Veterans

1. Schwartz, H. *Labor's Stronghold*, 4, 8.
2. Roediger, *Wages of Whiteness*; Saxton, *The Indispensable Enemy*.
3. Bullock, *Building California*, 165.
4. Ibid., 211.
5. Interview with Archie Green, April 14, 2006.
6. Vlach, "Always on Stolen Time," in author's files.
7. Ibid.
8. Interview with Archie Green, April 19, 2006.
9. Interview with Louanne Green, Oct. 19, 2006.

10. Interview with Archie Green, March 27, 2008.
11. Ibid.
12. Ibid.
13. On February 18, 1943, Japan issued the Proclamation Concerning Restriction of Residence and Business of Stateless Refugees, which set the terms for Jewish confinement.
14. Interview with Archie Green, March 27, 2008.
15. Brokaw, *The Greatest Generation*, xxv–xxxviii.
16. Saxe, *Settling Down*, 15. See chapter 3, "Kiss the Blood Off My Hands," for an examination of how film noir expressed social attitudes toward veterans.
17. Ibid., 50.
18. Ibid.
19. Bolte, *The New Veteran*, 74.
20. *AVC Bulletin* (National), box 1, folder 1, American Veterans Committee, San Francisco Area Council Records, 1945–51, Bancroft Library, University of California, Berkeley (hereafter Bancroft AVC Papers).
21. Archie Green to Bernard Bellush, New York, Oct. 20, 1948, Political Correspondence, carton 2, folder 7, Bancroft AVC Papers.
22. Mission Scrapbook, box 1, folder 1, Bancroft AVC Papers.
23. The only significant study is Saxe's *Settling Down*.
24. National Planning Committee Correspondence, carton 2, folder 4, Bancroft AVC Papers.
25. Ibid.
26. The *New York Herald*'s syndicated columnist Westbrook Pegler wrote a series of articles in 1946 critical of the AVC's purported radicalism. Saxe, *Settling Down*, 137.
27. The best resource on the politics of AVC leadership is found in Bolté, *The New Veteran*. Bolté was the organization's first president.
28. Ibid., 138.
29. National Planning Committee Minutes and Notes, 1945–47, carton 1, folder 26, Bancroft AVC Papers. See "Statement on Communism by the National Planning Committee of the AVC," Nov. 11, 1946.
30. Saxe, *Settling Down*,149.
31. Norman Leonard, "What Happened at Milwaukee: A Report of the Second Annual Convention of the American Veterans' Committee," National Convention, Milwaukee—Politics, carton 1, folder 23, Bancroft AVC Papers.

Part 3. A Decent Philosophy: Culture, Politics, and American Folk Revivalism

1. Archie Green to Pete Seeger, June 20, 1956, Pete Seeger file, Archie Green Papers, Wilson Library, UNC.
2. Archie Green to Pete Seeger, April 19, 1965, Pete Seeger file, Archie Green Papers, Wilson Library, UNC.

3. Pete Seeger to Archie Green, Nov. 19, 1963, Pete Seeger file, Archie Green Papers, Wilson Library, UNC. Emphasis added.

4. Pete Seeger to Archie Green, March 23, 1965, Pete Seeger file, Archie Green Papers, Wilson Library, UNC.

5. Archie Green to Pete Seeger, April 19, 1965. Emphasis added.

6. Seeger did not openly denounce Joseph Stalin until the early 1990s. Wakin, "This Just In."

7. Archie Green to Pete Seeger, April 19, 1965.

8. Green uses "People's Songs partisans" as a reference to the larger Popular Front and its legacy. People's Songs was a folk song performance collective founded by Seeger, Irwin Silber, and others in 1945 to promote folk song as a tool in empowering progressive social change. Likewise, Green speaks of the "*Broadside* writers of today" to refer to the prevailing fashion of folk revival during the sixties.

9. This question is considered in Part 4.

10. Cantwell, *When We Were Good*; Cohen, *Rainbow Quest*; Denning, *The Cultural Front*; Lieberman, *"My Song Is My Weapon"*; Reuss and Reuss, *American Folk Music and Left-Wing Politics.*

11. Denning, *The Cultural Front*, 5.

12. Denisoff's *Great Day Coming*, although having other shortcomings, does not fall into this category. Denisoff had political roots in Trotskyism and therefore did not share the more common optimistic appraisals of the Popular Front.

Chapter 8. Folk Music and the American Communist Party

1. The *Daily Worker* was the popular Communist Party newspaper published in New York City.

2. For detailed discussions of the Composers Collective see Reuss and Reuss, *American Folk Music and Left-Wing Politics*, chs. 3, 4; Denisoff, *Great Day Coming*, ch. 3, and Romalis, *Pistol Packin' Mama*, ch. 4.

3. Cowell's rejection of music that combined "revolutionary lyrics with traditional music" is a transparent criticism of Aunt Molly Jackson, who by 1933 had sung her political songs many times for members of the Composers Collective.

4. Green was proud of the piano-playing Wobbly on the cover of *The Big Red Songbook*. Interview with Archie Green, Nov. 12, 2007.

5. Sochor, *Revolution and Culture*, 3, 10.

6. Ibid., 8. Part of the significance of Sochor's research is her insistence that histories of cultural Marxism that most often begin with discussions of Lukács and Gramsci need to pay closer attention to A. A. Bogdanov, the author of *Red Star* (1907). Another important perspective on the history of Marxist thinking in relation to culture appears in Limon, "Western Marxism and Folklore."

7. Interview with Archie Green, Nov. 12, 2007.

8. Denning, *The Cultural Front*; Lieberman, *"My Song Is My Weapon"*; Reuss and Reuss, *American Folk Music and Left-Wing Politics*. The Third Period refers to the

years from 1928 to 1935, when the Communist International officially promoted a strict revolutionary political strategy, including noncooperation with other sectors of the left commonly labeled "social fascists." The Popular Front, often symbolized in the figure of Earl Browder, president of the CPUSA during this time, emphasized a politics of coalition-building with other sectors of the radical and liberal left. It was during the Popular Front period that the CPUSA achieved its greatest degree of middle-class and mainstream acceptance. The two periods are associated with very different cultural programs and aesthetics.

9. Reuss and Reuss, *American Folk Music and Left-Wing Politics*, 128.

10. Denisoff, *Great Day Coming*, 9–10, 50.

11. Ibid., 9–10.

12. Archie Green to Pete Seeger, April 19, 1965, Pete Seeger file, Archie Green Papers, Wilson Library, UNC.

13. Author interview with Bill Friedland, May 28, 2006, and Joe Gladstone, Dec. 13, 2005.

14. For a full account of the Almanac Singers see Reuss and Reuss, *American Folk Music and Left-Wing Politics*, ch. 7; Lieberman, *"My Song Is My Weapon,"* 52–59; and Denisoff, *Great Day Coming*, ch. 4. See also Cohen R., *Rainbow Quest.*

15. I identify Nelson and Kelley specifically for their respective books that address, critically and successfully, aspects of CP history: *Workers on the Waterfront* and *Hammer and Hoe.*

16. Burns, "Going Public."

17. Denning, *The Cultural Front*, xi.

18. Cantwell, *When We Were Young*, 7, 40.

19. Denning, *The Cultural Front*, 41.

20. Cohen, *Rainbow Quest*, 12. For information on Gordon see Kodish, *Good Friends and Bad Enemies.*

21. Folkways Records' *Anthology of American Folk Music* (1952), edited by the eccentric filmmaker and abstract expressionist Harry Smith, was a major milestone for the popular appreciation and study of American old-time music.

22. Cantwell, *When We Were Young*, 100.

23. Seeger quoted in Denisoff, *Great Day Coming*, 40–41.

24. Green, *Only a Miner*; Dennisoff, *Great Day Coming*; Lieberman, *"My Song Is My Weapon"*; Reuss and Reuss, *American Folk Music and Left-Wing Politics*, especially ch. 5; Romalis, *Pistol Packin' Mama.*

25. Romalis, *Pistol Packin' Mama*; Ardery, *Welcome the Traveler Home.*

26. Linear notes, Sarah Ogan Gunning, *Girl of Constant Sorrow*, Folk-Legacy Records, 1965, 1.

27. Green, "The Death of Mother Jones," 68–80.

28. Reuss and Reuss, *American Folk Music and Left-Wing Politics*, 90.

29. Ibid.

30. Anon., "Revolutionary Music," 27.

31. Green, *Only a Miner*, 78.

32. Cited in Reuss and Reuss, *American Folk Music and Left-Wing Politics*, 48.

33. Joe Hill was the famous revolutionary bard of the Wobblies assassinated by the state of Utah in 1915. Mike Gold's fervent advocacy of folk music and its revolutionary potential was certainly influenced by his connection to and respect for Elizabeth Gurley Flynn. A Wobbly in the first quarter of the century, Flynn celebrated the song craft of her comrade, Joe Hill. Reuss and Reuss, *American Folk Music and Left-Wing Politics*, 36; Romalis, *Pistol Packin' Mama*, 161. Flynn later became a prominent member of the Communist Party. The definitive study of Joe Hill is Rosemont's *Joe Hill.*

34. Romalis quotes Tillman Cadle, *Pistol Packin' Mama*, 88.

35. Ibid.

36. The relationship of Mary Elizabeth Barnicle and Alan Lomax to these traditional artists and others is a complicated and controversial story in itself. For an indication of these controversies see Romalis, *Pistol Packin' Mama*, 115, 146. Green knew Aunt Molly Jackson well before he met Alan Lomax, and it seems reasonable that Jackson's opinions of Lomax would have influenced Green's attitude toward Lomax.

37. Ibid., 49.

38. Reuss and Reuss, *American Folk Music and Left-Wing Politics*, 98–103. Denisoff, *Great Day Coming*, 26–34.

39. Reuss and Reuss, *American Folk Music and Left-Wing Politics*, 66.

40. Ibid., 224.

41. Ibid., 206–7.

42. Ibid., 208.

43. Reuss's argument that in this era "communist-associated musicians were clearly marching to their own tune, not Moscow's" should be seen as an early work in what many social movement scholars consider a profound shift in the historiography of the CP (ibid., 69). Authors such as Reuss, Maurice Isserman, Robin D. G. Kelley, and Mark D. Naison have significantly contributed to what Denning identifies as the need for scholarship that breaks from a "core-periphery" analysis of the party. See also Brown, ed., *New Studies in the Politics and Culture of U.S. Communism*. Friedland and other former Trotskyists refer to the new histories as a "Stalinist Renaissance."

44. Sharp, *English Folksongs from the Southern Appalachians*.

45. Cantwell, *When We Were Young*, 28; see also Whisnant, *All That Is Native and Fine.*

46. Reuss and Reuss, *American Folk Music and Left-Wing Politics*, 269–70.

47. Interview with Archie Green, Nov. 12, 2007.

48. Conversation with Archie Green, Oct. 8, 2007. Green's use of "Age of the CIO" is a reference to Denning's *The Cultural Front*.

49. Reuss and Reuss, *American Folk Music and Left-Wing Politics*, 197.

50. David Roediger makes three main challenges to Denning's portrayal of the popular Front. He refuses to wholly celebrate the racial politics of the movement on the grounds that Native Americans were unaddressed and there was no acknowl-

edgment of the legitimacy of an autonomous black radical politics. Furthermore, Roediger asks, where is surrealism? A question fundamental to his argument that Denning's Cultural Front "is not the story which ought to ground our imaginations of new movements." Roegider, "Radical Culture without Surrealism."

51. Botkin, *A Treasury of American Folklore*, xxv–xxvi.

52. Another of Green's mentors, the song scholar George Korson, maintained a significant suspicion toward Communist influence on coal-mining songs.

53. Lieberman raises this point in *"My Song Is My Weapon,"* 53.

Chapter 9. Moments in the Making of a Laborlorist

1. Green's 1965 essay "Hillbilly Music: Source and Symbol" became one of the early cornerstone texts for Appalachian studies and the history of country and western music.

2. In 1986 Green helped Kathleen Tamony, Peter's sister, with the transfer of her brother's collection to the Western Historical Manuscript Collection at the University of Missouri-Columbia. It is through that experience that he met his long-time friend and collaborator David Roediger. Green, "Peter Tamony," in *Torching the Fink Books*, 183–98.

3. Green, "John Neuhaus, Wobbly Folklorist," in Green et al., *The Big Red Songbook*, 400.

4. One of Green's few regrets was that he never could convince Neuhaus to make a recording of his performance of Wobbly songs.

5. Interview with Archie Green, Oct. 9, 2006.

6. Machado, "Eugene Earle"; Porterfield, *Exploring Roots Music.*

7. "When I wrote, it was impossible to publish a book for the general public that spoke out frankly on the subject [folksingers and the Communist Party], and since I thought at the time that it was more important to get Guthrie to the attention of the receptive public than to be entirely honest, I omitted it. But I knew about it right enough." Greenway to Richard Reuss, Jan. 19, 1967, Richard Reuss file, Archie Green Papers, Wilson Library, UNC.

8. Interview with Archie Green, Oct. 27, 2006.

9. These interviews eventually proved important to Green's dissertation and first book *Only a Miner* (77–88) as well as Shelly Romalis's definitive book on Aunt Molly Jackson.

10. John Edwards file, Archie Green Papers, Wilson Library, UNC. The capitalization is Edwards's.

11. John Edwards file, Archie Green Papers, Wilson Library, UNC, Aug. 9, 1957. Edwards refers to a 1924 Columbia recording of Georgia farmer Gid Tanner, billed as a "Famous Southern Fiddler."

12. Quoted in Earle, "A Tribute to John Edwards," n.p., John Edwards file, Archie Green Papers, Wilson Library, UNC.

13. For an understanding of how important the John Edwards Collection (and the

JEMF Quarterly it inspired) became to early country music scholarship see Porterfield's *Exploring Roots Music*. From 1965–85 the *Quarterly* served as a groundbreaking public forum for the emergent field of country music and vernacular music scholarship. Academic and nonacademic authors alike were encouraged to contribute. In a miraculous feat of will, intellect, and logistics, Green wrote sixty-eight columns—one in every issue of the *Quarterly* from number six in 1967 until its final 1985 publication—for a series he called "Commercial Music Graphics." The series is a significant contribution to the integration of music scholarship, history, visual studies, and folklore.

14. Interview with Archie Green, Oct. 27, 2006.

15. Green, "The Death of Mother Jones," 68–80; Green, "John Neuhaus, Wobbly Folklorist," in Green et al., *The Big Red Songbook*, 189–217; Green, "*Dutchman*," 27074.

16. Green, "The Death of Mother Jones," 77.

17. Interview with Robert Sayers, Aug. 28, 2006.

18. *Green Fields of Illinois*, Campus Folksong Club, CFC 201, May 1963.

19. In 2007 the archivist and oral historian Tracy Wilson compiled an oral history of the University of Illinois Campus Folksong Club. Her impressive collection of interviews, including two with Archie Green, can be found at http://www.library.uiuc.edu/edx/folklore/cfc.htm.

Chapter 10. Vernacular Music and Cultural Pluralism

1. Shelton, "Students Import Folk Art to Chicago." The article marked the first time that Green's name appeared in a major national paper.

2. Cited in Storey, *Inventing Popular Culture*, 2–3, 4.

3. Green, "Vernacular Music: A Naming Compass," 35–46.

4. Denning, *The Cultural Front*, 285–95.

5. Quoted in Green, "Vernacular Music: A Naming Compass," 37.

6. Ibid., 38.

7. Denning, *The Cultural Front*, 287.

8. Green, "Vernacular Music: A Naming Compass," 39, 44.

9. Seeger, "Music in America," 411–13, 435–36. For Green's discussion of Seeger see "Vernacular Music: A Naming Compass," 40.

10. Interview with Nick Spitzer, Sept. 18, 2006.

11. Green, "Winding Down," 101.

12. Green, "Industrial Lore: A Bibliographic-Semantic Query," 215.

13. Cantwell, *When We Were Good*, 182.

14. Interview with Bob Sayers, Aug. 28, 2006.

15. Ron Cohen suggests reading Allen, *Gone to the Country*, in which Allen discusses real versus revival musicians.

16. Interview with Archie Green, March 27, 2008. "Mickey Mouse music" was a favorite phrase Green picked up from his good friend and founder of Arhoolie Records, Chris Strachowitz.

17. Ibid.

18. "People's Songs and Singers," 8.

19. Storey, *Inventing Popular Culture*, 104, emphasis added.

20. Strategic essentialism is a major concept in postcolonial theory and was introduced by Gayatri Spivak. My use of the concept follows her idea that when a subaltern group uses strategic essentialism it is explicitly understood as a construct. When I employ the concept to explain Green's privileging of "vernacular music," however, I recognize that he used the term as an outsider in description of others. That use is different from how Spivak observes strategic essentialisms being defined and used by subaltern groups themselves. Spivak, "Subaltern Studies: Deconstructing Historiography," in *The Spivak Reader*, 203–6.

21. Interview with Nick Spitzer, Sept. 18, 2006.

22. Interview with Archie Green, Oct. 27, 2006.

23. Storey, *Inventing Popular Culture*, 94.

24. Green, "Four 78-rpm Album Covers," 118.

Part 4. "Always on Stolen Time": Folklore, Labor History, and Cultural Studies

1. In the late 1980s, John Vlach wrote an introductory essay, "Always on Stolen Time: The Sources and Rationale for the Graphics Series," for a collection of Green's Graphics writing that he hoped to edit. The book was never published, but the title of this part of the volume is drawn from that essay. I am grateful to John Vlach for sharing his work with me. For information on the development of public folklore see Feintuch, ed., *The Conservation of Culture*; Baron and Spitzer, eds., *Public Folklore*; Hufford, ed., *Conserving Culture*; and Bauman and Paredes, eds., *Toward New Perspectives in Folklore*. Gross-Bressler specifies ("Culture and Politics," 16) that the Folklife Festival initially owed much to Jim Morris, a director of the Smithsonian's Division of Performing Arts. Morris hired Rinzler to direct the festival.

2. McCarl, "Occupational Folklife in the Public Sector,"139.

3. Green developed his doctoral dissertation from University of Pennsylvania into *Only a Miner: Studies in Recorded Coal-Mining Songs*, an interdisciplinary laborlore study that remains a key text in American music scholarship, cultural studies, Appalachian studies, folklore, and working-class history.

4. The nine ironworkers came from locals throughout the country (e.g., Local 1, Chicago; Local 84, Houston; and Local 433, Los Angeles) and had been selected and brought together by the Ironworker's International. Smithsonian intern Ron Stanford worked closely with Preston George of Local 5 to coordinate the logistics of the Ironworker's exhibit.

5. Jacobson, "At the Folklife Festival," B1.

6. Unlike the prevailing historiographies of new labor history and American cultural studies, narratives of the development of public folklore consistently figure Green as integral to the transformation of the discipline. Feintuch, ed., *The Conser-*

vation of Culture; Baron and Spitzer, eds., *Public Folklore*; Hufford, ed., *Conserving Culture*. On the question of alternative directions for new labor history in the United States, it is useful to look abroad to other traditions of workers' history as represented, for example, in Alesandro Portelli's work and the work of Circolo Gianni Bosio in Rome.

Chapter 11. Alternative Popular Front Imaginary

1. Green, *Wobblies, Pile Butts, and Other Heroes*, 5.
2. Green, "John Neuhaus," 189–217.
3. Green, "American Labor Lore," 51–58.
4. "The long fetch" is a term Peter Linebaugh, Marcus Reddiker, and George Lipsitz use to help people visualize how historical dynamics take shape like ocean waves and play out over long periods of time. Lipsitz, *Footsteps in the Dark*, vii–xxv.
5. Interview with Debora Kodish, Aug. 23, 2006.
6. Lipsitz notes that "it makes a difference for our work in the present when we acknowledge that the origins of American Studies lie both inside and outside the academy, that the social movements of the thirties were both an inspirational stimulus and an empirical site for the construction of the field." Lipsitz, "'Sent for You Yesterday, Here You Come Today,'" 214.
7. Green, *Only a Miner*, viii.
8. Antonio Gramsci makes a similar recommendation in his *Prison Notebooks*.
9. Interview with Peter Rachleff, Aug. 13, 2006.
10. Denning, the *Cultural Front*, 74, 109, 124.
11. Green, *Only a Miner*, 12, 15 (on Korson); xii, 412 (on methodology). Green held enormous admiration for Korson.
12. Ibid., 214.
13. Denning, *The Cultural Front*, 95–114.
14. Ibid., 110.
15. Green, *Only a Miner*, 432.
16. This paraphrases an important work by another of Green's laborlore students. Finnegan, "Only a Folklorist, or Cult Stud?" 43–63. My thanks to John Vlach for drawing my attention to Finnegan's work.
17. Interview with Robert McCarl, Aug. 8, 2006.
18. Interview with Julie Ardery, Sept. 22, 2006.
19. Denning, *The Cultural Front*, 107.
20. Abrahams, "Phantoms of Romantic Nationalism in Folkloristics," 3, 21.
21. Bauman and Paredes., eds., *Toward New Perspectives in Folklore*; Shuman and Briggs, "Theorizing Folklore," 109–34.
22. Green, "Industrial Lore," 238.
23. Green, "Dutchman," 74.
24. Hufford, ed., *Conserving Culture*, 249.
25. Green, *Torching the Fink Books*, 134–50.

26. Green always had a good laugh when he recalled Dorson's line "debasing the coin of scholarship." U.S. Senate, Hearings, 85.

27. Green is best known for his monumental role in this achievement. Bressler covers the legislative history of the act thoroughly and Green's central role in its success.

28. U.S. Senate, Hearings, 83–85.

29. Interview with Robert McCarl, Aug. 8, 2006.

30. Syllabus in Archie Green file, American Folklife Center; Library of Congress.

31. Interview with Nick Spitzer, Aug. 18, 2008.

32. "Stitching Patchwork in Public," in Feintuch, ed., *The Conservation of Culture*, 31.

33. Interview with Archie Green, July 29, 2008.

34. Bressler, "Culture and Politics," iv. By "cultural diversity" Bressler specifically refers to artistic cultural diversity.

35. "P.L. 94–201—A View from the Lobby," in Feintuch, ed., *The Conservation of Culture*, Green notes that "members of Congress and their aides knew not only that our bill made a symbolic statement about the intrinsic value in folklife, but also that it might make positive contribution to internal reforms needed within the NEA-NEH." Willett illustrates the enormous national expansion, in part based on the bill, of NEA programming and funding for folklife. "In 1966," he observes, "the first state folklorist position was created in Pennsylvania. There were no additional positions created for the next eight years. . . . At present there are state folk cultural programs in over forty states, with another half dozen or so states at various stages in the development of such programs. The vast majority of those programs were initially established through matching funds provided by the Folk Arts Program of the National Endowment for the Arts." Willett, "A Survey of State Folk Cultural Programs," 3.

36. An excellent introduction to these accomplishments is found in Graves, *Cultural Democracy*.

Chapter 12. New Labor History and American Cultural Studies

1. Green also considered working under Wayland Hand (UCLA) or Bertrand Bronson (UC Berkeley), but their West Coast locations made doing so logistically difficult.

2. Green, *Only a Miner*, 170.

3. Green, "American Labor Lore," 53.

4. The term *history from below* was originally coined by the French social historian Georges Lefebvre in his many books on the origins of the French Revolution. British Marxist historians including E. P. Thompson, Christopher Hill, Erich Hobsbawn, and Raphael Samuel popularized the notion, and it is through their influence on American social historians that the concept became wedded with new labor history in the United States.

5. For an insightful reflection on the continuities and discontinuities between new labor history and the Wisconsin School see Brody, "The Old Labor History and the New" and "Reconciling the Old Labor History and the New." Green studied under Ira Cross, a student of John Commons, at UC Berkeley.

6. Brody, "The Old Labor History and the New"; Brody, "Reconciling the Old Labor History and the New"; MARHO, *Visions of History*.

7. Thompson, *The Making of the English Working Class*; Gutman, "Work, Culture, and Society in Industrializing America"; Montgomery, "Worker's Control of Machine Production in the Nineteenth Century."

8. *Only a Miner* was immediately reviewed in journals focused on music, folklore, and anthropology as well as *The Nation*, and Staughton Lynd reviewed it in *The American Historical Review*. As David Whisnant, one of central figures in the founding of Appalachian studies, said of Green's influence on the early days of the field, "Everyone knew and respected Archie, and he talked with them/us as he always did, with enthusiasm, amazing political insight, the ability to make connections and draw conclusions no one else was making or drawing, connecting people with each other, praising their work and helping them to take the next step, helping us all to see the implications and possibilities of what we were trying to do or might do." Author's notes, interview with David Whisnant, Sept. 6, 2006.

9. Kelley, *Race Rebels*, 6.

10. Interview with David Roediger, Sept. 29, 2006.

11. Ibid.

12. Lynd and Lynd, *Rank and File*. The American Social History Project produced the two-volume *Who Built America? Working People and the Nation's History* and continues its work in collaboration with CUNY's Center for Media and Learning.

13. Ibid., 152–94.

14. None of these lists of individuals should be read as exclusive; they are only representative.

15. In the first chapter of *The Wages of Whiteness* (14–15), Roediger uses Archie Green, along with Mikhail Bakhtin and Raymond Williams, to help make a distinction between a kind of historical, materialist, and social cultural studies that has long taken language seriously and the poststructuralist literary theories (most closely associated with Jacques Derrida) that gained popularity in the eighties. Roediger sees his work in the tradition of the former and says of that tradition, "Meaning is thus always multifaceted and socially contested, but it is neither absent nor unconnected with social relations. Indeed, for Bakhtin and for such brilliant modern, but not poststructuralist, students of language as Raymond Williams and Archie Green, the ambiguity of language affords its meaning."

16. Finnegan, "Only a Folklorist, or Cult Stud?"

17. Ibid., 58–59.

18. Cohen, "JEMF and the *Quarterly*," 92; Porterfield, *Exploring Roots Music*.

19. Green, "Columbia's Jigs, Reels, and Banjo Tunes," 128.

20. Green, "Edison Envelope Stuffer," 23.

21. Green, "Buell Kazee Folk Song Recital," 25.

22. Green, "Winding Down," 101.

23. Ibid., 102.

24. Green's background in ethnography and oral history gave him important insight into the difference between "meaning" and "fact" in terms of how people interpret their world. He took interest in how meaning often traveled in ways quite independent from fact and how the significance that meaning had on people's lives raises questions about what constitutes veracity. Green, *Calf's Head and Union Tale*, 17; Green, *Only a Miner*, 58. Green's emphasis on how audiences make sense of and appropriate cultural objects situates him as an early proponent of "reception theory" in cultural studies.

25. Green, "Edison Envelope Stuffer," 25.

26. "In one sense" acknowledges that folklore also had much to learn from cultural studies. Briggs and Shuman, "Theorizing Folklore."

27. Green, "J. E. Mainer's Liza and Sambo," 73.

28. Interview with Debora Kodish, Aug. 23, 2006.

29. Hufford, ed., *Conserving Culture*, 251, emphasis in the original.

30. Kahn, "Early Days at JEMF," 92.

Chapter 13. Laborlore: A Pedagogy of the Working Class

1. Cantwell, "Foreword," x.

2. Interview with Archie Green, Dec. 22, 2007.

3. Ibid.

4. My phrasing reflects language that a variety of thinkers use who are concerned with the relationship between pedagogy, culture, and liberation struggles. See, for example, the work of Paula Allman, Paulo Freire, Bell Hooks, Ivan Illich, Peter McLaren, Chandra Mohanty, and Francesca Polletta.

5. On Alexander Bogdanov, see Sochor, *Revolution and Culture*; Gramsci, *Prison Notebooks*; James, *American Civilization*; Freire, *Cultural Action for Freedom*; and Horton and Freire, *We Make the Road by Walking*. For an excellent article on the Marxism and folklore see Limon, "Western Marxism and Folklore."

6. "Solidarity Forever" by Ralph Chaplin, Jan. 17, 1915; "The Preacher and the Slave" ("Pie in the Sky" or "Long Haired Preachers") by Joe Hill, July 6, 1911.

7. Green's ally Staughton Lynd has been a long-time proponent of the centrality of workers' culture to workers' power. "Another missing dimension in most rank-and-file movements is, I think, a cultural dimension," he says. "At the St. Thérèse General Motors plant what became a sit-down had its origins in an insistence of French-speaking workers that their language be respected; that is, the group that formed around that demand became the group that sparked the sit-down. And, of course, in the short-lived Black Revolutionary Union movement in Detroit, one sensed that extra dimension. It was the dimension that the church contributed to the southern civil rights movement . . . I sense the absence of that in movements that call themselves rank and file, and I think it is absolutely critical. We are talking about something that gives people the courage to say, 'Hey! I have two kids and I'm

going to risk my job for this.' That has got to come from somewhere. That has got to have deep roots." MARHO, *Visions of History*, 160–61.

8. For a discussion of how the "politics of the everyday" redefines traditional conceptions of the political, see Kelley, *Race Rebels*, 9–11, 229–33.

9. Hufford, ed., *Conserving Culture*, 249.

10. Green, *Torching the Fink Books*, xxvii.

11. Green, "The Folklorist as Cultural Critic," cited in Finnegan, "Only a Folklorist, or Cult Stud?" 54.

12. Green, "Another Tool in the Carpenter's Chest," 43.

13. More information on the Copra Crane Labor Landmark Association is available at www.laborculture.org.

14. Laborlore Conversation VI (2008), held in Chicago, was an exception to this format. Toward the aim of making links with new scholars and activists it was held in collaboration with the Labor and Working Class History Association's yearly conference.

Bibliography

Research Archives

American Folklife Center, Library of Congress, Washington, D.C.
Archie Green Papers, Southern Folklife Collection, Wilson Library, University of North Carolina at Chapel Hill
Bancroft Library, University of California, Berkeley
Holt Labor Library, San Francisco
International Longshoremen and Warehouse Union Library, San Francisco
Labor Archives and Research Center, San Francisco State University
National Archives, Washington, D.C.

Interviews

Roger Abrahams (email), Aug. 17 and 21, 2007
Julie Ardery, Sept. 22, 2006
Peggy Bulger, Aug. 25, 2006
Carl Fleishauer, Aug. 24, 2006
William Friedland, May 28 and Oct. 27, 2006; June 12, Aug. 21, and (email) Sept. 2, 2007
Joseph Gladstone, Dec. 13 and 14, 2005 (both two parts)
Archie Green, Feb. 10, Feb. 21, March 3, March 22, and April 14 (all two parts), April 19, May 8, Oct. 9, Oct. 27 (two parts), and Dec. 22, 2006; Jan. 17, July 20, Oct. 8, and Nov. 12, 2007; Jan. 8, March 27, July 28, and Sept. 26, 2008.
Louanne Green, Oct. 19, 2006
Mitzie Green, Dec. 22, 2006
Joseph Hickerson, Aug. 30, 2006
Alan Jabbour, Aug. 29, 2006

Paula Johnson, Aug. 24, 2006
Debora Kodish, Aug. 23, 2006
Robert McCarl, Aug. 8, 2006
Judith McCulloh, Aug. 17, 2006
Bernard Mergen, July 14, and (email) July 15, 2007
Peter Rachleff, Aug. 13, 2006
David Roediger, Sept. 29, 2006
Robert Sayers, Aug. 28, 2006
Harvey Schwartz, Feb. 28, 2007; interview with Archie Green in author's possession, Sept. 29, 1998.
Nick Spitzer, Sept. 18, 2006
John Vlach, Aug. 25, 2006
David Whisnant, Sept. 6, 2006
Steve Winick, Aug. 25, 2006

Primary and Secondary Sources

Abrahams, Roger. "Phantoms of Romantic Nationalism in Folkloristics." *Journal of American Folklore* 106 (Winter 1993): 3–37.

Adamic, Louis. *Dynamite: The Story of Class Violence in America.* New York: Chelsea House, 1958.

Allen, Ray. *Gone to the Country: The New Lost City Ramblers and the Folk Music Revival.* Urbana: University of Illinois Press, 2011.

Allen, Robert L. *The Port Chicago Mutiny.* New York: Amistad Press, 1993.

Allman, Paula. *Critical Education against Global Capitalism: Karl Marx and Revolutionary Critical Education.* Westport: Bergin and Garvey, 2001.

Anon. "People's Songs and Singers." *The New Masses,* July 16, 1946, 9–12.

———. "Revolutionary Music." *The New Masses,* Feb. 1933, 27.

———. "The Trade Union Movement and the Immediate Tasks of the Party in Development of Mass Work." *Socialist Workers Party Internal Bulletin* 3 (April 1940): 4–8.

Ardery, Julie. *Welcome the Traveler Home: Jim Garland's Story of the Kentucky Mountains.* Lexington: University Press of Kentucky, 1983.

Avrich, Paul. *Sacco and Vanzetti: The Anarchist Background.* Princeton: Princeton University Press, 1991.

Baron, Robert, and Nicholas R. Spitzer. *Public Folklore.* Washington, D.C.: Smithsonian Institution Press, 1992.

Bauman, Richard, and Americo Paredes, eds. *Toward New Perspectives in Folklore.* Austin: University of Texas Press, 1972.

———, and Roger Abrahams, *And Other Neighborly Names.* Austin: University of Texas Press, 1981.

Bimba, Anthony. *The History of the American Working Class.* New York: International Publishers, 1927.

Bogdanov, Alexander. *Red Star: The First Bolshevik Utopia*. Reprint. Ed. Loren R. Graham and Richard Stites. Bloomington: Indiana University Press, 1984.

Boggs, Grace Lee. *Living for Change*. Minneapolis: University of Minnesota Press, 1998.

Bolté, Charles. *The New Veteran*. New York: Reynal and Hitchcock, 1945.

Botkin, B.A., ed. *A Treasury of American Folklore*. New York: Crown Publishers, 1944.

Briggs, Charles, and Amy Shuman. Eds. "Theorizing Folklore: Toward New Perspectives on the Politics of Culture." *Western Folklore* 52 (April–Oct. 1993): 109–34.

Brodkin, Karen. *How Jews Became White Folks and What That Says about Race in America*. New Brunswick: Rutgers University Press, 1998.

Brody, David. "The Old Labor History and the New: In Search of an American Working Class." *Labor History* 17 (1976) 485–509.

———. "Reconciling the Old Labor History and the New." *Pacific Historical Review* 62 (Feb. 1993): 1–18.

Brokaw, Tom. *The Greatest Generation*. New York: Delta Press, 1998.

Brown, Michael E., ed. *New Studies in the Politics and Culture of U.S. Communism*. New York: Monthly Review Press, 1993.

Brundage, David. *The Making of Western Labor Radicalism: Denver's Organized Workers, 1878–1905*. Urbana: University of Illinois Press, 1994.

Buhle, Paul, and Nicole Schulman, eds. *Wobblies: A Graphic History of the Industrial Workers of the World*. New York: Verso Press, 2005.

Bullock, Paul. *Building California: The Story of the Carpenters' Union*. Los Angeles: Institute of Industrial Relations, 1982.

Burns, Sean. "Going Public: Archie Green's Lifelong Commitment to Laboring Culture." *International Labor and Working-Class History* 76 (Fall 2009): 164–79.

Cantwell, Robert. Foreword in Archie Green, *Torching the Fink Books and Other Essays on Vernacular Culture*. Chapel Hill: University of North Carolina Press, 2001.

———. *When We Were Good: The Folk Revival*. Cambridge: Harvard University Press, 1996.

Cherny, Robert. "Constructing a Radical Identity: History, Memory, and the Seafaring Stories of Harry Bridges." *Pacific Historical Review* 70(Nov. 2001): 571–99.

———. "Harry Bridges and the Communist Party: New Evidence, Old Questions; Old Evidence, New Questions." Presented at the Organization of American Historians, April 4, 1998, and in Stepan-Norris and Zeitlin, *Left Out*, 148.

———. "The Making of a Labor Radical: Harry Bridges, 1901–1934." *Pacific Historical Review* 64 (Aug. 1995): 363–88.

Clifford, James. *The Predicament of Culture: Twentieth-Century Ethnography, Literature, and Art*. Cambridge: Harvard University Press, 1998.

Cochran, Bert. *Labor and Communism*. Princeton: Princeton University Press, 1977.

Cohen, Lizabeth. *Making a New Deal: Industrial Workers in Chicago, 1919–1939*. New York: Cambridge University Press, 1990.

Cohen, Norm. "JEMF and the *Quarterly*: Reminiscences of a Shy and Retiring Editor." *JEMF Quarterly* 77–78 (Fall–Winter 1985): 91–98.

Cohen, Robert. *When the Old Left Was Young: Student Radicals and America's First Mass Student Movement, 1929–1941.* New York: Oxford University Press.

Cohen, Ronald. *Rainbow Quest: The Folk Music Revival and American Society, 1940–1970.* Amherst: University of Massachusetts Press, 2002.

Denisoff, R. Serge. *Great Day Coming: Folk Music and the American Left.* Urbana: University of Illinois Press, 1971.

Denning, Michael. *The Cultural Front.* New York: Verso Press, 1997.

Epstein, Barbara. *Political Protest and Cultural Revolution: Nonviolent Direct Action in the 1970s and 1980s.* Berkeley: University of California Press, 1991.

Feintuch, Burt, ed. *The Conservation of Culture: Folklorists and the Public Sector.* Lexington: University Press of Kentucky, 1988.

Feuerlicht, Robert Strauss. *Justice Crucified: The Story of Sacco and Vanzetti.* New York: McGraw-Hill, 1977.

Finnegan, Brian. "Only a Folklorist, or Cult Stud? Archie Green's Contributions to American Folklore and Cultural Studies." *Folklore Historian* 15 (1998): 43–63.

Flynn, Elizabeth Gurley. *Rebel Girl: An Autobiography, My First Life, 1906–1926.* New York: International Publishers, 1973.

Frankenberg, Ruth. *White Women, Race Matters: The Social Construction of Whiteness.* Minneapolis: University of Minnesota Press, 1993.

Freire, Paulo. *Cultural Action for Freedom.* Cambridge: Harvard University Press, 2000.

———. *Pedagogy of the Oppressed.* New York: Continuum, 1970.

Giroux, Henry. *Teachers as Intellectuals: Toward a Critical Pedagogy of Learning.* Boston: Bergin and Garvey, 1988.

Goldberg, Joseph P. *The Maritime Story: A Study in Labor-Management Relations.* Cambridge: Harvard University Press, 1958.

Gramsci, Antonio. *Prison Notebooks.* New York: Columbia University Press, 1992.

Graves, James "Bau." *Cultural Democracy: The Arts, Community, and Public Purpose.* Urbana: University of Illinois Press, 2005.

Green, Archie. "American Labor Lore: Its Meaning and Uses." *Industrial Relations* 4 (Feb. 1965): 51–58.

———. "Another Tool in the Carpenter's Chest." In *1973 Festival of American Folklife.* Ed. Ralph Rinzler and Gerald L. Davis, 40–43. Washington, D.C.: Smithsonian Institution, 1973.

———, with David Roediger, Franklin Rosemont, and Salvatore Salerno. *The Big Red Songbook.* Chicago: Charles H. Kerr Publishing, 2007.

———. "Buell Kazee Folk Song Recital." *JEMF Quarterly* 6 (Spring 1970): 23–27.

———. *Calf's Head and Union Tale: Labor Yarns at Work and Play.* Urbana: University of Illinois Press, 1996.

———. "Columbia's Jigs, Reels, and Banjo Tunes." *EMF Newsletter* 4 (Dec. 1968): 126–30.

———. "The Death of Mother Jones." *Labor History*, no. 1 (Winter 1960): 68–80.

———. "*Dutchman*: An On-the-Job Etymology." *American Speech* 35 (Dec. 1960): 270–74.

———. "Edison Envelope Stuffer." *JEMF Quarterly,* no. 22 (Spring 1971): 23–26.

———. "Four 78-rpm Album Covers." *JEMF Quarterly* 2 (Autumn 1971): 116–21.

———. *Harry Lundeberg's Stetson and Other Nautical Tales.* Crockett, Calif.: Carquinez Press, 2006.

———. "Hillbilly Music: Source and Symbol." *Journal of American Folklore* 78 (July 1965): 204–28.

———. "Industrial Lore: A Bibliographic-Semantic Query." *Western Folklore* 37 (July 1978): 213–44.

———. "J. E. Mainer's Liza and Sambo." *JEMF Quarterly,* no.22 (Summer 1971): 72–75.

———. "John Neuhaus: Wobbly Folklorist." *Journal of American Folklore* 73 (July 1960) 189–217.

———. *Only a Miner: Studies in Recorded Coal-Mining Songs.* Urbana: University of Illinois Press, 1972.

———. "Raven, Mallard, and Spotted Owl: Totems for Coalition." In *Conserving Culture: A New Discourse on Heritage.* Ed. Mary Hufford, 245–52. Urbana: University of Illinois Press, 1994.

———, ed. *Songs about Work: Essays in Occupational Culture.* Bloomington: Indiana University Press, 1993.

———. *Torching the Fink Books and Other Essays on Vernacular Culture.* Chapel Hill: University of North Carolina Press, 2001.

———. "Vernacular Music: A Naming Compass." *Musical Quarterly* 77 (Spring 1993): 35–46.

———. "Winding Down." *JEMF Quarterly,* nos. 77–78 (Fall–Winter 1985): 99–115.

———. *Wobblies, Pile Butts, and Other Heroes: Laborlore Explorations.* Urbana: University of Illinois Press, 1993.

Green, James. *Taking History to Heart: The Power of the Past in Building Social Movements.* Amherst: University of Massachusetts Press, 2000.

Gross, Sandra Bressler. "Culture and Politics: A Legislative Chronicle of the American Folklife Preservation Act." Ph.D. diss., University of Pennsylvania, 1995.

Gutman, Herbert. "Work, Culture, and Society in Industrializing America." *American Historical Review* 78 (1973): 277–85.

Harer, Asher. "The Trouble with Harry Bridges." *International Socialist Review,* no. 34 (Sept. 1973): 9.

Hinton, James. *The First Shop Steward's Movement.* London: G. Allen and Unwin, 1973.

Horton, Myles, and Paulo Freire. *We Make the Road by Walking: Conversations on Education and Social Change.* Philadelphia: Temple University Press, 1990.

Hufford, Mary, ed. *Conserving Culture: A New Discourse on Heritage.* Urbana: University of Illinois Press, 1994.

Illich, Ivan. *Deschooling Society.* New York: Harper and Row, 1971.

Isserman, Maurice. *Which Side Were You On? The American Communist Party during the Second World War.* Urbana: University of Illinois Press, 1982.

Jacobson, Aileen. "At the Folklife Festival: Hard Hats and Hard Songs of Union Dues and Blues." *Washington Post,* July 3, 1971, B1.

Jacobson, Matthew Frye. *Whiteness of a Different Color: European Immigrants and the Alchemy of Race.* Cambridge: Harvard University Press, 1998.

James, C. L. R. *American Civilization.* Oxford, U.K.: Basil Blackwell, 1993.

Kahn, Ed. "Early Days at JEMF." *JEMF Quarterly,* no.77–78 (Fall–Winter 1985): 89–98.

Kelley, Robin D. G. *Hammer and Hoe: Alabama Communists during the Great Depression.* Chapel Hill: University of North Carolina Press, 1990.

———. *Race Rebels: Culture, Politics, and the Black Working Class.* New York: Free Press, 1994.

Kerry, Tom. *Workers, Bosses, and Bureaucrats: A Socialist View of Labor Struggles since the 1930s.* New York: Pathfinder Press, 1980.

Kimeldorf, Howard. *Reds or Rackets? The Making of Radical and Conservative Unions on the Waterfront.* Berkeley: University of California Press, 1988.

Kodish, Debora. *Good Friends and Bad Enemies: Robert Winslow Gordon and the Study of American Folksong.* Urbana: University of Illinois Press, 1986.

Kundera, Milan. *The Book of Laughter and Forgetting.* Trans. Michael Helm. New York: A. A. Knopf, 1980.

Kutler, Stanley L. *The American Inquisition: Justice and Injustice in the Cold War.* New York: Hill and Wang, 1982.

Larrowe, Charles P. *Harry Bridges: The Rise and Fall of Radical Labor in the United States.* New York: Lawrence Hill, 1972.

Lenin, V. I. *What Is to Be Done?* Trans. Joe Fineberg and George Hanna. Harmondsworth, U.K.: Penguin Books, 1988.

Levi, Margaret, et al. "Union Democracy Reexamined." *Politics and Society* 36 (June 2009) 203–28.

Lieberman, Robbie. *"My Song Is My Weapon": People's Songs, American Communism, and the Politics of Culture, 1930–1950.* Urbana: University of Illinois Press, 1995.

Limon, Jose. "Western Marxism and Folklore: A Critical Introduction." *Journal of American Folklore* 96 (Jan.–March 1983): 34–52.

Lipset, Seymour Martin, Martin Trow, and James S. Coleman. *Union Democracy: The Internal Politics of the International Typographical Union.* Glencoe: Free Press, 1956.

Lipsitz, George. *Footsteps in the Dark: The Hidden Histories of Popular Music.* Minneapolis: University of Minnesota Press, 2007.

———. *A Life in the Struggle: Ivory Perry and the Culture of Opposition.* Philadelphia: Temple University Press, 1995.

———. *"A Rainbow at Midnight": Labor and Culture in the 1940s.* Urbana: University of Illinois Press, 1994.

———. "'Sent for You Yesterday, Here You Come Today': American Studies Scholarship and the New Social Movements." *Cultural Critique,* no. 40 (Autumn 1998): 203–25.

Lynd, Alice, and Staughton Lynd. *Rank and File: Personal Histories by Working-Class Organizers.* Princeton: Princeton University Press, 1981.

———. Review of *Only a Miner. American Historical Review* (Feb. 1973): 169–70.

Machado, Adam. "Eugene Earle: A Lifetime Affair Collecting Old-Time Country Music." *Old-Time Herald* 10 (Dec. 2006) 24–33.
Maclean, Iain. *The Legend of Red Clydeside.* Edinburgh: John Donald, 1983.
MARHO—the Radical Historians Organization. *Visions of History.* Ed. Henry Abelove et al. New York: Pantheon Books, 1983.
Markholt, Ottilie. *Maritime Solidarity: Pacific Coast Unionism, 1929–1938.* Tacoma: Pacific Coast Maritime History Committee, 1998.
McCarl, Robert. "Occupational Folklife in the Public Sector." In *The Conservation of Culture: Folklorists and the Public Sector. Ed.* Burt Feintuch, 132–54. Lexington: University Press of Kentucky, 1988.
McLaren, Peter. *Capitalists and Conquerors: A Critical Pedagogy against Empire.* Lanham: Rowman and Littlefield, 2005.
Mergen, Bernard. "A History of the Industrial Union of Marine and Shipbuilding Workers of America, 1933–1951." Ph.D. diss., University of Pennsylvania, 1968.
Michel, Robert. *Political Parties: A Sociological Study of the Oligarchical Tendencies of Modern Democracy.* Glencoe: Free Press, 1949.
Mohanty, Chandra. *Feminism without Borders: Decolonizing Theory, Practicing Solidarity.* Durham: Duke University Press, 2003.
Montgomery, David. "Worker's Control of Machine Production in the Nineteenth Century." *Labor History* 17 (1976): 485–509.
Morrison, Toni. *Playing in the Dark: Whiteness and the Literary Imagination.* Cambridge: Harvard University Press, 1992.
Naison, Mark. *Communists in Harlem during the Depression.* Urbana: University of Illinois Press, 1983.
Nelson, Bruce. *Workers on the Waterfront: Seaman, Longshoremen, and Unionism in the 1930s.* Urbana: University of Illinois Press, 1990.
Oaxley, Howard. *Education Activities in CCC Camps.* U.S. government research document. Washington, D.C., 1938.
O'Conner, Jessie Lloyd, Harvey O'Conner, and Susan Bowler. *Harvey and Jessie: A Couple of Radicals.* Philadelphia: Temple University Press, 1988.
Ortiz, Paul. *Emancipation Betrayed: The Hidden History of Black Organizing and White Violence in Florida from Reconstruction to the Bloody Election of 1920.* Berkeley: University of California Press, 2005.
Painter, Nell Irvin. *The Narrative of Hosea Hudson: The Life and Times of a Black Radical.* New York: W.W. Norton, 1979.
Palmer, David. *Organizing the Shipyards: Union Strategy in Three Northeast Ports, 1933–35.* Ithaca: ILR Press, 1998.
Polletta, Francesca. *Freedom Is an Endless Meeting: Democracy in American Social Movements.* Chicago: University of Chicago Press, 2002.
Portelli, Alessandro. *The Battle of Valle Giula: Oral History and the Art of Dialogue.* Madison: University of Wisconsin Press, 1997.

Porterfield, Nolan, ed. *Exploring Roots Music: Twenty Years of the* JEMF Quarterly. Lanham, Md.: Scarecrow Press, 2004.

Preis, Art. *Stalinists on the Waterfront.* New York: Pioneer Publishers, 1947.

Quam-Wickham, Nancy. "Who Controls the Hiring Hall? The Struggle for Job Control in the ILWU during World War II." In *The CIO's Left Led Unions.* Ed. Steven Rosswurm, 47–68. New Brunswick: Rutgers University Press, 1992.

Quinn, Michael. *The Big Strike.* Olema, Calif.: Olema Publishing, 1949.

Ransby, Barbara. *Ella Baker and the Black Freedom Movement: A Radical Democratic Vision.* Chapel Hill: University of North Carolina Press, 2003.

Rawick, George, ed. *The American Slave: A Composite Autobiography.* Santa Barbara: Greenwood Press, 1977.

"Recognition of Archie Green." Extensions of Remarks E1741. *U.S. Congressional Record,* Aug. 3, 2007.

Record, Jane C. "Ideologies and Trade Union Leadership: The Case of Harry Bridges and Harry Lundeberg." Ph.D. diss., University of California, Berkeley, 1955.

Reuss, Richard A., with Joanne C. Reuss. *American Folk Music and Left-Wing Politics, 1927–1957.* Lanham, Md.: Scarecrow Press, 2000.

Richmond, Al. *A Long View from the Left: Memoirs of an American Revolutionary.* Boston: Houghton Mifflin, 1973.

Ripley, B. J., and John McHugh. *John Maclean.* New York: Manchester University Press, 1989.

Robinson, John V. *Spanning the Strait: Building the Alfred Zampa Memorial Bridge.* Crockett, Calif.: Carquinez Press, 2004.

Roediger, David. *History against Misery.* Chicago: Charles H. Kerr Publishing, 2006.

———. *The Wages of Whiteness: Race and the Making of the American Working Class.* New York: Verso Press, 1991.

Romalis, Shelly. *Pistol Packin' Mama: Aunt Molly Jackson and the Politics of Folksong.* Urbana: University of Illinois Press, 1999.

Rosemont, Franklin. *Joe Hill: The IWW and the Making of a Revolutionary Working-class Counterculture.* Chicago: Charles H. Kerr Publishing, 2003.

Rossman, Harold. "Brother Archie Green: S.F. Carpenter Helps Preserve Labor's History and Lore." *Organized Labor,* Nov. 17, 1957, 1.

Rosswurm, Steve, ed. *The CIO's Left Led Unions.* New Brunswick: Rutgers University Press, 1992.

Sanchez, George. "'What's Good for Boyle Heights Is Good for the Jews': Creating Multiracialism on the Eastside during the 1950s." *American Quarterly* 56 (Sept. 2004): 633–61.

Saxe, Robert Francis. *Settling Down: World War II Veterans' Challenge to the Postwar Consensus.* New York: Macmillan, 2007.

Saxton, Alexander. *The Indispensable Enemy: Labor and the Anti-Chinese Movement in California.* Berkeley: University of California Press, 1971.

———. *The Rise and Fall of the White Republic: Class Politics and Mass Culture in Nineteenth Century America.* New York: Verso Press, 1991.

Schwartz, Harvey. "Harry Bridges and the Scholars: Looking at History's Verdict." *California History* 59 (1980): 66–79.

———. *Labor's Stronghold: 120 Years of Local 22, UBCJA in San Francisco, CA. 1882–2002.* San Francisco: UBCJA, 2002.

———. *The March Inland: Origins of the ILWU Warehouse Division, 1934–1938.* San Francisco: ILWU, 2000.

———. Review of *Maritime Solidarity. California History* 80 (Spring 2001): 65.

Schwartz, Stephen. *Brotherhood of the Sea: A History of the Sailors' Union of the Pacific, 1885–1985.* New Brunswick: Transaction Books, 1986.

Seeger, Charles. "Music in America." *Magazine of Art* 31 (July 1938): 411–13.

Sharp, Cecil. *English Folksongs from the Southern Appalachians.* 2 vols. New York: Oxford University Press, 1966.

Shelton, Robert. "Students Import Folk Art to Chicago." *New York Times,* Feb. 12, 1961, 17.

Shuman, Amy, and Charles Briggs. "Theorizing Folklore: Toward New Perspectives on the Politics of Culture." *Western Folklore* 52 (April–Oct. 1993): 109–34.

Sochor, Zenovia A. *Revolution and Culture: The Bogdanov-Lenin Controversy.* Ithaca: Cornell University Press, 1988.

Spivak, Gayatri. "Subaltern Studies: Deconstructing Historiography." In *The Spivak Reader: Selected Works of Gayatri Spivak.* Ed. Donna Laudry and Gerald MacLean, 203–36. New York: Routledge, 1995.

Stepan-Norris, Judith, and Maurice Zeitlin. *Left Out: Reds and America's Industrial Unions.* New York: Cambridge University Press, 2003.

Storey, John. *Inventing Popular Culture.* New York: Blackwell Publishing, 2003.

Terkel, Studs. *Hard Times: An Oral History of the Great Depression.* New York: Pantheon Books, 1986.

Thomas, C. "West Coast Longshoremen and the 'Bridges Plan.'" *Fourth International* 3 (Dec. 1942): 362–68.

Thompson, E. P. *The Making of the English Working Class.* New York: Vintage Books, 1963.

Trotsky, Leon. *The History of the Russian Revolution.* Ann Arbor: University of Michigan Press, 1957.

U.S. Civilian Conservation Corps. Miscellaneous Publications, 1933–41. SD 143 A296. Main Library, University of California, Berkeley.

U.S. Senate. Hearings before the Subcommittee on Education of the Committee on Labor and Public Welfare. American Folklife Foundation Act, Senate Bill 1591. May 18, 1970.

Vlach, John. "Always on Stolen Time." Unpublished essay, author's possession, n.d.

Wakin, Daniel J. "This Just In: Pete Seeger Denounced Stalin over a Decade Ago." *New York Times,* Sept. 1, 2007, B7.

Weintraub, Hyman. "The I.W.W. in California, 1905–1931." M.A. thesis, University of California, Los Angeles, 1947.

Weir, Stan. *Singlejack Solidarity.* Ed. George Lipsitz. Minneapolis: University of Minnesota Press, 2004.

Whisnant, David E. *All That Is Native and Fine: The Politics of Culture in an American Region.* Chapel Hill: University of North Carolina Press, 1983.

Willett, Henry. "A Survey of State Folk Cultural Programs." Public Programs section, American Folklore Society, in conjunction with the Folk Arts Program, National Endowment for the Arts, Jan. 1986.

Index

Sean Burns (www.seanburns.net) is a teacher, musician, and gardener. Since graduating from Georgetown University in 1995 he has taught a wide range of humanities and social science courses at both the high school and university level. His research and teaching interests center on the history, culture, and politics of progressive social movements. He earned his Ph.D. in the history of consciousness department at the University of California, Santa Cruz. His band, Professor Burns and the Lilac Field, is rooted in Berkeley, Calif.

Nick Spitzer is the voice and creator of public radio's *American Routes.* He is professor of anthropology and American studies at Tulane University in New Orleans.

The University of Illinois Press
is a founding member of the
Association of American University Presses.

Designed by Kelly Gray
Composed in 10.5/13 Adobe Minion
with DIN 30640 and 1451 display
by Jim Proefrock
at the University of Illinois Press
Manufactured by Sheridan Books, Inc.

University of Illinois Press
1325 South Oak Street
Champaign, IL 61820-6903
www.press.uillinois.edu